Knowledge at Work

Additional praise for *Knowledge at Work*

"A very impressive account of 'knowledge at work' on several levels of analysis: individual, organization, industry, and community; that successfully connects with managerial practice."

Joerg Sydow, Free University of Berlin

"This book provides unique insights into the drivers behind the knowledge economy, showing how individuals, groups, organizations, and industries create and use knowledge. It provides an important and highly readable contribution to contemporary understanding of knowledge and learning processes."

David Gann, Imperial College London

"For those of us wilting under the weight of new publications on knowledge and knowledge management this book provides a welcome refuge in what is a busy, crowded, and often confusing zone. Not only does it provide a broad ranging and thorough review of the key issues, but it also challenges the reader to reflect on them chapter by chapter. The book recognizes what too many others don't that all the company procedures and IT-based knowledge management systems are just tools and that people are at the centre of the knowledge-based economy. The strength of the book lies in its grounding in real work examples and in its consistent use of a framework – the knowledge diamond – which highlights the interdependencies of four key participants in knowledge work: individuals, communities, organizations, and industries. It should be useful to both knowledge workers themselves and those that study them."

Tim Brady, University of Brighton

ROBERT J. DEFILLIPPI
Suffolk University, Boston

MICHAEL B. ARTHUR
Suffolk University, Boston

VALERIE J. LINDSAY
Victoria University, Wellington, New Zealand

KNOWLEDGE AT WORK

CREATIVE COLLABORATION IN THE GLOBAL ECONOMY

Blackwell
Publishing

© 2006 by Robert J. DeFillippi, Michael B. Arthur and Valerie J. Lindsay

BLACKWELL PUBLISHING
350 Main Street, Malden, MA 02148-5020, USA
9600 Garsington Road, Oxford OX4 2DQ, UK
550 Swanston Street, Carlton, Victoria 3053, Australia

First published 2006 by Blackwell Publishing Ltd

1   2006

Library of Congress Cataloging-in-Publication Data

DeFillippi, Bob.
Knowledge at work : creative collaboration in the global economy / Robert J
DeFillippi, Michael B Arthur, Valerie J Lindsay.
p.   cm.
Includes bibliographical references and index.
ISBN-13: 978-1-4051-0755-6 (hardback : alk. paper)
ISBN-10: 1-4051-0755-3 (hardback : alk. paper)
ISBN-13: 978-1-4051-0756-3 (pbk. : alk. paper)
ISBN-10: 1-4051-0756-1 (pbk. : alk. paper)   1. Intellectual capital.
2. Knowledge and learning.   3. Knowledge management.   4. Organizational
learning.   5. Interpersonal communication.   6. Interpersonal relations.
I. Arthur, Michael B. (Michael Bernard), 1945–   II. Lindsay,
Valerie J.   III. Title.

HD53.D44 2006
658.4′038—dc22
2006002734

A catalogue record for this title is available from the British Library.

Set in 10/12.5pt Baskerville
by Graphicraft Limited, Hong Kong
Printed and bound in Singapore
by Markono Print Media Pte Ltd

The publisher's policy is to use permanent paper from mills that operate a
sustainable forestry policy, and which has been manufactured from pulp
processed using acid-free and elementary chlorine-free practices. Furthermore,
the publisher ensures that the text paper and cover board used have met
acceptable environmental accreditation standards.

For further information on
Blackwell Publishing, visit our website:
www.blackwellpublishing.com

CONTENTS

FIGURES

TABLES

CASE STUDIES

Dedicated to the memory of two devoted teachers:

Peter Arthur
and
Mary Mallon

PREFACE

The origins of this book date back to 1993, when Bob DeFillippi and Michael Arthur first collaborated in examining the dynamics of knowledge-based careers. This collaboration led to our further exploring the organization of knowledge work in temporary, project-based enterprises. Along, the way, we began to communicate with others looking at knowledge work through a variety of different lenses, and to broaden our own appreciation in response to those communications. Val Lindsay first joined the conversation in 1995, adding her particular interests in international business and industry clusters.

Our collaboration unfolded through a series of projects, addressing a variety of interdependent subjects including boundaryless careers, project-based enterprise, distributed knowledge systems, career communities, project-based learning, and the changing practice of human resource management. As we dug deeper into these subjects, we saw the potential associated with a rich variety of separate approaches. We also saw more clearly how approaches that assumed traditional "levels of analysis" could interfere with a broader appreciation of knowledge work dynamics. This book offers an alternative, more integrative approach.

Knowledge At Work focuses on the processes through which knowledge is created, accumulated and put to use in the knowledge-driven economy. The book examines four types of knowledge work participant – the individual, the community, the organization and the host industry – and the connections among them. The four participants are represented in an underlying framework – the knowledge diamond – highlighted throughout the book. Coverage is also provided on the key topics of project-based, virtual, and global knowledge work and intellectual property. Throughout the book we emphasize the practices through which knowledge workers perform their work, and we illustrate these practices through relevant examples drawn from a variety of industries and international settings.

This book is not another book on "knowledge management," in the sense that the term has been adopted by information technology writers. Instead, it offers an alternative perspective grounded in the behavioral and social sciences. However, our book does acknowledge the role of information technology in contributing to the social processes through which knowledge is generated, transmitted and retained. It may therefore be seen as a complement to mainstream information technology approaches.

Knowledge at Work is written to appeal to three distinct audiences: scholars, graduate students, and managers seeking to extend their prior education. It is our hope that all three audiences will benefit from both the material in the book and its organization, and by the tying together of ideas as the chapters unfold. Questions for individual reflection are provided at the end of each chapter. A companion website provides further support for both scholars teaching from the book and independent readers. You may visit this website at the url: www.knowledgeatwork.info

We are deeply indebted to Lars Lindkvist and Joerg Sydow, who read the entire first draft of our manuscript and subsequently commented on specific revisions. Pat Keck read the full second draft and greatly improved the prose that went to press. Tim Brady, Sushil Bhatia, Andrew Davies, Nick Marshall, Andrea Prencipe, Jonathan Sapsed, David Silverstein, Sherry Sullivan, and Fredrik Tell all read selected chapters related to their expertise and offered helpful commentary. Michael Hobday and Howard Rush hosted Bob DeFillippi on several occasions as a Visiting Fellow to the Center for Research in Innovation Management (CENTRIM) at University of Brighton and at the Science Policy Research Unit (SPRU) at the University of Sussex. John Bessant, David Gann, Ammon Salter, Tim Venables and Jennifer Whyte, all now at the Tanaka Business School of Imperial College of London, also supported this work, most recently by hosting Bob DeFillippi in 2005–2006 as an Advanced Institute of Management (AIM) international visiting fellow.

We are also directly indebted to a number of co-authors, book editors, journal special issue collaborators, symposium conveners and valued colleagues who have helped along the way. Thanks to Virginia Aacha, Pierpaolo Andriani, Yochanan Altman, N. Anand, Steve Armstrong, Charles Baden-Fuller, Lotte Bailyn, Michael Best, Max Boisot, Mike Bresnan, Jim Brown, Loic Cadin, Paul Carlile, François Dany, Linda Edelman, Anne Keegan, Gernot Grabher, Rob Goffee, Tobias Gosling, Tim Hall, Chris Hendry, Herminia Ibarra, Rob Jansen, Candace Jones, Kerr Inkson, Svetlana Khapova, Henrik Holt Larsen, the late Mary Mallon, Tim Morris, Susan Newell, Leon Oerleans, Maury Peiperl, Polly

Parker, Judith Pringle, Joe Raelin, Maxine Robertson, Denise Rousseau, Harry Scarborough, Jackie Swan, Charles Wankel, and Celeste Wilderom.

Journal editors James Walker and William Stopper (Human Resource Planning), Christopher Grey and Elena Antonacopoulou (Management Learning), Michael Poole (International Journal of Human Resource Management), Haridimos Tsoukas (Organization Studies), and David Vogel (California Management Review), all supported special issues or extended debate on topics related to this work. Tom Davenport, Lucia Garcia-Lorenzo, and Mary Lakis all helped in providing case study materials.

We benefited from the constructive observations of those who attended presentations about ideas in this book at meetings of the Academy of Management, the European Group for Organizational Studies, the Organizational Knowledge, Learning and Capabilities conferences, the annual University of Lecce workshops in Otranto and Brindisi, Italy, and the annual Multi-Organizational Partnerships, Alliances and Networks conference. Bentley College, Cambridge University, City University, Copenhagen Business School, University of Derby, Erasmus University, Harvard Business School, Rotterdam School of Management, Free University of Berlin, Linkoping University, London Business School, Manchester Business School, Stockholm School of Economics, University of Auckland, University of Brighton, University of Hull, University of Lecce, University of Lyon, University of Otago, University of Sussex, University of Tilburg, and Vienna University of Economics and Business Administration all hosted presentations by one or more of the authors that contributed to the development of this book.

Bob and Michael are grateful to Dean Bill O'Neill for his continuing support, the Suffolk Business School Research Committee, and three groups of MBA or Executive MBA students with whom we were able to teach successive drafts of this book. Val is grateful for the support of colleagues in the School of Marketing and International Business at Victoria University, New Zealand, over the course of this project. Thanks to Zack Blake for both timely literature reviews and help in the development of our website. Thanks also to Jeevan Kamble, an information technology student Bob DeFillippi met on the web, who contributed to our understanding of blogging and other virtual tools. We also acknowledge the financial support received from the European Social Science Research Council and the Social Science Research Council to fund Bob DeFillippi's one-year UK visiting fellowship during 2004–2005.

We have benefited from the support of our team at Blackwell Publishing. We thank our senior editor Rosemary Nixon for never losing faith in us. We also thank Jean Ashford (editorial controller), Linda Auld (project manager), Brian Goodale (copy editor), Katherine Wheatley (marketing), Karen Wilson (editorial controller), and Desirée Zicko (marketing) for helping bring this manuscript to you the reader.

Not least, we would each like to thank our respective partners, Jane, Pat and John and our children for their love and support while this book was being written. The responsibility for the contents and any short-comings of this manuscript remains with us.

Robert J. DeFillippi
Michael B. Arthur
Boston, Massachusetts
and
Valerie J. Lindsay
Wellington, New Zealand
June 2006

ACKNOWLEDGMENTS

The authors and publisher gratefully acknowledge the permission granted to reproduce the copyright material in this book:

Michael Arthur, Robert DeFillippi, and Candace Jones for "Projects as Episodes in Knowledge Work," derived from "Project-based learning as the interplay of career and company non-financial capital," from *Management Learning* 32 (1), pp. 99–117. © 2001 Sage Publications. Reprinted by permission of Sage Publications Ltd.

Thomas H. Davenport for "Teltech: the business of knowledge management case study," http://www.mccombs.utexas.edu/kman/telcase.htm. Reprinted with kind permission of the author.

Every effort has been made to trace copyright holders and to obtain their permission for the use of copyright material. The publisher apologizes for any errors or omissions in the above list and would be grateful if notified of any corrections that should be incorporated in future reprints or editions of this book.

CHAPTER 1

KNOWLEDGE WORKERS AND KNOWLEDGE WORK

[W]hile the modern world often appears increasingly imper-
sonal, in those areas where knowledge really counts, people
count more than ever.

John Seely Brown and Paul Duguid[1]

Today's economy is a knowledge-based economy where the ability to create, distribute and apply knowledge are key drivers of worker productivity, company competitive advantage, and regional and industry growth. Knowledge workers are dispersed around the globe and connected through the Internet. Intellectual property challenges often arise over who owns what knowledge, and when knowledge may be traded for personal gain. Knowledge workers are continuous learners, and are typically engaged in both applying and adding to their stock of knowledge. Over time, knowledge workers develop specialized work practices and an important challenge in knowledge work is to foster effective communications between these practices. However, knowledge workers frequently differ in how open they are to sharing what they know with potential collaborators.

There are four key types of participant in knowledge work – namely individuals, communities, organizations and industries. Each of these interacts with the other three participants as knowledge work unfolds. The four participants may be best understood as interdependent actors within a larger system of knowledge application and creation. This book will consider each participant in turn, and also the project-based, virtual, global and intellectual property communications and collaborations among participants.

Let us look at the world of film-making.

An episode in film-making[2]

In the summer of 1996, the popular British actor, director and screen-writer, John Cleese, started work on a new movie with the American producer, Michael Shamberg. The two individuals had previously worked together on the surprise box-office hit *A Fish Called Wanda*. Popular opinion had seen this as an ideal outlet for Cleese's comic genius, and Cleese, Shamberg, and key members of the cast and crew had been eager to develop a follow-up. Cleese had the screenplay ready, and Shamberg and other influential readers were delighted with it.

Word went out to Cleese's and Shamberg's favorite collaborators. Three star actors from the first movie (Jamie Lee Curtis, Kevin Kline, and Michael Palin) all agreed to return. So too did many of the crew members. For example, a camera operator from *Wanda* put together a new crew from people he had already worked with or heard about. Shamberg confirmed some of his closest allies on the production side would also join in. A senior crew member summarized the recruiting philosophy by saying: "The first project was a success . . . We had a good collaboration . . . In the film industry, like all businesses, you tend to work with people . . . with whom you are comfortable."

On the set of the movie, crew members described their motivations for joining the new venture. Many had joined out of an admiration for Cleese and his distinguished body of earlier work. As one sound mixer suggested, "I consider simply being on a project with John a success." Others were attracted to the project because it provided a high-profile opportunity to demonstrate their competence and possibly gain further recognition through industry awards. Others were attracted by the opportunity to apply their expertise in a novel application. For example, one senior crew member had a distinguished career training animals for Disney shows, and saw the project as an occasion to adapt her expertise for a more adult audience.

Almost all of the crew members had worked with other crew members on either *Wanda* or another movie. Many of the crew members were already anticipating working with each other on future projects after the new film – to be titled *Fierce Creatures* – was made. The present collaboration added to the shared work experience that would serve them later on. For the crew as well as the actors, the movie set was the stage on which motivations were played out, knowledge was shared, and relationships were developed.

A Fish Called Wanda had been made on a shoestring budget, but this time the director and producer had more bargaining power. There was a successful previous collaboration to boast about, and since then each of the principals had enhanced their reputation. Important actors and crew members were already in place. Shamberg went to his Hollywood contacts and arranged for a major "studio" to finance the full cost of the new movie. *Fierce Creatures* would be made on a budget five times larger than the two friends' earlier venture in return for the studio getting the distribution rights.

Film-making is a high-risk business, and in this particular case the movie was not a financial success. A first cut did not sit well with a preview audience, key sequences were hastily reshot, and the film subsequently opened to mixed reviews. However, the risks are well understood within the industry, and most members of the crew and cast moved on with their reputations intact and their personal knowledge enriched from the shared experience. There were other movies to be made.

The main title of this book, *Knowledge at Work*, suggests two distinct meanings. The first meaning is the knowledge people bring to their work, as is illustrated by Cleese's and Shamberg's efforts to get their sequel film project under way. The two leaders needed to recruit and tap into the knowledge of a wide range of specialists – actors, camera operators, sound mixers, electricians, script supervisors, makeup artists, costume designers, and many more. The distinctive knowledge of each type of specialist was necessary if the film was to get made. The specialists were also expected to be creative – that is to apply their knowledge in new ways – in responding to the unique circumstances of the new film. According to this first meaning, knowledge is located in the talents of individual workers, or groups of workers, and those talents are put to work in accomplishing the task at hand.

The second suggested meaning of *Knowledge at Work* is that knowledge spreads through social interaction. In the film-making example, it was not enough for the diversity of film crew specialists to merely come together. Knowledge held by one group of specialists had to be shared with other groups of specialists – for example camera operators, electricians and boom operators needed to collaborate closely – for the film to get made. Knowledge also needed to be shared between more experienced and less experienced workers, if the less experienced workers were to become more effective film crew contributors. In this second sense, the stock of knowledge can spread to more people, and grow to address new problems, as a result of overlapping work experiences.[3]

The point to be made at the outset of this book is that both meanings are important. The first meaning invites questions about individual or group knowledge, how it is accumulated, and the contribution it makes to how work gets done. In this sense knowledge is an asset to the people who possess it, the companies that recruit or hire it and the industries in which it is applied. The second meaning points to a fundamental difference between knowledge and other kinds of assets, such as cash. If one person shares cash with another person, the total amount of cash is the same. However, if one person shares knowledge with another person, both can have all of the knowledge. Moreover, each person is in a position to share the knowledge again, so that the pace of knowledge transfer can, in theory, be exponential.

A further observation here is that both meanings of *Knowledge at Work* point to a dynamic, and frequently cyclical, picture. The knowledge resources that crew members brought to the film-making episode came out of the knowledge created in previous film-making endeavors. Later films would provide fresh opportunities for participant workers to make specialized investments in their own knowledge assets, and shared investments in each film's overall success. The experience of putting knowledge to work also provides an opportunity to gain new knowledge along the way. This is the essence of what the subtitle of this book refers to as creative collaboration. The subtitle also refers to the global economy, to which we turn next.

KNOWLEDGE WORK IN
THE GLOBAL ECONOMY

Peter Drucker first coined the term "knowledge work" in 1959 to refer to a growing set of work roles requiring education, qualifications, and "the ability to acquire and to apply theoretical and analytical knowledge."[4] Today, knowledge has a central place in the global economy. For example, the UK government aspires to a knowledge-driven economy "in which the generation and exploitation of knowledge play the predominant part in the creation of wealth."[5] The World Bank describes a knowledge economy as one that provides incentives for the efficient use of existing and new knowledge, sustains an educated and skilled workforce to successfully create and share knowledge, provides an infrastructure to facilitate effective communication and dissemination of knowledge, and hosts an efficient innovation system – of firms, research centers, universities, consultants, etc. – to further tap into, apply and expand knowledge.[6]

What is the evidence of the trend towards knowledge work that Drucker predicted? A Canadian study over a thirty-year period from 1971 to 2001 showed so-called knowledge workers – defined as post-secondary educated professional workers, management workers and technical workers – growing from 14% to 25% of the national labor force. In business services the ratio grew to 66%, in finance and insurance to 42%, and in wholesale trade and mining, quarrying, oil and gas to around 25%. Even using restrictive definitions based on post-secondary education, the trend toward much higher levels of knowledge work amongst the workforce is clear. Estimates of the proportion of knowledge workers in the US economy range from 28% to 34%. The 28% estimate is derived from defining knowledge work as the following occupational categories of the Bureau of Labor Statistics (BLS): management; business and financial operations; computer and mathematical; architecture and engineering; life, physical and social scientists; legal; health care practitioners; community and social services; education, training and library services.[7] The 34% estimate counts knowledge workers as those in the broad BLS category of "managerial, professional and technical workers," which constituted 34% of the US workforce in 2003.[8]

Evidence in business and economic statistics suggests the relative magnitude of the economic value of knowledge in publicly owned firms. It has become commonplace for the stock price of publicly owned companies to largely reflect intellectual assets rather than physical assets. For example, any comparison of physical assets on a balance sheet (book value) to stock market valuations will reveal a large discrepancy between the share prices to book value per share. Those companies with the highest market to book value (suggesting not all market value is captured by physical assets) are typically companies in knowledge intensive industries, where intellectual assets are a key driver of competitive advantage. It is the intangible value of these intellectual assets, including brands, trademarks, patents, trade secrets and other forms of intellectual property, that accounts for a far greater proportion of the share price valuations than the physical asset valuations.[9]

Knowledge also figures powerfully in international trade statistics. For example, despite a cumulative trade deficit of $3.4 trillion during 1990 –2003, the US economy enjoyed a trade surplus of over $243 million in advanced technology products during the same time period.[10] Knowledge, embedded in high-technology products and sophisticated financial and business services, was one of the US economy's leading exports. Much knowledge related to global trade now flows across the World Wide Web. The United States and the countries of Western Europe were early leaders in "connectivity," with up to two out of every three workers expected to have access to the web by the year 2007 (Table 1.1). However, Eastern European and Asia-Pacific countries were already surpassing the US and Europe in their raw numbers of connected workers, and in investments in web-related infrastructure.[11] Knowledge work and knowledge workers are everywhere, and knowledge flows substantially transcend traditional geographic or government boundaries.

Table 1.1 Internet users worldwide[12]

Geographic region	Internet users (millions)	
	2005	2007 (est.)
North America	178,530	254,350
Western Europe	151,999	290,999
Eastern Europe and Russia	34,155	98,151
Asia-Pacific	237,922	615,571
South and Central America	39,146	110,893
Middle East and Africa	23,922	96,287
Total Internet users	665,674	1,466,251

WHAT DO KNOWLEDGE WORKERS DO?

Tom Davenport defines knowledge workers as having "high degrees of expertise, education and or experience" and where "the primary purpose of their jobs involves the creation, distribution or application of knowledge."[13] Others have similarly seen knowledge workers as people involved with abstractions or symbols, and engaging with mental rather than physical work activities.[14] In sum, you are a knowledge worker if you work primarily with your head rather than your hands. Although it is tempting to presume knowledge workers possess higher levels of education, it may be more accurate to see knowledge work arising from accumulated experience and skill mastery. In the film-making example, people were recruited for their ability to reproduce what they had done before, as well as to help out in solving new challenges. These capabilities were largely based upon their work experience and accumulated know-how and proven mastery, or what contemporary writers have termed "deep smarts."[15]

Moreover, knowledge workers need not be involved with the development of new products or services. Knowledge workers can also help improve ongoing operations, as for example in continuous improvement projects within Toyota's Total Quality Management teams and General Electric's Six Sigma programs. These programs reflect a wider trend to push responsibility for both knowledge and learning directly onto the person or group responsible for the work. Knowledge workers can also cooperate with each other on their own volition, exchanging relevant information and enhancing existing products – as for example computer programmers often do in software development.[16] Knowledge workers may also listen to, learn from, and apply lessons in response to feedback from suppliers or users, leading to improved products, services or business processes.

Business writer Thomas Stewart notes that North Sea oil rig workers perform cold, dangerous, work twelve hours at a time, but only spend two of those hours on physical activities. The rest of their time is spent "checking manuals, making sure the rigs have the right permits, preparing such permits, testing and measuring, and so on," that is, performing knowledge work. We find people like oil rig workers everywhere, on production lines, doing construction work, and managing delivery schedules. These kinds of workers are increasingly evident even within traditional manufacturing and construction industries.[17] Most workers are knowledge workers at least some of the time in the work assignments that they undertake, and knowledge work is less identified by job titles than by the way people perform work.

There is still cause for concern with the so-called "McDonaldization of work," that is, the shift in low-skill repetitive work from the blue-collar to the white-collar sector.[18] Many jobs in food services and retailing appear resistant to evolving into knowledge worker roles. Telephone call centers have been called "the faceless factories of the Internet Age, complete with over supervision and limited autonomy."[19] The extent of such arrangements will vary according to other economic variables. It nevertheless seems likely that the economic health of regions, states and localities will depend on the proportion of knowledge workers employed, and in turn on the further learning opportunities made available to those workers.[20]

EXPLICIT AND TACIT KNOWLEDGE

A useful analytical distinction involves explicit versus tacit knowledge. Explicit knowledge refers to knowledge that is codified and thereby directly available to others. Explicit knowledge is made available through replication of written instructions, mathematical equations or scientific formulae that summarize the knowledge content. In this way anyone possessing the "code" or recipe for the explicit knowledge can create an imitative or duplicative product without having mastery of the underlying knowledge behind the available instructions, equations or formulae. It is for this reason that industries whose product or service offerings are based upon explicit knowledge (e.g. prescription drugs, computer software, engineering designs, artistic images or literary documents) go to great lengths to protect their intellectual property.

By contrast, tacit knowledge means, "We know more than we can tell."[21] For example, knowledge of piano playing does not reside in the music theory summarized in books, but is created from the persistent act of playing the piano. In other instances, activities may create tacit skills in the absence of any explicit theoretical knowledge, as in Michael Polanyi's classic example of when a person learns to ride a bicycle, in some cases with the assistance of training wheels, in other cases with human assistance by a more experienced teacher, but ultimately through repeated practice and the direct experience of performance feedback. Tacit knowledge cannot be reduced to written instructions or code, nor can it be easily transferred from one person to another. Tacit knowledge is acquired through personal effort, involving the accumulation of experience and learning by doing, and becomes manifest in skilled performance.

Although explicit and tacit knowledge are distinct analytical concepts, in practice they typically interact with one another. Knowledge workers often employ tacit knowledge that complements previously explicit knowledge and leads to enhanced products or services. For example, research scientists frequently engage in "thought experiments" about the product or service possibilities of a new breakthrough (explicit knowledge) that they have read about in the scientific journals. However, these thought experiments also rely on the participants' deep, frequently unspoken knowledge of the underlying science or technology involved (tacit knowledge). As the research process moves from exploratory concepts towards product development, the underlying tacit knowledge will take on an increasingly concrete form, perhaps as a computer model or an engineering design. At this point the original concept may be in a sufficiently explicit form to qualify for registration with the patent or copyright office as a form of intellectual property.[22]

WHO OWNS THE KNOWLEDGE?

An important issue in knowledge work is the determination of ownership, as covered by patents, copyrights, trade secrets and other aspects of intellectual property legislation. The story of the Napster file-sharing program illustrates the kind of conflicts that can occur.

Napster and its aftermath[23]

In 1998, eighteen-year-old Shawn Fanning, a freshman at Northeastern University in Boston, developed a file-sharing program in his spare time. The program, named Napster, allowed users to type in the name of a band or tune, and the software would search the websites and the hard drives of all users connected over the World Wide Web. Once Napster found the music, it would be downloaded automatically onto the search initiator's own hard drive. By 1999, Napster and related file-sharing technologies had become so popular that college campuses reported major slowdowns in their computer systems because of the volume of music downloading. Meanwhile, established music industry companies raised a series of complaints that the copying of digital music files was a breach of copyright.

The Recording Industry Association of America (RIAA), representing five major record labels and many smaller labels, sued Napster for copyright infringement. "We love the idea of using technology to build artist communities, but that's not what Napster is all about. Napster is about facilitating piracy, and trying to build a business on the backs of artists and copyright owners," claimed Cary Sherman, senior executive vice-president and general counsel for RIAA.[24] The band Metallica launched its own lawsuit using a similar argument.

In its defense, Napster interim CEO Hank Barry retorted: "the Napster community says loudly and clearly that it wants artists and songwriters to be paid. I think that the license you create should include a direct Internet rights payment to the artist."[25] This argument did not directly address the issue of intellectual property rights of the companies that held the rights to the artists' work. Instead, it suggested a disintermediation of these companies in favor of direct artist remuneration based on downloads over the web.

In 2001, judgments against Napster required it to stop the distribution of copyright material, and to block all files infringing copyright. In 2002, after several years of costly legal battles with the RIAA, Napster filed for bankruptcy and sold its file-sharing programs to another company, Roxio. In 2003, Apple Computer started selling tunes over the web for $0.99 per song and $9.95 per album. Other online vendors, including Roxio, quickly imitated Apple's pay-per-tune approach. However, in 2005 Fanning tried again, this time with a new file-sharing company named Snocap, whose software also provided peer-to-peer technology, but was designed to respect, and collect royalties on, copyright holders' property.

Although the music industry has become an active partner with Apple and other online music distributors, the fight over access to digital content is far from over. Companies such as Apple wish to restrict digital content to their proprietary hardware player platforms, such as iPod. In

contrast, the Electronic Frontier Foundation, a San Francisco-based advo-
cacy group, favors fewer restrictions on digital technology.[26] The battle has
shifted from free access to freedom to transfer digital content between
computers. Fanning's 2005 technology would still require cooperation among
recording industry companies, music publishers, and music retailers as
well as favorable rulings by the courts on the new copyright implications.[27]

Meanwhile, a wide range of industries are imitating the recorded music
industry in transforming knowledge into intellectual property governed
by copyrights. These "copyright industries" include advertising, computer
software, design, photography, film, video, performance arts, music, radio,
TV and video games.[28] In all these industries, major conflicts arise over
the free access versus restricted use of those explicit cultural products that
are subject to copyright protection. We will return to these conflicts over
the course of this book, and examine them directly in Chapter 9.

KNOWING AND LEARNING

Knowledge may be broadly defined as "familiarity, awareness or understanding gained through experience or study."[29] This accommodates the
discussion so far that knowledge accrues to people – individuals or groups
– and can be explicit or tacit. However, we use "knowing" here in a more
selective sense than it is commonly applied. Specifically, we use the term
knowing to mean the act of putting knowledge to work. Thus, knowing
refers to "work that is done as part of action or practice, like that done
in the actual riding of a bicycle or the actual making of a medical diagnosis."[30] In this sense, knowledge is something that people possess, whereas
knowing is something that they do.

As we saw in the opening film-making example, crew members were
called on to utilize their knowledge in contributing to film production
requirements. However, crew members also needed to insure that their
contributions were compatible with those of other members of the crew.
There was an ongoing interaction among crew members whereby each
contributed what he or she knew, that is performed the act of knowing,
and thereby contributed to the film production work being undertaken.

Knowing is often a prelude to *learning*, which is the process through which
new knowledge is created or acquired. Learning is frequently experiential,
in that it arises from performance of work rather than through formal study
or instruction. Returning to the film-making example, interactions on the
set not only facilitated the film-making process, but also offered people
insights into how their contributions affected and were affected by others
on the film crew. These insights served to deepen people's knowledge of

their related crafts, and to expand the crew's overall knowledge resources. Knowing and learning are intertwined over time, as knowledge work interactions create the conditions for new learning to arise.[31]

As already noted, work roles vary in their capacity to provide learning opportunities. At one extreme, mass-production manufacturing plants and their service industry offspring – fast-food restaurants and call centers – are not rich in opportunities for learning. Greater learning can occur if workers participate around principles of "continuous improvement" that call on rather than resist worker feedback.[32] However, the ideal of broadly harnessing workers' capacity to learn, and thereby to add economic value in employment arrangements, has yet to be realized.[33]

THE INTERPLAY OF KNOWING AND LEARNING

The following story of scientific research illustrates the complex interplay in knowledge work between putting current knowledge to work (knowing) and the processes of acquiring or creating new knowledge (learning).

Chemistry in academia[34]

John, a theoretical chemist, had a chance conversation with Susan, an experimental chemist who worked in a different department of the same university. They were surprised to realize that they both believed the National Bureau of Standards' published statistics about the magnesium dioxide molecule were incorrect. John used his theoretical knowledge to compute what the numerical measure of the property in question ought to be. Susan used her experimental knowledge to design a way to confirm whether this measure was accurate.

Frank was a radio astronomer from yet another department, who heard about the experiment and saw it was relevant to his own work on star formation. The three scientists then began a triangular collaboration. This collaboration persisted for decades, and became a basis for the further learning by each of the three scientists individually, as well as for their joint investigations.

John's, Susan's and Frank's collaboration also gave rise to separate and parallel collaborations with people at other universities as the original work became known. This brought further research questions to the surface, and generated new arenas of inquiry at the intersection of what were previously separate fields. These collaborations and others like them throughout a globally dispersed research community collectively fostered the emergence of a new field of research.

The learning cycle began when John and Susan had a chance conversation, and shared what each of them already knew. Through that conversation the scientists discovered an opportunity to work together. Learning occurred when the two scientists started to collaborate, and continued as they gathered and wrote up their results. This gave rise to a further cycle of knowledge work activity, beginning with Frank's unanticipated interest. There followed a series of further cycles of knowing, giving rise to learning as word of the collaborators' work spread. The story illustrates how an initial collaboration can have widespread effects through successive cycles of knowing and learning among a rapidly widening group of knowledge work participants.

A related interpretation of the chemistry story can be developed from evolutionary principles of variation, selection and retention.[35] The initial collaboration between John and Susan created *variation* in the existing stock of scientific knowledge. Members of the scientific community exercised *selection* by adopting research problems suggested by John and Susan's work. The publication of John and Susan's and their followers' work in scientific journals assured the *retention* of their cumulative knowledge for use by future members of their scientific community. We will return to this evolutionary view of learning later in this book.

KNOWLEDGE WORK AS PRACTICE

Practice refers to the application of a body of knowledge, and is usually associated with a particular type of work or occupational specialization.[36] Practice may be reflected in the repetition of individual or collective activities. From the perspective of the individual, the practice of engineers, accountants, physicians or violin makers draws on a specific body of knowledge that distinguishes one type of practice from another. Part of how people engage in their work is related to their formal education. Engineers, accountants and physicians each undertake specialized occupational education to gain fundamental knowledge of their professions and the skills to apply that knowledge. Accordingly, occupations function as social systems that impart a set of practices to their individual members through formal education and training.

However, another element of practice involves "learning the ropes" of being a practitioner. Learning how to be a practitioner is more than formal education and study; it requires participation with experienced practitioners. Research into the real work experiences of professional workers (e.g. doctors, lawyers, accountants, engineers) and technical workers (e.g. machine repair specialists) demonstrates that much of what

we learn about being a practitioner derives from our experiences of interacting with others. In the course of these real-world interactions, we fill
in gaps in our theoretical knowledge and learn things not to be found
in textbooks or classrooms. We learn the subtleties of how experienced
practitioners interact with other practitioners, with clients and with the
public at large.[37]

Our practitioner status evolves over time as we cross the sometimes
visible and sometimes invisible boundaries that distinguish varying
levels of expertise and status as a practitioner. At work, we may receive
formal recognition of our expertise and status in the form of a promotion,
a change of job title, new responsibilities, or perhaps a pay raise. We
may also receive informal confirmation of our competence from the feedback of respected work peers. In the best of work situations, we experience both formal and informal acknowledgement of our expertise.
In sum, knowledge work is embedded in the emergent practice of
knowledge workers over the course of their careers. This practice is
based on both the workers' formal education and their informal practical
experience through work-related interactions with others.[38]

COMMUNICATION BETWEEN PRACTICES

Knowledge work does not lend itself to any simple separation of different practices. Rather, the segregation of expertise into separate com-
partments can be a significant barrier to success in a fast moving,
knowledge-based, economy. Much knowledge work requires people to
extend themselves beyond the comfort zones of like-minded peers, and
to collaborate with practitioners whose skills and experiences may be
largely foreign. Hence, knowledge work is often performed in teams whose
members have a wide variety of expertise and practical experience. This
was evident in our opening story of the multiple teams involved in film-
making and the requirements for close interaction and coordination
between different specialist film crews and their individual members.

Perhaps the most general expertise required of all knowledge workers
is the ability to work effectively with others representing different but
complementary practices. Dorothy Leonard-Barton refers to the need
for knowledge workers to develop a "T form" of expertise.[39] The stem
of the T represents a knowledge worker's investment in becoming a deeply
expert practitioner of a specialized body of knowledge and skill.
However, the top of the T refers to the requirement that knowledge
workers develop a knowledge base and set of skills for collaborating
productively with people possessing complementary expertise. For

example, it would be useful for an engineer designing new products to know something about manufacturing and marketing (and maybe even finance), in order to work productively with other specialists on a product development team.

From a career perspective, it can be argued that those technical practitioners who become successful managers complement their expert knowledge with a broad capacity to appreciate and integrate the contributions of a range of complementary practices. Additionally, there are explicit roles in organizations for knowledge workers who can serve as boundary spanners or integrators of diverse types of practice. These different roles in knowledge work projects will be further explored later in this book.

Some organizations are designed to capitalize on the diverse practices of their workforce and to facilitate "creative abrasions," defined as the creative insights that can arise when different practices and perspectives are brought to bear on a common task or problem.[40] At Microsoft, the development of multimedia products has been facilitated by clashes between the practices of software code developers and the more artistically driven practices of designers responsible for user interfaces, screens, and icons. These two groups think, communicate and problem-solve differently from one another. The challenge for Microsoft has been to somehow blend and integrate these diverse practice perspectives in order to produce new creative possibilities. Similar collaborative challenges face companies in a wide variety of knowledge-based industries.

TOOLS FOR KNOWLEDGE WORK

In every profession and occupation, there are so-called "tools of the trade" that are associated with everyday practice. In accounting and financial services there are spreadsheets, and in construction critical path analyses, to support the practices of professional workers. However, knowledge work also employs a range of tools that facilitate the integration of skills and expertise across a range of different practices. Those tools allow knowledge work participants – individually or collectively, and in single or diverse employment settings – to combine separate pools of knowledge to accomplish knowledge work. Knowledge work tools are the means by which diversely trained knowledge workers communicate and collaborate across the specialized boundaries of their separate practices.

Tools for knowledge work fall into two major categories: information technology (IT) tools and behavioral tools. IT tools combine hardware and software to support knowledge work practices in a wide variety of industries and occupations. Some IT tools – for example client–server systems, the Internet, and telecommunications networks – are universally available to a wide range of knowledge workers and knowledge work practices. A growing number of other tools support more specialized practices.[41] Three major families of IT tools focus on content (e.g. document management and best practice repositories), computation (e.g. data search and data mining) and collaboration (e.g. cooperative document creation and virtual team tools).[42]

A second set of knowledge work tools involves behavioral tools, developed to facilitate effective and efficient knowledge work processes. These behavioral tools may be applied within or between organizations by specialist employees or may be used in interventions by external consultants. Behavioral tools exist for a variety of clients and purposes, for example to help individuals develop a knowledge-based career, or to help teams work more effectively together.[43] Organizations often promote company-wide behavioral tools, such as the widely noted "learning culture" tools employed by General Electric (which we will examine more closely in Chapter 4). Behavioral tools are also used within whole industries to disseminate knowledge and innovation. In the film-making industry, these include the many awards ceremonies and processes by which aspects of film-making are annually reviewed, evaluated and recognized.

The film-making project described earlier involved a number of examples of IT and behavioral tools in use. For example, every production team member utilized a pager and cell phone to stay in close communication with other geographically dispersed production team members. Additionally, the results of each day's shooting were codified and compiled by an editing team into an unfolding record ("the Dailies"). Every evening, members of the film crew met to review the Dailies and to offer commentary and feedback to the director, producer and other core project team members. The behavioral process of reviewing the day's shooting provided closure on the day's work by making use of the IT tools for digital editing now available to film production crews.

The chapters that follow will illustrate the role of tools, both IT and behavioral, to foster effective communication and collaboration between different types of knowledge work participants. For some writers the field of "knowledge management" is mainly or completely associated with IT hardware and software tools.[44] However, our emphasis here is not on the tools themselves but on the way that people are able to use them. This book therefore offers a complementary perspective to those taking an IT-based approach.

CLOSED VERSUS OPEN PERSPECTIVES

The creation and use of knowledge have arisen within two distinct and frequently conflicting perspectives, involving either open systems or closed systems.[45] Closed systems place primary importance on control over who has access to existing knowledge and who participates in the creation of new knowledge. Closed systems at their extreme reduce to the solo inventor jealously guarding his or her secrets from the prying eyes and ears of others. Within work groups, closed systems strictly prohibit group members from disclosing their work in progress to non-group members. At the organization level, closed systems prohibit employees from disclosing knowledge work projects and their results to non-employees. These closed systems assume that sharing knowledge outside a tightly circumscribed membership is dangerous and will result in net losses for those inside relative to those outside the knowledge work system. Traditional systems of intellectual property (patenting, licensing, and especially trade secrecy) are premised in part on closed systems of knowledge work. Similarly, vertically integrated approaches to knowledge work share a bias toward closed systems of knowledge work practice.

By contrast, open systems place primary importance upon maximizing access to relevant sources of new knowledge and to external opportunities for creating value from knowledge. Open systems emphasize lowering barriers to participation in knowledge creation and increasing access to the new knowledge that results from knowledge work. Open systems approaches are giving rise to new models of intellectual property, which foster access to knowledge created by others, and offer legal mechanisms to support such access. The previously noted royalty-collecting file-sharing program, developed by Shawn Fanning after his failed Napster venture, is one example. Open systems are also increasingly influencing the way that globally dispersed approaches to knowledge work are being pursued. For example, as we will discuss later in this book, IBM has made a major shift in its own approach to more substantially favor open system ideals.

There are inherent tensions between closed and open systems in the global knowledge-based economy. A closed system can reduce both access to external sources of knowledge and external opportunities to put that knowledge to work. An open system can increases the risk of economic free riding – that is, producing knock-off products and services based on proprietary knowledge. At the same time, knowledge work practices must come to terms with the disparate legal, cultural and organizational attitudes and behaviors associated with knowledge access and disclosure and the political and legal controversies that arise over intellectual property rights, which were previously illustrated in the Napster case.

PARTICIPANTS IN KNOWLEDGE WORK

Knowledge work is neither created nor used in a social vacuum. The participant in knowledge work has to be able to deal with a "complex web" of relationships among people and activities.[46] Moreover, the film-making example with which we started this chapter illustrates that knowledge work involves a variety of participants. These participants include individual knowledge workers, the occupational communities that join together on the film set, the company or organization that makes the film, other organizations providing specialized services and the overall industry that will absorb the film crew, and any new learning that has been gained, once their work on the present film has been completed.

The individual

First, and most fundamentally, there is the individual. In film-making this participant is the singular actor or crew member who brings know-ledge to and has the opportunity to take knowledge from the film-making activity. Most film projects involve the creative recombination of actors and crews with previous experience in the industry. In turn, when a new film is completed, each individual participant and his or her know-ledge investments are returned to the industry and become available for new film-making endeavors seeking new combinations of expertise. Certain key individuals (like Cleese and Shamberg in the film project) serve as champions who attract and integrate necessary people, ideas and resources. However, the power of the film-making example is that it demonstrates how a broad range of people can both contribute to and learn from knowledge work activities.

The community

Second, knowledge work cannot be understood as simply collaboration among individuals. In the film-making example, people's community attachments fall largely along occupational lines. For example, Jim the camera operator was recruited for both his individual photographic expert-ise and his relationship with other camera operators and camera assist-ants. These occupationally based communities serve as repositories of knowledge about their craft and advances in its application. As a result, community attachments tend to prevail over successive project invest-ments. Jim stays in touch with his community of fellow professionals and informally shares with them lessons learned from the latest application of his craft. These communities also provide a place for newcomers to learn from experienced workers as the film-making unfolds.[47]

The organization

Third, knowledge work typically involves one or more organizations that provide the infrastructure through which the work gets done. Most obviously in the film-making example is the independent film-making company itself, often a temporary entity to provide the infrastructure to make a single film. However, there are other companies, too, such as the so-called "major studio" that often finances a new film, and the specialist companies that provide special effects. These kinds of organizations serve as repositories of particular kinds of specialized knowledge, and often seek to both apply and expand their knowledge by attending to the task at hand. Organizations thus participate with one another, as well as with individuals and communities, in performing knowledge work – and in turn in creating the preconditions for future collaborations.

The industry

Finally, the industry itself may be seen as both a participant in and a contributor to the knowledge-based economy. To make *Fierce Creatures*, Cleese and Shamberg needed to attract a variety of specialized resources. Many of these were to be found in Hollywood, California, or in similar locales of film-making activity, such as London. These locales typically provide finance, actors, distribution and marketing capabilities, film production studios, production support staff, and much of the creative talent. The film industry's geographic clustering of its individual, community and organizational participants fosters the dissemination and sharing of best practices (knowing) and innovative contributions (learning) as industry opportunities attract new combinations of participants. The industry is thus the ultimate repository for knowledge that is created and put to work by other knowledge work participants.

THE KNOWLEDGE DIAMOND

Many discussions of knowledge work tend to focus upon a single type of participant, thereby seeking to advise individuals and organizations in particular, and sometimes communities, how to create and use

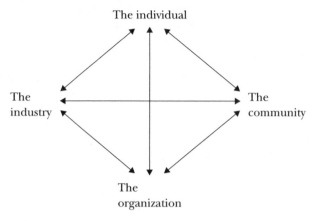

The individual

The
industry

The
community

The
organization

Figure 1.1   The knowledge diamond

knowledge.[48] An alternative, more economically focused perspective involves looking at entire industries.[49] We aspire here to do something different, which is to explain how each of these participants in knowledge work influences, and is in turn influenced by, one another. In so doing, we seek to help the individual knowledge worker gain a fuller picture of the process in which he or she is engaged.

The relationships among the different types of knowledge work participant may be represented in the form of a knowledge diamond, as shown in Figure 1.1. Each of the four points of the diamond corresponds to a focal participant, whose knowledge work activity both influences and is influenced by each of the other three points of the diamond. The lines interconnecting each of the four points represent the possible types of interaction and influence that may arise between any pair of knowledge work participants.

The knowledge diamond thus suggests that the individual participant in knowledge work activities can be expected to interact with three other types of participant – community, organization and industry – through the kind of work he or she takes on. Communities, notably but not exclusively occupational communities, also engage with their individual members – as well as organizations and industries – through trade, professional and industry associations. Organizations engage with individual workers, occupational communities (through company employment and/or outside contracting practices) and industry associations. Industries engage with all of the individuals, communities and organizations as the hosts of knowledge work activities.

The representation of the knowledge diamond needs to be accompanied by two important caveats. First, the model does not imply that each participant has any equal influence on each of the other types of participant. In some knowledge work situations a sponsoring company might be a dominant source of influence on the knowledge work activities of a project team. In other situations the involvement of industry representatives as potential co-sponsors, for example in determining industry standards, may be critical. In further situations an external community, such as an online user group involved with a computer software program, may be most influential. Not all interactions among participants are equally important in all knowledge work situations.

A second caveat is that the knowledge diamond will never represent a closed system. Rather, it will always be a "diamond among diamonds" where individuals, communities, organizations and whole industries are in further communication with other knowledge work participants, and where simultaneous, frequently interdependent, knowledge work activities are unfolding at the same time. The knowledge diamond represents one particular piece of a much larger open system of knowledge application and creation. The value of the model is to emphasize that for any identifiable activity, all four types of knowledge work participant are likely to be involved.

THE CHAPTERS TO FOLLOW

Each of the next four chapters of our book will focus on one of the four participants depicted in the knowledge diamond. In Chapter 2 we will examine how knowledge workers personally engage in knowledge work with other individuals and how those interactions influence and are influenced by interactions from other points of the knowledge diamond. Chapter 3 then examines the various kinds of community attachments that knowledge workers have with people inside and outside their immediate work environment. Chapter 4 examines the organization as the sponsor of knowledge work activities and details a variety of organizational strategies for fostering knowledge work. Chapter 5 next describes how the host industry can provide institutionalized support for fostering productive interactions among the other types of knowledge work participants.

These four chapters on the knowledge diamond are followed by five additional chapters that take up important themes about knowledge at work. Chapter 6 examines the role of projects for organizing knowledge work and fostering learning among its various participants. Chapter 7 examines the virtual organization of knowledge work and dispersed knowledge workers made possible by advances in information technology and virtual collaboration tools. Chapter 8 examines global knowledge work as pursued by multinational companies and through international collaborative ventures. Chapter 9 examines the role of intellectual property in facilitating the distribution of economic returns to creators and users of knowledge at work. Chapter 10 concludes our journey with a summation of lessons learned and some implications for effective participation in the knowledge economy.

QUESTIONS FOR REFLECTION

1   In what types of industries or organizations do you see the demand for knowledge workers growing? Do you anticipate that the overall demand for knowledge workers in your national economy will go up or go down?

2   What is the role of tacit knowledge in your work? What is your organization's approach to tacit knowledge?

3   What situations have you experienced in your own life, as a worker or a consumer, that reflect competing claims to the ownership of knowledge?

4   Chapter 1 suggests that knowing provides a platform for learning. Does this apply to your own work experience? If so, how or how not?

5   How can organizations promote greater learning from their knowledge workers? What policies and practices are likely to constrain knowledge work and learning?

6   What kind of behavioral tools have you used or seen used in your own work experience? What about IT tools? How have these tools helped you or your organization promote knowledge generation or learning?

7   Can you name and briefly describe at least one of each of the four types of knowledge work participant active in an industry that is familiar to you?

NOTES

1   Brown, J.S. and Duguid, P. (2002) .The Social Life of Information, Boston, Harvard Business School Press.
2   Source of the case study: fieldnotes by Robert DeFillippi.
3   DeFillippi, R.J. and Arthur, M.B. (1998) "Paradox in project-based enterprise: the case of film-making," California Management Review, 40 (2), 125–39.

4   Drucker, P. (1959) *Landmarks of Tomorrow*, New York, Harper Collins, p. 210.
5   UK Department of Trade and Industry (1998) *Building the Knowledge-Driven Economy*, White Paper.
6   See "Framework for a knowledge-based economy," World Bank website, www.worldbank.org/wbi/knowledgefordevelopment.
7   Davenport, T.H. (2005) *Thinking for a Living*, Boston, Harvard Business School Press.
8   Ibid.
9   Grant, R. (2002) *Contemporary Strategy Analysis*, Malden, MA, Blackwell, pp. 141–3.
10 US Census Bureau Foreign Trade Statistics, *US International Trade in Goods and Services*, compiled by APS Office of Public Affairs, www.futureofinnovation.org.
11 The Economist Intelligence Unit (2005) *The 2005 e-Readiness Rankings*.
12 Adapted from Exhibit 8.1 "Growth in Internet activity," in G.G. Dess, G.T. Lumpkin and M.L. Taylor (2005) *Strategic Management*, 2nd edn, McGraw-Hill Irwin.
13 Davenport, *Thinking for a Living*, p. 10.
14 Bell, D. (1976) *The Coming of Post-Industrial Society: A Venture in Social Forecasting*, New York, Basic; Fuller, S. (1992) "Knowledge as product and property," in N. Stehr and R.B. Ericson (eds), *The Culture and Power of Knowledge: Inquiries into Contemporary Societies*, Berlin, de Gruyter, pp. 773–96; Davis, G.B., Collins, R.W., Eirman, M. and Nance, W. (1991) *Conceptual Model for Research on Knowledge Work*, Management Information Systems Research Center Working Paper 91-10, University of Minnesota, Minneapolis; Davis, G.B. and Nauman, J.D. (1997) *Personal Productivity with Information Technology*, New York, McGraw-Hill.
15 Leonard, D. and Swap, W. (2005) *Deep Smarts*, Boston, Harvard Business School Press.
16 DeFillippi, R. and Arthur, M. (2002) "Career creativity to industry influence: a blueprint for the knowledge economy?," in M.A. Peiperl, M.B. Arthur and N. Anand (eds), *Career Creativity: Explorations in the Remaking of Work*, Oxford, Oxford University Press.
17 Stewart, T.A. (2003) *The Wealth of Knowledge: Intellectual Capital and the 21st Century Organization*, New York, Random House, p. 10.
18 Kanter, R.M. (2001) *Evolve! Succeeding in the Digital Culture of Tomorrow*, Boston, Harvard Business School Press, p. 223.
19 Ibid.
20 Atkinson, R.D. (2003) *The Innovation Economy: A New Vision for Economic Growth in the 21st Century*, Washington, DC, Progressive Policy Institute, http://www.ppionline.org/ppi_ci.cfm?knlgAreaID=107&subsecID=123&contentID=252104.
21 Polanyi, M. (1966) *The Tacit Dimension*, London, Routledge and Kegan Paul, p. 4.
22 Dalkir, K. (2005) *Knowledge Management in Theory and Practice*, Oxford, Elsevier Butterworth-Heinemann.

23 Derived from a variety of public materials including Wingfield, N. and Smith, E. (2003) "With the web shaking up music, a free-for-all in on-line songs," *Wall Street Journal*, 11 (19); Wingfield, N. and Smith, E. (2003) "Microsoft plans to sell music over the web," *Wall Street Journal*, 11 (17); www.roxio.com; also Howkins, J. (2001) *The Creative Economy*, New York, Penguin, pp. 61–5.

24 McManus, Sean (2003) *A Short History of File Sharing*, blog, http://www.sean.co.uk/a/musicjournalism/var/historyoffilesharing.shtm, accessed July 21, 2005.

25 *The Napster Controversy*, http://iml.jou.ufl.edu/projects/Spring01/Burkhalter Napster%20history.html.

26 Ibid.

27 Hansell, S. (2005) "Putting the Napster genie back in the bottle," *New York Times*, November 20, 2005, http://www.nytimes.com/2005/11/20/business/yourmoney/20fanning.html?pagewanted=1.

28 Howkins, J. (2001) *The Creative Economy*, New York, Penguin, pp. xii–xiii.

29 *The American Heritage Dictionary of the English Language* (2000), Boston, Houghton Mifflin.

30 Cook, S.D.N. and Brown, J.S. (1999) "Bridging epistemologies: the generative dance between organizational knowledge and organizational knowing," *Organization Science*, 10 (4), 381–400.

31 Similar views on the relationship between knowing and learning may be found in Amin, A. and Cohendet, P. (2004) *Architectures of Knowledge*, Oxford, Oxford University Press; Newell, S., Robertson, M., Scarbrough, H. and Swan, J. (2002) *Managing Knowledge Work*, London, Palgrave; and Orlikowski, W.J. (2002) "Knowing in practice: enacting a collective capability in distributed organizing," *Organization Science*, 13 (3), 249–73.

32 Hammer, M. (2004) "Deep change: how operational innovation can transform your company," *Harvard Business Review*, April, 85–93.

33 Prichard, C., Hull, R., Chumer, M. and Willmott, H. (2000) *Managing Knowledge: Critical Investigations of Work and Learning*. London: Macmillan.

34 Robinson, D. and Miner, A. (1996) "Careers change as organizations learn," in Arthur, M.B. and Rousseau, D.M. (eds) *The Boundaryless Career*, New York, Oxford University Press, pp. 76–94.

35 Campbell, D. (1969) "Variation and selective retention in sociocultural evolution," *General Systems*, 16, 69–85.

36 Cook and Brown, "Bridging epistemologies."

37 Argyris, C. and Schon, D.A. (1974) *Theory in Practice: Increasing Professional Effectiveness*, San Francisco, Jossey-Bass.

38 Wenger, E. (1998) *Communities of Practice: Learning, Meaning and Identity*, Cambridge, Cambridge University Press.

39 Leonard-Barton, D. (1995) *Wellsprings of Knowledge*, Boston, Harvard Business School Press.

40 Barton, D. and Swap, W.C. (2005) *When Sparks Fly: Igniting Creativity in Groups*, Boston, Harvard Business School Press.

41   Awad, E.M. and Ghaziri, H.M. (2004) *Knowledge Management*, Upper Saddle River, NJ, Pearson Prentice Hall.
42   Rao, M. (2005) *Knowledge Management Tools and Techniques*, Oxford, Elsevier.
43   See subsequent chapters of this volume.
44   Rao, *Knowledge Management.*
45   Portions of the following argument were inspired by H.W. Chesbrough (2003) *Open Innovation*, Boston, Harvard Business School Press.
46   Gherardi, S., Nicolini, D. and Odella, F. (1998) "Toward a social understanding of how people learn in organizations: the notion of situated curriculum," *Management Learning*, 29, 274.
47   We owe a major debt of gratitude to the groundbreaking work of John Seely Brown and Paul Duguid, whose stream of work on communities of practice has deeply influenced the co-authors of this volume.
48   See C. Argyris and D. Schön (1978) *Organization Learning: A Theory of Action Perspective*, Reading, MA, Jossey-Bass, for an exemplar of an individual perspective on knowledge and learning, albeit within organizations; see J.S. Brown and P. Duguid (1991) "Organizational learning and communities of practice: toward a unified view of working, learning and innovation," *Organization Science*, 2 (1), 40–57, for an exemplar of a community perspective on knowledge and learning; and see R.R. Nelson and S.G. Winter (1982) *An Evolutionary theory of Economic Change*, Cambridge, MA, Harvard University Press, for an exemplar of an organization perspective on knowledge and learning.
49   See J.C. Spender (1989) *Industry Recipes: An Enquiry into the Nature and Sources of Managerial Judgment*, Oxford, Blackwell, for an exemplar of an industry perspective on knowledge and learning.

CHAPTER 2

INDIVIDUAL KNOWLEDGE AT WORK

The opportunities are clear: an adaptive workforce for which getting ahead means getting better – growing in skills, growing ideas, or finding ever more challenging arenas in which to apply skills and ideas.

Rosabeth Moss Kanter[1]

The skilled, adaptive and learning-driven individual knowledge worker is fundamental to the contemporary economy. Each worker brings a unique combination of individual motivation, expertise and personal relationships to the workplace. Each worker also interacts with various peers, mentors, protégés, community members, organizational colleagues and fellow industry travelers in going about his or her work. As those interactions unfold, individual workers influence and are influenced by other knowledge work participants. Understanding individuals, and the roles that they play, is fundamental to any wider appreciation of how knowledge work gets done.

A necessary but insufficient view of individuals sees them as free agents, representing their own interests in the unfolding knowledge economy. However, individuals' value to themselves and the economy also depends on their willingness and ability to build trusting relationships with others. Trust building in turn calls into question the nature of an individual's networks. These can take two complementary forms, involving strong ties with few people or weak ties with many people. These forms have contrasting implications for how individual knowledge workers collaborate.

Let us now turn to our opening example.

Mary Lakis[2]

From an early age, Mary enjoyed performing for her family in Sunday afternoon plays. Her love of theater persisted through high school and university, where she was a commuter student at Long Island University, New York. On her family's advice she majored in English, but she took elective classes in theater when she could.

At university, Mary maintained links with her high school drama coach, who ran a small professional theater. She would work lights, paint sets, do anything that needed doing just to stay involved. After graduation she set her sights on professional acting, waited on tables to pay the bills, and signed up for classes at two New York drama schools. One acting coach was particularly inspirational, not only for his talent, but also because "he would take this skill and he would go and do seminars at large corporations . . . on how to give presentations." Mary saw in her coach's behavior "a neat way to have business and theater in balance."

Mary arranged with the package delivery company FedEx to work on Mondays and Saturdays, keeping the rest of her time available for auditions, rehearsals and performances. FedEx soon recognized Mary's potential as a responsible and creative worker (especially in helping with clip-art and presentations), and had already offered her a full-time job when she was involved in a serious car accident. While her acting friends were calling and sending flowers, it was FedEx that was paying the bills. She took the job, determined to apply what her new coach had described as the Jimmy Stewart theory of acting: "Plant your feet, look them in the eye, and tell the truth."

She began in customer service, applying the Jimmy Stewart theory to customer relations, and later to a temporary assignment for the regional director. She applied for a position specializing in hazardous materials, wore a lab coat at the interview, and described how she was going to "bring a little biology, a little chemistry and a little physics" to the role. She toured the country training couriers and service agents, and imagined herself as one of the senior managers with whom she interacted. She became a company expert on dangerous goods coordination, filled in for a colleague unable to visit the Far East, and determined she wanted to work overseas. However, she needed management experience back in the US first.

Mary accepted a management position in New England. In the language of the theater, she worked on "adding dimensions" to her character as a manager, in for example financial analysis, technical awareness, and inter-department coordination, and simultaneously began to study part-time for a Master of Business Administration (MBA) degree. She applied theater concepts to package delivery, which she saw involving "an entire troupe or acting company" working to get a package to its destination.

Just as good theater companies would share scripts and swap parts to make better use of everyone's talents, so could FedEx team members collaborate in getting the work done, and helping one another in the process.

Two years and two jobs later Mary was "digging her way to China" interviewing for an operations management position in Guangao. This would be "the next layer to the character" in terms of helping to grow an office, learning to work in a different culture, and building new relationships not only within FedEx but also with expatriates, local farmers, chamber of commerce members, legal and government representatives, and more. Meanwhile, Mary was scheduling her leave time "to get back to the home office, keep in touch with your peers [and] your old bosses, because they are going to have to help you find a job when this is wrapped up."

On one of her trips home Mary was introduced to a headhunter at a party. Several months later she was offered two positions, one to relocate with FedEx to Mexico, the other to stay in New England as Director of Customer Service for the sporting goods company Spalding. The customer service role involved the greater learning curve, and made Mary anxious. However, she returned to her lessons from theater: "Choose your roles carefully . . . [Each will] craft the next layers for [your] character to bring to the next role." She had experience in a service-driven company, in conflict resolution, and in the operational issues behind customer service. She determined to "leave the size and security [of FedEx] and jump into something small."

The FedEx President of Asia impressed upon Mary to call him "if ever there's a blip on the radar screen." FedEx, he said, would always welcome her back. She has kept in touch with him as well as with other friends from old company, customer, acting and MBA circles, and the National Association of Female Executives. She was enjoying making new friends at Spalding, where there was "some comedy, some tragedy and a little bit of everything thrown in." She had already shared the Jimmy Stewart theory of acting – she used it in her interview!

There is much in Mary's story that reflects the distinction between knowing and learning introduced in the first chapter. Mary engaged in knowing, that is acting on the knowledge she already held, when she drew on her theater background to help her succeed in FedEx customer relations, and later to promote the kind of teamwork she sought for effective package delivery. She later used her knowledge about operations and conflict resolution in taking the customer service director's job at Spalding. However, at the same time Mary was also engaged in learning. She was ready to try new things, in learning about transportation of hazardous materials, national and international package delivery systems, living in a foreign culture, and directing customer services as part of a senior management team.

The example of Mary also helps us to see how knowing and learning are interdependent with each other. What Mary knew (for example, about acting) informed what she learned (for example, about teamwork in package delivery), which in turn informed what she came to know about FedEx operations. Yet, to see knowledge and learning as interdependent is insufficient. How much we learn from a job is likely to hinge, for example, on the enthusiasm with which we perform that job. Our enthusiasm may wax or wane according to the kind of feedback we receive from a boss or from our workmates. How do we act on what we know, and how do our actions spur new learning activities?

THREE WAYS OF KNOWING

Let us look again at Mary's story. This time we will use it to suggest that knowledge workers invest in three "ways of knowing," each of which the story illustrates.

Knowing-why

First, knowing-why may be described as the individual's response to the question: *why* do we work? Knowing-why investments reflect our underlying motivation to participate in knowledge work, and the related interests, values, sense of identity, and any further lifestyle or family concerns that we bring to the workplace. In Mary's case her knowing-why investments can be traced to a love of acting, moderated by a desire for some level of security in her adult life. This resulted in her taking her first part-time position with FedEx while continuing to pursue theater work. She later drew fresh motivation from the realization that she could apply her theatrical training to help her make sense of her work as she moved through subsequent career positions.[3]

Knowing-how

Second, knowing-how may be described as the individual's response to the question: *how* do we work? Knowing-how investments reflect the skills and expertise that we bring to the workplace, and on which we draw in performing the work that we do. In Mary's case her initial knowing-how investments largely reflected her theatrical talents and related interpersonal skills. As her career progressed, she persistently used her existing talents to open up the opportunity to develop new ones: in operations management, regional management, international operations, and then as a customer services director. In taking this last job she was explicit about how her knowing-how experiences in operations could help her, as well as about the opportunities for new learning.

Knowing-whom

Third, knowing-whom may be described as the individual's response to the question: with *whom* do we work? Knowing-whom investments reflect the relationships that we build around the workplace, and the reputation, trust and access to information embedded in those relationships. In Mary's case the knowing-whom connection that introduced her to FedEx was a family friend. However, she quickly made new friends as people got to know her and to see what she could do. Internal, knowing-whom contacts were important in helping her gain her next three promotions, although it was an external contact made through her neighbor that led Mary to the Spalding opportunity. Mary kept in touch with former company, customer, MBA, and other network contacts as her career progressed.

INTERDEPENDENCE AMONG THE WAYS OF KNOWING

The three ways of knowing do not function independently. Rather, they are continually influencing one another as our careers unfold. Let us look again at the Mary story.

Knowing-why and knowing-how

Mary's enthusiasm for the theater influenced her choice to take her first position with FedEx, and also influenced the skills – borrowed from her stage experience – that she demonstrated. Her identity as an actor also shaped the underlying metaphor, of adding dimensions to her "character," that she used in choosing what new learning to pursue. Conversely, Mary's work experiences also influenced her motivation – for example in imagining she could become a senior manager at FedEx, and in determining that she could succeed in the job at

Spalding. Mary's knowing-why and knowing-how career investments emerged interdependently.

Knowing-why and knowing-whom

Mary's motivation also influenced the relationships that she developed. Her enthusiasm for her work led to lasting friendships with employees and customers of FedEx, with fellow alumni of her MBA program, and with the contacts that helped her to succeed in China. On the other hand, Mary's connections also influenced her motivation. A family friend encouraged her to apply for her first position at FedEx. Later, friends in FedEx and in her MBA program encouraged her career aspirations, and a friend of Mary's neighbor encouraged her to apply for the job at Spalding. Mary's knowing-why and knowing-whom investments also evolved interdependently.

Knowing-how and knowing-whom

Furthermore, Mary's skills and expertise influenced the kind of contacts that she made. First there were people she met because of her talents as an actor, then there were the contacts she made as a direct result of the work roles she took on – in New York, New England, China, and back in New England – as well as from her MBA program. In the other direction, Mary's contacts also influenced her skill development, through her mentors in the theatrical world and later in FedEx and in Spalding. Mary's knowing-how and knowing-whom investments also unfolded interdependently with one another.

We all work through these three ways of knowing. Through knowing-why, we all develop identities and motivations that underlie the choices we make in formal education, and in choosing which jobs we will undertake. Through knowing-how, we all proceed as Mary did to apply existing skills and expertise to our work, as well as to gather new learning to add to our knowledge "portfolios." Through knowing-whom, we all have relationships with other people that may introduce us to a new job, or be the basis of our reputation for future jobs, or provide valuable sources of further information. Through the interplay among knowing-why, knowing-how and knowing-whom, we all develop preferences, seek new challenges, make new contacts, and adapt to the changing world of work over time. We all engage in knowledge work through our own individual ways of knowing.[4]

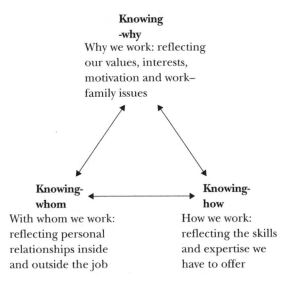

Knowing
-why
Why we work: reflecting
our values, interests,
motivation and work–
family issues

Knowing-   **Knowing-**
whom   **how**
With whom we work: How we work:
reflecting personal   reflecting the skills
relationships inside   and expertise we
and outside the job   have to offer

Figure 2.1   The individual's three ways of knowing

The various links suggested above are represented in Figure 2.1. The interdependent relationships among the three ways of knowing bring us back to the earlier discussion about learning. Learning, like knowing, can be understood to involve more than absorbing new skills or expertise. Learning can also involve shifts in our knowing-why motivation to work, and in our knowing-whom relationships around work. Moreover, learning something that affects any one way of knowing is likely to affect the other two ways of knowing as well. Learning is any act that leads to change in any one or more of the three ways of knowing.

THE INDIVIDUAL AND THE KNOWLEDGE DIAMOND

As we will explore next, individual knowledge work, and learning that stems from it, can involve other individuals or any of the three further participants in the knowledge diamond described in Chapter 1. In the next part of this chapter, we will offer a series of examples of knowledge at work that links the individual worker with another worker, a community, an organization or an industry.

One individual and another

A first link in the knowledge diamond is between like participants, that is, between two individuals with related knowledge investments. These kinds of relationships often prevail beyond the circumstances that brought the individuals together.

Harris's new friend[5]

Harris, a thirty-nine-year-old regulatory affairs director at the health care firm Pharmaco, returned from an executive development program ready for a new job. However, his assignment as a business unit manager was cut short by a corporate merger. Harris and some of his long-serving peers became disenchanted. He agreed with one such peer, Georgina, that Pharmaco had become "more structured, more political and bureaucratic" and understood why she chose to leave the firm for what she saw as a better opportunity.

Georgina later helped Harris to find an offer as Chief Executive Officer of a technology start-up, but the risk and cost of relocating his family were too high. Similar offers followed, but again Harris felt the risks were too high. He determined to keep developing his local contacts, and soon met Gerry, the founder of a regional health care start-up and inventor of a non-competing product. Gerry sought Harris's advice about the regulations affecting the product, and Harris was forthcoming in offering the value of his experience. Gerry seemed grateful, and Harris was glad to help his new friend. Each quickly grew to like and trust the other.

One day Gerry surprised Harris with an offer to become Chief Operating Officer of Gerry's company. Moreover, Gerry had done his homework. He knew how highly Harris was thought of at Pharmaco and was sympathetic about his family situation. Impressed, and encouraged by Georgina and other members of his network, Harris took the job.

Many of us will have seen or directly experienced something similar to Harris's story. The network and support system he built at Pharmaco migrated beyond that company's boundaries. Encouraged by Georgina and other long-standing colleagues, Harris put more energy into developing further outside contacts. The early stages of his relationship with Gerry brought reciprocal rewards, where Gerry gleaned helpful regulatory information, and Harris gained respect as a valued source of industry knowledge. Reciprocity, where each party gains something from the other, is fundamental to any enduring interpersonal relationship. As we will discuss later, the kind of rapid trust building in which both Harris and Gerry invested may be critical in the knowledge-driven economy. The job offer was a surprise to Harris, but job offers frequently do stem from network contacts like Gerry, rather than from formal job postings.[6]

Interpersonal relationships also involve mentor–protégé relationships, where the protégé has the opportunity to draw on the mentor's knowledge and experience. Much has been written about mentoring over the years, but three observations seem particularly important. First, in a world of relatively high job mobility it can make sense for individuals to find mentors outside the present workplace.[7] Second, the mentor's role can often be distributed across more than one person, that is across multiple developmental relationships.[8] Third, few writers have focused on the benefits to the mentor. These include making good use of the knowledge and skill one has accumulated, learning in ways that would otherwise not be possible, and gaining affirmation and respect from a different generation.[9] Mentoring, like other interpersonal relationships, works because there is reciprocity between the two parties.

The individual and the community

A now classic case of the links between individual and community endeavors comes from California's Silicon Valley.

The Homebrew Computer Club[10]

In 1975, Fred Moore, a "vagabond activist" who believed that most problems could be solved by bringing people together, got talking with Gordon French, a consulting engineer who – in the language of local technology enthusiasts – had just "homebrewed" an early microcomputer based on recent Intel chip technology. The pair placed the following notice on a few regional high-school technology company billboards in what is now widely known as California's "Silicon Valley:"

AMATEUR COMPUTER USERS GROUP
HOMEBREW COMPUTER CLUB . . . you name it
Are you building your own computer? Terminal? TV? Typewriter?
I/O device? or some other digital black magic box? Or are you buy-
ing time on a time-sharing service? If so, you might like to come to

a gathering of people with likeminded interests. Exchange information, swap ideas, help work on a project, whatever . . .

The meeting was called for March 5, 1975, at French's home address in
Menlo Park, California.

As the announcement implied, the underlying idea was to start up a
group of people interested in building computers. This would be "[t]heir
own hardware group, and it would be full of good computer talk, shared
electronic technique, maybe a demonstration or two of the latest stuff you
could buy. Just a bunch of hardware hackers seeing what might come of
a somewhat more than random meeting." With the possible exception
of social activist French, "every person in the garage was passionate about
hardware" and about "getting computers into their homes to study, to
play with, [and] to create with." Thirty-two people attended the first meeting, including a number of people later recognized as Silicon Valley high-
technology pioneers.

French later described the group assembled as "the damned finest
collection of engineers and technicians that you could possibly get under
one roof." Among them were a Hewlett-Packard engineer named Alan
Baum, who dragged along his friend and fellow employee Stephen
Wozniak. The group "discussed what they wanted in a club" and concluded
that they were most interested in the free exchange of ideas and information. As one of their number, Lee Felsenstein, later recalled, they were
"a bunch of escapees, at least temporary escapees from industry, [who]
got together and knew this was [their] chance to do something the way
[they] thought it should be done."

Within months of the first meeting, the club's membership had grown
to several hundred. It served as the incubator for a number of Silicon Valley
businesses, including Apple Computer, which was founded by Wozniak
in conjunction with his friend and fellow member Steve Jobs. Meetings
frequently spilled over into informal conversations in local "watering
holes," and the Homebrew Computer Club became the prototype for other
Silicon Valley communities based on similar collaborative principles.

The story of the Homebrew Computer Club is a story of how people
with overlapping motivations and interests can create a community
from the bottom up, and in turn contribute to the unfolding knowledge economy. The Club is now disbanded, but many similar com
munities formed in Silicon Valley in its wake. We will return to the
combined effects of those communities, and the emergent outcomes for
the host industry, in later chapters.[11]

The individual and the organization

A further link in the knowledge diamond is that between individuals and organizations. Here, the behavior of partners in small professional service firms, and how those partners contribute to the knowledge work of their firms, provides an interesting example.

Partners in architectural practice[12]

A study of twenty small architectural firms examined how those firms' partners went about their careers, and how those careers contributed to each firm's survival and development. It emerged that the partners were not equally attracted to all work opportunities. Instead, partners commonly identified with and become personally excited about the work they took on. One partner reported, "We are doing a visitors' center that's very unique architecturally. It's a once-in-a-lifetime building, truly an architectural piece." By contrast, partners were disinclined to perform what they saw as humdrum work: "I did a jail . . . I have the skills for it . . . but jails are not a real fun project . . . They're so dreary . . . so depressing . . . the materials are just real basic."

Partners were concerned to both apply and develop their own and their firms' architectural skills. One approach was to take on small projects to build customer confidence: "The State agency is a tough place to break into. We did it by going after little projects – little by little we got larger projects." A second approach was for the partners to recruit people who possessed specialist skills. A third approach was to team up with and learn from another firm that held distinctive expertise: "I think anybody starting into the business cannot be successful unless they do teaming . . . Teaming brings new skills and a new understanding of how to do projects."

Partners were also deeply aware of the role of relationships in determining whether they would receive further work. One informant spoke of the need for clients to "feel that you are on their side on the job and that if there is a question or a situation that you are available and anxious to talk about it." Another spoke of the importance of staying closely connected to key institutional decision-makers: "Public relations is very, very important . . . You have to get to know the people in the industry, the State for example . . . You need to get to know institutions, their people and the people who finance a building, and building people [such as contractors]."

The study suggests that partners in architectural firms made distinctive career investments. These involved (1) bringing particular kinds of motivation to their practice (knowing-why), (2) exercising distinctive choices about the kind of work they took on and the complementary skills they sought (knowing-how), and (3) building relationships either to get closer to particular clients or to build more diverse social contacts (knowing-whom). Moreover, not only did partners make distinctive career investments, but also those investments evolved into three patterns or "dominant logics" that drove the knowledge-based investments of the partners' firms. One logic was grounded in the idea of distinctive *competence*, that is, in the firm's particular design skills and experience. A second logic was *relational*, concerned with developing relationships with key clients or sponsoring agencies. A third logic was *calculative*, focusing on the firm's prospective markets, and switching between clients and collaborators to better compete in those markets (Table 2.1).

Table 2.1   Dominant logics of architectural firms and their partners' knowledge investments[13]

Dominant logic of the firm	Partners' individual career investments		
	Knowing-why	Knowing-how	Knowing-whom
Competence: involving a focus on the firm's professional capabilities and their development	Push the technical or aesthetic envelope; develop unique solutions to complex problems	Cultivate state-of-the-art expertise; develop this through smaller projects or external collaborations	Seek out key clients, decision-makers; build long-term, performance-based relationships
Relational: involving a focus on the firm's relationships with clients and other relevant players	Emphasize helping key clients; seek to become liked and trusted by those clients	Identify and understand client needs; expand into new areas in response to client needs	Empathize with clients; build reciprocity by taking smaller, less profitable jobs
Calculative: involving a focus on the firm's markets, with frequent switching of clients, collaborators	Meet the business challenges that emerge from the firm's changing markets	Develop skill sets in project management and negotiation; hire outside experts as needed	Learn about different contractor systems; promote the firm's image in the industry

The architectural firms' study suggests that partners pursue their careers in a way that influences the dominant logic of their firms. Similar dominant logics can be found in other professional service firms, such as in law or management consulting.[14] The more general point is that people's career investments often influence the strategies of their employer organizations, even if those organizations' strategies simultaneously influence people's careers.

The individual and the industry

A final link in the knowledge diamond that concerns us here is that between individuals and the host industry. An example of how individual knowledge investments can lead to industry outcomes comes from a study of successful women in the entertainment industry.

Women in entertainment[15]

Interviews were conducted with a group of fifteen executive women who were recognized as successful players in the entertainment industry. The women were all college educated, but none of them began their careers with any significant industry contacts.

All of the women had to find a way to break into what they saw as a male-dominated industry. They did so by being motivated to move to where the industry was located, and to find a first position, usually by taking on volunteer work, or performing temporary, low-paid labor as secretaries or assistants. For example, one of the women took a job as a restaurant hostess, and volunteered to work on a Hispanic television marathon. When the assistant producer quit she was asked to do cue cards. Despite her lack of Spanish, she was able to figure out what to do over the twelve hours that the show was broadcast. The appreciative producer then offered her a job as a production assistant, making her "happy to be getting donuts and building sets" in return for enjoying the opportunity to learn more about the industry.

The women's low status and lack of experience in the industry meant that each of them had to pursue career strategies involving rapid movement through on-the-job learning experiences. One woman described spending a year with Creative Artists Agency as a "year of hell," but one that served her well: "[Y]ou learn so much and the resources available to you are so broad that you can really educate yourself very quickly. The contacts you make are lifelong. My goal was not to get tracked as an assistant. [It was] to get . . . so good, so fast that you get out. I was up-front with my boss about my goals and she told me that if I stayed for a year, she would help me find my next (and better) position."

Personal networks appear critical to success in the entertainment industry. Most of the women relied heavily on informal networks that extended from their work situations to their social environments. These networks provided both psychological support and practical assistance. One woman was fired on the same day as a scheduled party to celebrate the start of a new show she had bought. She went to the party, told everyone she was fired and "was touched by the amount of support and help that I got." A prominent company president guided her to get-ting into the media network he oversaw, which led in turn to her next position.

All of the women came to hold influential positions in their adopted industry. Eleven became high-status vice-presidents, senior vice-presidents or presidents in large entertainment companies – television networks, affiliates, cable stations or production companies. The other four owned and managed their own independent production companies or were highly placed "show runners" – freelancers in charge of all aspects of a show's management, including creative decisions and budgetary accountability.

The interplay of the women's commitment to the industry (knowing-why), to learning about it through on-the-job experience (knowing-how) and to building interpersonal networks (knowing-whom) led to them each holding influential positions in their adopted entertainment industry. All of the women attained their latest positions through knowledge invest-ments, but were not focused on or subordinated to any particular occupa-tional group or company. Rather, all of the women sought to work in and learn about the overall industry of their choice. In turn, all of them became prominent and influential industry players.

KEEPING THE INDIVIDUAL IN VIEW

Let us review the story of this chapter so far. The channels through which individuals participate in the knowledge diamond are highlighted in Figure 2.2. These involve simultaneous, two-way communications between individuals and all four of: (1) other individuals, (2) work-related communities, (3) one or more organizations and (4) a host industry. The individual invests in these communications on behalf of his or

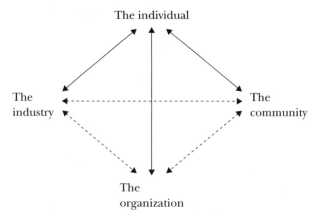

The individual

The industry

The community

The organization

Figure 2.2 The individual and the knowledge diamond

her career. In the process, knowledge generation and transfer occur among all four knowledge diamond participants. It is worth reemphasizing that the view of knowledge work offered here is distinct from any view grounded in orderly "levels of analysis" from the individual to the work group to the organization and in turn to the industry. The evidence presented suggests that any presumption of levels of analysis will provide only a partial picture, and distort our view of how knowledge work unfolds.

The story of the individual knowledge worker is also a story about personal networks, where the knowledge diamond invites us to ask what purpose an individual's network connections may serve. Does a network contact involve a straightforward case of reciprocity between two people? Or does the contact connect a person to a distinctive community (like the Homebrew Computer Club), an organization (like an architectural firm) or an industry (such as the entertainment industry)?

The story also involves the World Wide Web, as a vehicle for people to participate in knowledge work through virtual as well as physical interactions. How do people use the web for developing personal networks, contributing to professional communities, working with fellow employees and tracking industry developments? What does the web mean for the overall pace of knowledge exchange across all four knowledge diamond participants? These kinds of questions will be more fully addressed in later chapters.

OTHER WAYS OF KNOWING?

I keep six honest serving-men
(They taught me all I knew)
Their names are What and Why and When
And How and Where and Who
Rudyard Kipling, Just So Stories, 1902

The three ways of knowing described earlier in this chapter suggest an integrative way to think about individual knowledge investments. To put it another way, the three ways of knowing offer a framework for "personal knowledge management," that is, for systematically building personal knowledge around our individual interests and aspirations.[16] However, Kipling's poem suggests there may be other ways of knowing, other "wise men" that we have so far not considered. How can we reconcile Kipling's suggestion with what we previously described?

A distinction is offered in some writing between what is described as formal knowledge (most usually called knowing-what, but also called knowing-that or knowing-about) and practical knowledge (commonly called knowing-how).[17] This distinction can be useful, for example, to highlight the difference between classroom learning and later application of that learning, or between formal instructions and people's ability to follow those instructions. However, the distinction may be more useful in theory than in practice.

Henry Mintzberg draws an analogy with the skilled potter, who "knows exactly what has not worked for [him or] her in the past," and who gathers new learning through the further application of [his or] her craft.[18] The analogy suggests that formal knowledge is embedded in the further practice through which work gets done. That is, in the world of practice, knowing-what gets embedded in and expressed through knowing-how. Embedding formal knowledge within a person's knowing-how investments also allows us to examine complementarities with other knowledge diamond participants, as we will see in later chapters.

Knowing-where and knowing-when may be related to the location and timing of work arrangements respectively. Regarding knowing-where, the location of work arrangements involves issues about where potential employers are to be found, and where sought-after industries are concentrated. These issues include the potential for overseas location of manufacturing and service work, and telecommuting opportunities, all now greatly enhanced by the emergence of the World Wide Web.

Regarding knowing-when, it is necessary not only to be in the right place but also to be there at the right time. This involves such issues as an individual's visibility to prospective employers, and readiness to take on a job when it needs to be done.[19] However, once issues of location and timing are resolved, the framework of knowing-why, knowing-how and knowing-whom provides an effective way of examining individual knowledge work activities.[20]

FREE AGENCY AND TRUST

The chapter so far suggests two things. First, "free agency" is good – in the sense that we need to take charge of our careers, know where we are trying to go, and trade knowledge that will help us get there. Second, trust building is also good – in the sense that trust can open up the opportunities through which to succeed in the knowledge economy.[21] Yet, most readers will have been in situations where they felt badly let down by a trusted other, where they determined their mistake was to trust too easily, or where they picked up credible clues that the other party could not be relied upon. Moreover we live in a society that appears to encourage distrust. Our economic systems seem to encourage person-to-person competition, and our legal systems assume an adversarial relationship between the parties. When asked, most people say they don't trust most other people.[22] How are we to make sense of free agency and trust together?

If we reduce free agency to the simple idea of investing in the three ways of knowing, and doing so on our own terms, then free agency appears to work. For example, a study of University of Georgia alumni demonstrated that people who worked most through the three ways of knowing reported higher levels of career success than their counterparts.[23] One key to this kind of result may lie in the link between professional identity (knowing-why) and reputation (knowing-whom). A person's identity – of being a plain dealer, a dependable friend, a true professional, etc. – can be a powerful driver of trust building behavior.[24] A second key may be in the process through which interpersonal trust is built. A University of Toronto experiment in negotiation found that a simple "tit-for-tat" approach – trust the person a little, see if he or she trusts you back, if so trust the other person a little more, and so on – can outperform more complicated approaches.[25] Moreover, once a reputation has been gained, trust is further encouraged by the "embeddedness" of that relationship within larger social ties.[26] Trust can also provide the flexibility to adapt to changing times in a way that legal contracts do not allow.[27]

Yet some have argued that free agency can be socially harmful, leading to what Richard Sennett has described as a "corrosion of character." Sennett argues that this corrosion needs to be addressed "by loyalty and mutual commitment, or through the pursuit of long-term goals, or by the practice of delayed gratification for the sake of a future end." In contrast, however, Karl Weick has argued that individual agency and interpersonal communion – that is, making communal social investments – need to function together. Communion "enables organizing, learning, and trust" and allows for continuity in the face of shifting formal arrangements. The payback for knowledge workers is that people who can integrate agency and communion should "develop faster because they learn more."[28] The earlier examples about Mary's continued support from former FedEx colleagues, the collaborations through the Homebrew Computer Club, and the women in entertainment where interpersonal relationships opened new learning opportunities, all support Weick's argument.

NETWORKS AND SOCIAL CAPITAL

Networks among people are commonly represented as a set of points or nodes (representing individuals) and a series of links or ties between pairs of nodes (representing relationships between individuals). These kinds of networks typically involve both bridging and bonding.[29] *Bridging* involves making a new tie or sustaining an existing tie between individuals, across what would otherwise be a "hole" in the overall social structure. *Bonding* involves the development of strong ties, based on the time spent, trust built and degree of reciprocal services established between two people. Both bridging and bonding can contribute to a person's social capital, which may be defined simply as "the advantage created by a person's location in a structure of relationships."[30]

Figure 2.3 illustrates both bridging and bonding activities. Ann is an employee of a large software company working closely with one of her employer's corporate customers. Ann has several bridges into two main groups, one of fellow software programmers in her own company, the other of software users at the customer site. Ann also provides a medium for communications between these two groups. Liz, in contrast, performs similar work to Ann and is connected to her fellow employees and customers. However, Liz also has bridges to other groups, to other local professionals, to an online group of software writers, and to a friendship group representing a range of companies and occupations. Let us assume for the sake of illustration that Liz and Ann both invest equally in the overall set of five relationships represented for each of them.[31]

The contrast between Ann and Liz invites a series of questions. Ann has multiple contacts in each of only two groups, while Liz has single contacts in five groups. Does this mean that Ann has bonded better with people in her two groups than Liz? If so, can Ann benefit from the more trusting relationships she has built? Or are the bonds so strong, and the communications lines so repetitive, that there is a risk of "groupthink" inhibiting alternative ideas? In contrast, do Liz's bridges into five different groups provide her with access to a wider range of information? If so, is the level of trust between Liz and her contacts sufficient for her to rely on what she hears? Each of us makes choices about bridging and bonding with direct consequences for our access to personally useful knowledge, and our capacity to share that knowledge with others.

The knowledge diamond suggests we need both bridging and bonding behavior. Bridging allows for the initiation of contacts between individual parties representing themselves, or their communities, or their organizations, or their host industries through which knowledge transfer can occur. Bonding allows for the kind of interpersonal trust building that is likely to sustain the relationships that have been previously

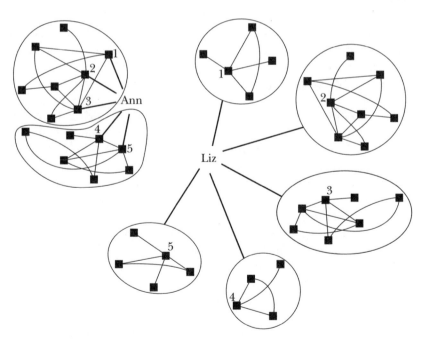

Figure 2.3 Example network maps for two knowledge workers[32]

initiated. Bridging can span existing "holes" in the social structure, while bonding can encourage the flow of information and ideas across bridges.[33] The challenge is to seek to optimize both functions – that is to most effectively leverage one's overall social capital – in contributing to knowledge work activities.

TOOLS FOR INDIVIDUALS

What kind of tools exist to help people manage their careers in the knowledge-based economy? One prominent set of tools seeks to link individual personality, interests or values (all aspects of knowing-why) to the choices we make to enter into, continue with, or transition out of a particular line of work (knowing-how). For example, the Strong Interest Inventory (SII) is often used to guide a person toward the kind of occupations in which he or she is likely to feel satisfied. Tools based directly on personality theory, such as the Myers–Briggs Type Indicator (MBTI), can guide people to better appreciate the effect of their own personalities on their everyday work behavior.[34] Another set of tools offers "360 degree feedback" from relevant co-workers about an individual's job performance, thereby making a link from knowing-whom to knowing-how.[35] Tools concerned with "emotional intelligence" examine both self-awareness and awareness of others, suggesting both personal (knowing-why) and reference group (knowing-whom) data likely to affect an individual's work performance (knowing-how).[36]

The web has provided a means for individuals to communicate and share with others their interests (knowing-why), skills (knowing-how) and relationships (knowing-whom). Many knowledge workers have personal and/or organizationally sanctioned websites for connecting with like-minded others. An increasing number of people have developed "web logs," a term now commonly reduced to "blogs," which are websites that permit periodic postings and provide a venue for visitors to read and post comments.[37] Blogs are created to serve a variety of purposes, including relationship building, branding, selling, knowledge sharing and collaboration.[38] Blogs can greatly extend the reach of individual knowledge workers, and contribute to the greater circulation of knowledge and knowledge work collaboration across time and space, a topic further explored in Chapter 7.

Additional tools invite us to focus on the knowledge and skills we possess (that is, knowing-how) and to consider ways to upgrade what we can do, or to make what we can do applicable in alternative employment settings.[39] Organizations frequently provide "performance appraisals," which invite a particular focus on the jobs we perform, and on how job performance might be improved.[40] Frequently, useful data can be gained by simply asking others. Our friends and colleagues often know a great deal about what excites us, how we tend to work, and how we behave toward other people.[41] Another set of tools involves mapping and interpreting personal networks (knowing-whom), either to examine the sources of information we have or to examine the guidance and support we have access to in managing our future careers. One such tool is social network analysis, through which we can examine our overall set of career-relevant contacts and look for patterns within it.[42] Another tool is the developmental network questionnaire, through which we can examine the influence of the key mentors and supporters we listen to in developing our careers.[43]

The Intelligent Career Card Sort® (ICCS®), so named after the title of an early article describing the three ways of knowing, is a career exploration exercise that allows for the examination of individual career investments in each of the knowing-why, knowing-how and knowing-whom arenas. Individuals are invited to use an online instrument to select and rank seven important statements about their careers for each of the three ways of knowing. The individuals may then work with a career coach or consultant directly, or under supervision in small groups, to interpret their selections and develop future action plans. A variation of the exercise allows groups or communities with shared career interests to participate in online focus groups, and to examine shared career investments and future agendas. The ICCS® can also be used with other tools, since the underlying three ways of knowing allow for a variety of career-relevant data to be integrated within the same theoretical framework.[44] Moreover, there is firm evidence that people who make the greater investments in the three ways of knowing report higher levels of career success than their counterparts.[45]

SUMMARY

Individuals participate in the knowledge economy through three ways of knowing – *knowing-why, knowing-how* and *knowing-whom* – concerning why, how and with whom we work, respectively. The three ways of knowing are interdependent as we each, for example, bring our motivation to work to our present job, meet others through that job, and reflect on the feedback that they provide. The three ways of knowing also link individual knowledge work to other participants in the knowledge diamond, that is to other individuals, to the communities to which we get attached, to the organizations that provide work, and to the industries that host our work.

Part of the story of the unfolding knowledge economy involves how individuals influence these other participants, as was illustrated in the examples about Harris finding a new job, Homebrew Computer Club members' launching and shaping their community, architects influencing their organizational practice, and executive women contributing to the entertainment industry. There is no necessary tradeoff between free agency and trust building, or between bridging and bonding, in interpersonal behavior. However, there are persistent challenges in managing the level of trust in interpersonal relationships, and the pace at which that trust develops, to maximize individual learning. A variety of tools, many of them web based, can help individuals to engage in knowledge work on their own terms.

QUESTIONS FOR REFLECTION

1   *Why* do you work? How do your own personal identity, values, talents, life and family situation affect your overall motivation to work? What examples can you provide?
2   *How* do you work? How do your education, training, skills, and work and life experience affect the way you work and learn? What examples can you provide?
3   With *whom* do you work? How do your relationships both inside and outside the workplace affect your work experience? What examples can you provide?
4   What *connections* do you see in the three accounts above? How do your knowing-why, knowing-how and knowing-whom investments affect one another? Can you provide examples of each kind of connection (for example from knowing-why to knowing-how), that is of six one-directional connections overall?
5   Assume your place as an individual in the knowledge diamond. How do your own knowledge investments relate to those of (a) other individuals, (b) communities, (c) organizations and (d) the industry in which you work? Again, can you provide examples?
6   What is your own experience of (a) the relationship between free agency and trust building, and (b) how each of bridging and bonding affects your present career situation?
7   What tools have you used in your own knowledge work activities? How have these helped or hindered your career to this point?

NOTES

1 Kanter, R.M. (1989) *When Giants Learn to Dance*, New York, Simon & Schuster, p. 320.

2 Source: case notes taken by Michael Arthur.

3 We use the term "career" to mean a person's – any person's – sequence of work experiences over time. This intentionally avoids any social attribution, and leaves any further interpretation of the meaning of career or career success to the person. See Arthur, M.B., Khapova, S.N. and Wilderom, C.P.M. (2005) "Career success in a boundaryless career world," *Journal of Organizational Behavior*, 26, 177–202.

4 See for example Arthur, M.B., Claman, P.H. and DeFillippi, R.J. (1995) "Intelligent enterprise, intelligent careers," *Academy of Management Executive*, 9 (4), 7–22; DeFillippi, R.J. and Arthur, M.B. (1996) "Boundaryless contexts and careers: a competency based perspective," in M.B. Arthur and D.M. Rousseau (eds), *The Boundaryless Career*, New York, Oxford University Press, pp. 116–31; Inkson, K. and Arthur, M.B. (2001) "How to be a successful career capitalist," *Organizational Dynamics*, 30 (1), 48–61.

5 Ibarra, H. (2003) *Working Identity*, Boston, Harvard Business School Press, pp. 114–19.

6 Various claims on the web state that a "hidden job market" accounts for between 60% and 80% of job openings being filled by way of networking rather than formal job posting. However, it is difficult to find current or systematic data, and any data will vary by country, region and occupation. A 1999 survey by Drake, Beam and Morin has been a popularly cited source, and that company's website currently claims "2/3 of us find our next jobs through networking:" http://www.dbm.com/content1.aspx?main=10&item=12.

7 De Janasz, S.C., Sullivan, S.E. and Whiting, V. (2003) "Mentor networks and career success: lessons for turbulent times," *Academy of Management Executive*, 17 (4), 78–91.

8 Higgins, M.C. and Kram, K.E. (2001) "Reconceptualizing mentoring at work: a developmental network perspective," *Academy of Management Review*, 26 (2), 264–88.

9 Levinson, D.J. (1978) *The Seasons of Man's Life*, New York, Knopf, pp. 251–6.

10 Levy, Steven (2001) *Hackers: Heroes of the Computer Revolution*, revised edition, New York, Penguin.

11 Saxenian, A.L. (1996) "Beyond boundaries: open labor markets and learning in Silicon Valley," in Arthur and Rousseau, *The Boundaryless Career*, pp. 23–39. The quote about meeting groups is from Delbecq, A. and Weiss, J. (1988) "The business culture of Silicon Valley: is it a model for the future?," in J. Weiss (ed.), *Regional Cultures, Managerial Behavior and Entrepreneurship*, New York, Quorum.

12 Jones, C. and Lichenstein, B.M.B. (2000) "The 'architecture' of careers: how career competencies reveal from dominant logic in professional services,"

in M. Peiperl, M. Arthur, R. Goffee and T. Morris (eds), *Career Frontiers: New Conceptions of Working Lives*, Oxford, Oxford University Press, pp. 153–76.

13 Jones and Lichtenstein, "The 'architecture' of careers."

14 See for example Maister, D.H. (1997) *Managing the Professional Service Firm*, New York, Simon and Schuster; Starbuck, W.H. (1992) "Learning by knowledge-intensive firms," *Journal of Management Studies*, 29 (6), 713–40.

15 Ensher, E.A., Murphy, S.E. and Sullivan, S.E. (2000) "Boundaryless careers in entertainment: executive women's experience," in Peiperl et al., *Career Frontiers*, pp. 229–54.

16 Barth, S. (2005) "Self-organization: taking a personal approach to KM," in M. Rao (ed.), *Knowledge Management Tools and Techniques*, Oxford, Elsevier, pp. 347–61.

17 See for example Brown, J.S. and Duguid, P. (2002) *The Social Life of Information*, Boston, Harvard Business School Press, pp. 128–35.

18 Mintzberg, Henry (1987) "Crafting strategy," *Harvard Business Review*, 65 (4), 66–75.

19 Jones, C. and DeFillippi, R.J. (1996) "Back to the future in film: combining industry and self-knowledge to meet the career challenges of the 21st century," *Academy of Management Executive*, 10 (4), 89–103. Jones and DeFillippi (p. 90) use "knowing-what" in a more limited way than the other writers cited above, to emphasize the significance of an industry's "opportunities, threats and requirements for career success."

20 A seventh way of knowing, "knowing-if," has also been suggested in relation to people's capacity to consider alternative futures, as is attempted in scenario analysis. See Mason, J. (2005) "From e-learning to e-knowledge," in Rao, *Knowledge Management*.

21 For example Pink, D. (2002) *Free Agent Nation: The Future of Working for Yourself*, New York, Warner; Hakim, C. (2003) *We Are All Self-Employed: How to Take Control of Your Career*, San Francisco, Berrett-Koehler.

22 Dolliver, M. (2002) "I'll trust you not to be very trustworthy, buster," *Adweek*, 43 (32), 17–20.

23 Eby, L.T., Butts, M. and Lockwood, A. (2003) "Predictors of success in the era of the boundaryless career," *Journal of Organizational Behavior*, 24 (6), 689–708.

24 Granovetter, M. (1992) "Problems of explanation in economic sociology," in N. Nohria and R.G. Eccles (eds), *Networks and Organization*, Boston, Harvard Business School Press.

25 Axelrod, R. (1984) *The Evolution of Cooperation*, New York, Basic.

26 Granovetter, "Problems of explanation."

27 Uzzi, B. (1996) "The sources and consequences of embeddedness for the economic performance of organizations: the network effect," *American Sociological Review*, 61, 674–98.

28 Sennett, R. (1998) *The Corrosion of Character: The Personal Consequences of Work in the New Capitalism*, New York, Norton, p. 10; Weick, K.E. (1996) "Enactment and the boundaryless career," in Arthur and Rousseau, *The Boundaryless Career*, pp. 40–57.

29 Interview with Robert D. Putnam, *The Observer*, March 2004. The terms "bridging" and "bonding" are Putnam's, although we use them here to refer specifically to the behavior of one individual toward another.

30 Burt, R.S. (2005) *Brokerage and Closure: An Introduction to Social Capital*, New York, Oxford University Press, p. 4.

31 Raider, H.J. and Burt, R. (1996) "Boundaryless careers and social capital," in Arthur and Rousseau, *The Boundaryless Career*.

32 Based on Burt, R.S. (1992) *Structural Holes*, Cambridge, MA, Harvard University Press.

33 Bridging is related to the idea of "loose ties" which, in contrast to "strong ties," are seen as most important for information gathering and identifying new job opportunities. The original work was that of Granovetter, M. (1974) *Getting a Job: A Study of Contacts and Careers*, Cambridge, MA, Harvard University Press. Related to the idea of loose ties is the idea that only "six degrees of freedom" (six successive interpersonal ties) separate most of us from any other person in society: see Milgram, S. (1967) "The small world problem," *Psychology Today*, 2, 60–7. Both concepts were rejuvenated in Gladwell, M. (2002) *The Tipping Point*, 2nd edn, Boston, Little Brown.

34 For example, for the Strong Interest Inventory see Grutter, Judith (n.d.) *Making It Beyond Today's Organizations* and Grutter, J. and Lund, S.L. (n.d.) *Making It In Today's Organizations*; for the MBTI see Hammer, Allen L. (1993) *Introduction to Type® and Careers*; all Palo Alto, CA, CPP, Inc.

35 Peiperl, M.A. (2001) "Getting 360° feedback right," *Harvard Business Review*, 79 (1), 142–7.

36 Goleman, D. (1998) *Working with Emotional Intelligence*, New York, Bantam.

37 Dalkir, K. (2005) *Knowledge Management in Theory and Practice*, Oxford, Elsevier Butterworth-Heinemann.

38 Wacka, F. (2004) *Your Guide to Corporate Blogging*, http://www.corporateblogging.info/2004/08/six-types-of-business-blogs.asp; Stone, B. (2003) *Blogging: Genius Strategies for Instant Web Content*, Berkeley, CA, New Riders.

39 For example Bowes, B.J. (1999) *The Easy Resumé Book: A Transferable Skills Approach*, London, Bowes.

40 See for example Harvard Business Review (2005) *Appraising Employee Performance*, edited collection, Boston, Harvard Business School Press.

41 Amundson, N.E. (2003) *Active Engagement: Enhancing the Career Counseling Process*, 2nd edn, pp. 194–7.

42 Anklam, P. (2005) "Social network analysis in the KM toolkit," in Rao, *Knowledge Management*, pp. 329–46.

43 Higgins, M.J. (2004) *Developmental Network Questionnaire*, Case Study 404105, Boston, Harvard Business School Press.

44 The article is Arthur et al., "Intelligent enterprise, intelligent careers." Information on the ICCS® may be found at www.intelligentcareer.com.

45 See especially Eby et al., "Predictors of success."

CHAPTER 3

COMMUNITY KNOWLEDGE AT WORK

> We all belong to communities of practice. At home, at work, at school, in our hobbies – we belong to several communities of practice at any given time.
>
> *Etienne Wenger*[1]

This chapter extends the attention already paid to work practices in Chapters 1 and 2, but with a specific focus on communities. These are both informal and pervasive in the contribution that they make to knowledge work.[2] Communities serve as largely voluntary meeting-grounds for the individual ways of knowing described in the previous chapter, and facilitate people's pursuit of collective knowing and learning agendas. Increasingly, community members relate to one another through both physical and virtual means of communication. Communities interact not only with their individual members but also with organizations and industries, often with far-reaching consequences.

The meaning of the work-related communities under consideration here is not to be confused with other meanings of the term "community," such as those prescribing a place of residency or a formal membership obligation. Organizational and occupational communities are both prominent in knowledge work activities. Communities accumulate collective social capital, comparable to the individual social capital discussed in Chapter 2. This involves both internal bonding among and external bridging by a community's members. Knowledge work within communities tends to be based on shared knowledge, whereas knowledge work between communities tends to be based on the complementarity of knowledge possessed by each community.

Let us look at an example community of forensic accountants.

Forensic accountants[3]

The west coast Canadian community of forensic accountants is a relatively small group of accounting professionals that specializes in contributing to legal proceedings, focusing on such things as fraud, embezzlement, and other questionable financial practices. The forensic accountants' primary clients are lawyers and law enforcement officers. Most community members hold a formal qualification, usually as a chartered public accountant. However, the role of formal qualifications is relatively weak. Informal membership guidelines are more important, and especially guidelines concerning individual experience and personality.

Experience includes the forensic accountants' past performance in the courtroom. Their contribution as expert witnesses, privileged to offer opinions to both judge and jury, is often critical to the way a case plays out. It is the body of a forensic accountant's experience that signals his or her ability in such activities as inductive reasoning and presentational style. Lawyers who call on forensic accountants seek to know "how many times have you been before a court, what have you testified on for a court . . . what's your track record" and so forth. Moreover, courtroom performances are closely watched by the regional legal community, which provides a convenient although limited marketplace. It is a marketplace where reputation is both valuable and fragile, where "you screw up and word gets around."

Personality refers to the forensic accountants' aptitude to perform the required work. Curiosity is deemed essential, you have to be "a little bit of a Sherlock Holmes . . . interested in the academic challenge of trying to figure the puzzle out." You also need to be willing to "pay a lot of attention to detail" to work through the complexities of the cases in which you get involved. A further attribute in the assessment of personality, although it may also be driven by experience, is one of self-assurance in the courtroom. Neither "lions," who speak back too aggressively, nor "rabbits," who retreat from persistent questioning, fit the bill for courtroom performance. Personality assessments are further confirmed or disconfirmed by the word-of-mouth evaluations that follow after courtroom appearances.

The informal membership guidelines of experience and personality mean that employment for forensic accountants is largely determined by reputation. Although courtroom evidence is typically delivered individually, forensic accountants have a mutual interest in the legitimacy and standing of their field. This mutual interest is reinforced by the vulnerability of the field to degradation of reputation. Other non-specialist accountants may be readily attracted to the work, especially in an era where traditional public accounting services are seen as more of a commodity item, and less remunerative than they once were. This situation means that, for the specialist forensic accountants, "the biggest competition are the non-specialists within the [accounting] profession." As a result the forensic accountants work together in seeking to develop their own standards, and to control entry into their own specialization within the accounting profession.

Despite their obvious links to lawyers and law enforcement agencies, forensic accountants interact principally among themselves. They do so through special interest groups within one of two professional associations, by making direct contact through professional meetings, sustaining contacts outside of the meetings, and developing professional literature about their role. These interactions promote opportunities for mutual learning, which unfolds on a "case-by-case basis." Although there are certain recognized guidelines and "red flags," there is "no such thing as a canned program," and each case is unique. Getting inside the mind of a fraudster, building experience in interviewing, or seeing oddities in financial records derive largely from personal experience. In these circumstances, sharing experiences with sympathetic others can provide a powerful learning opportunity.

The learning to be gained from interacting with one another reinforces the bonds among the forensic accounting community. Members see a collective advantage in working to "start their own thing," by making their umbrella professional association more sensitive to their needs, and providing a focus for continuing education efforts. It is also felt that this self-organizing will lead to greater recognition, further improvement in standards, training, and "the quality of the product that is out there as forensic accounting." This aspiration for product or service quality stands in sharp contrast to how outside accountants are seen, as people likely to "lose their objectivity" in trying "to achieve as high an award [in the courtroom] as they can," and thereby failing to maintain credibility. One outcome of the learning process has been the greater involvement of forensic accountants in "upstream" preparations, which begin long before a case goes to trial.

The case of the forensic accountants illustrates how both knowing and learning are acted out in a collective setting. Instead of looking at knowing and learning as individual activities, we can see them as group activities. Our interest is drawn to how a community of workers both knows what it knows and learns what it learns.

THREE DIMENSIONS OF COMMUNITY ACTIVITY

We can describe the forensic accountants as a community because they exhibit what Etienne Wenger has described as three dimensions of a "community of practice." Those dimensions provide a framework for examining community knowledge work that is consistent with the idea of practice – as discussed in Chapter 1 – as the application of both explicit and tacit knowledge. The three dimensions are as follows.[4]

Joint enterprise

Wenger's first dimension is a sense of joint enterprise – a collective, negotiated response to the situation in which the community finds itself, typically involving common goals and mutual accountability. For the forensic accountants, this joint enterprise evolved from their shared appreciation of both the opportunities to promote their services and the threat from what were seen as inferior and disreputable imitators. The joint enterprise led to a self-organizing effort within a larger professional body that had been insensitive to the forensic accountants' needs, an effort that drew on the group's shared identification with their work, and allowed for the building of shared reputation.

Shared repertoire

The second dimension of a community of practice is one of a shared repertoire, covering the community's ways of doing things, the stories they exchange, the tools they develop and apply, and the actions and concepts they employ in performing their work. The shared repertoire provides a basis for both engaging in and learning from practice. For the forensic accountants, part of this repertoire involved the development of standards, and through them clarifying the community's purpose to the outside world. However, another part of this repertoire is relatively invisible to outsiders, drawing as it does on first-hand experience in the application of specialized accounting knowledge to a particular body of legal activity.

Mutual engagement

The third dimension of a community of practice is one of mutual engagement, that is of interacting with one another in their work. Within the forensic accountants' community, as is typical for occupational communities, this occurred through interaction around their field of specialization. This mutual engagement is at least in part volitional, stemming from the community members' efforts to get to know one another, exchange experiences, form a professional interest group, and so on. Mutual

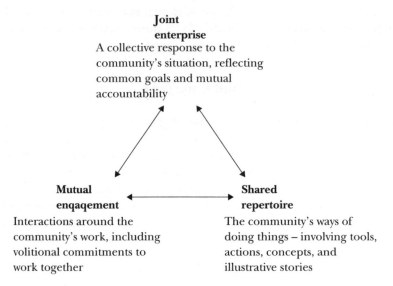

Figure 3.1 Three dimensions of community activity

engagement is also likely to involve complementary activities, of people playing different roles in their professional community, and of more experienced members tutoring or mentoring less experienced colleagues.

The three dimensions of community activity – joint enterprise, shared repertoire and mutual engagement – provide community counterpoints to the three individual ways of knowing introduced in the previous chapter. Joint enterprise provides a counterpoint to an individual's knowing-why investments, concerning the individual's identification with and motivation to perform the work. Shared repertoire offers a counterpart to an individual's knowing-how investments, reflecting the individual's skills and expertise to do the work. Mutual engagement represents a counterpart to an individual's knowing-whom investments, pertaining to the relationships an individual builds around the work.

The three dimensions of community activity are shown in Figure 3.1.

INTERDEPENDENCE AMONG THE DIMENSIONS

Another point of comparison with the previous chapter is that the three dimensions of community activity function interdependently. As with the three ways of knowing, the dimensions continually influence one another as the community's work unfolds. Let us look again at the forensic accountants.

Joint enterprise and shared repertoire

Participation in a joint enterprise, such as that pursued by the forensic accountants, can lead to greater collaborative investments in the community's shared repertoire. This is illustrated in the forensic accountants' joint enterprise to promote themselves inside the broader accounting profession, leading to the exchange of field experiences and new learning. In a reverse direction, the building of a shared repertoire of occupational skills – and in particular the focus on service quality – appeared to reinforce the accountants' greater identification with the joint enterprise on which they were embarked.

Joint enterprise and mutual engagement

Joint enterprise can also lead to mutual engagement in the affairs of the community. This is illustrated through the way that the forensic accountants responded to their competitive situation, and the level of self-organizing activity that followed. Mutual engagement can in turn reinforce a spirit of joint enterprise, for example when the forensic accountants collaborated to prevent non-specialists from taking over work in their field.

Shared repertoire and mutual engagement

A community's shared repertoire can be a powerful spur for further mutual engagement around that repertoire. This may be witnessed in the forensic accountants' considerable attempts to promote new learning in their field, and their use of collaborative workshops to achieve that learning. In a reverse direction, mutual engagement can inspire further development of the community's repertoire of services, as evidenced by the development of advanced or "upstream" services before cases came to trial.

A final point to be made here is that, unless otherwise indicated, we will be using the term "community" in the sense that Wenger implies. That is, a community is a group of individuals identifiable by a relatively high level of interaction among its members, and where those members exhibit a shared participation along all three community dimensions of joint enterprise, shared repertoire and mutual engagement. Management writer Phil Mirvis has similarly argued that communities involve "the emotive experience of feeling close to others" (as is likely with joint enterprise), the pursuit of shared obligations and commitments (predictably through a shared repertoire) and "living at least some of your life with others" (thereby reflecting mutual engagement).[5]

THE COMMUNITY AND THE
KNOWLEDGE DIAMOND

As was the case for individuals, community engagement in knowledge work can also involve another community, or any of the three further participants in the knowledge diamond – that is, individuals, organizations and industries. We turn next to offer examples of each kind of involvement.

One community and another

Our opening example of forensic accountants made reference to a parallel community of forensic lawyers – lawyers who specialize in forensic legislation. The lawyers are described to "also interact extensively with one another" and "to be quite frank in discussing [forensic accountants and other kinds of] experts with one another." Forensic lawyers and forensic accountants may be seen as two interdependent communities that each benefit from interaction with one another. This interaction takes place in four distinct ways: forensic accountants are hired by forensic lawyers to go to court; forensic accountants market their services to forensic lawyers; forensic accountants provide educational seminars for their lawyer counterparts; and forensic accountants and lawyers often work with the same evidence and in so doing "share a high level of awareness of each other."[6]

There are many examples of similar community-to-community links within the world of work. These include hardware and software engineers in high technology, architects and civil engineers in construction, surgeons and surgical nurses in operating rooms, the film-making communities described in Chapter 1, and many more. The point to be emphasized is that these inter-community relationships evolve from the overlapping investments of two or more separate communities. As we will see in the next two chapters, such relationships may be reinforced by other factors, such as organizational sponsors or the larger ecology of an industry. However, there is no reason to assume that such outside factors are principally responsible for the inter-community relationships that emerge. In the film-making example in Chapter 1, inter-community relationships are often firmly established before the producer organization – in this case the film-making company – is founded.

The community and the organization

It is common to read about examples of communities that are formed and shaped by employing organizations.[7] However, these kinds of examples neglect people's natural tendency to form communities that serve their own interests – communities that often precede any attempts at organizational cooptation. An interesting case is that of UK pub managers, who for centuries formed communities among themselves, or with their staff or immediate customers. The concept of a corporation – in the pub manager's case a conglomerate brewery – laying any claim over the pub managers' behavior is relatively new. Moreover, the kinks in the relationship between the organization and the pub managers are still being worked out.

British pub managers and their overlapping communities[8]

The British pub has a tradition going back centuries. It is as symbolic of the British social environment as the village green. However, management arrangements for the pub have evolved from a preponderance of sole owners, to growth in the number of tenant managers renting premises built and leased by breweries, and most recently to managers employed by the large corporations that now dominate the beer-making business.

Individual pub managers have traditionally maintained communities among themselves – a tradition that survives the change in ownership arrangements. This kind of community provides support from other managers who understand the grass roots problems and local issues that the community faces. As one manager stated: "If you ever get problems . . . [the] community of pub managers shares understanding and identity at a local level, and the managers engage in shared practices that benefit the whole community."[9]

Pub managers are also closely connected to two other kinds of community. One kind involves customers who "intrude deeply into the working environment of the manager;" the other kind involves the pub staff who are "enormously important sources of information about both customers and the competition." The unique, day-to-day interactions among managers, their customers and their staff are such that situational knowledge is not always transferable to the managers of other pubs, who are similarly embedded in their own unique environments.

Enter the large corporation – the brewery – as pub owner, and as a hierarchically controlled survivor of several waves of mergers and acquisitions in the UK brewing industry. It might be expected that the corporation's motivation to sell more product is closely aligned with the motivation of its pub managers. However, in at least one situation, early corporate attempts to communicate with the pub managers were relatively unsuccessful. Centralized guidelines about how to greet customers or serve drinks were at odds with established local practices and customer preferences, and corporate area managers, believing "knowledge is power," were reluctant to share profitability information with individual pub managers.

The later introduction of corporate trainers and point-of-sale record-keeping and feedback have perhaps improved the links between the corporate breweries and the pub managers, and in turn their staff and customers. However, relationships often remain fragile, reflecting the prospective tension between community practices and organizational policies.

In the pub example, we see the challenge faced by an organization in collaborating with a pre-existing community, that of the pub managers the brewery seeks to influence on its own behalf. We also see a simple illustration of the idea of a user community – in this case the pub's customers – whose joint enterprise, shared repertoire and mutual engagement revolve around gaining the best experience from the product or service on offer.[10] We will return to the idea of user communities in Chapters 7 and 8.

The community and the industry

Communities frequently evolve within a particular industry. As was discussed in Chapter 1, this is the case with the various communities of specialists that contribute to the film industry. Similar communities often emerge among scientists, where the joint enterprise involves pursuing a particular research question, or finding a solution to a mutually recognized problem. Biotechnology provides an interesting example.

Scientists in biotechnology[11]

The development of an animal model for Alzheimer's disease was reported in the journal *Nature*. There were thirty-four authors affiliated with two biotech companies, one pharmaceutical firm, a research university, a federal research laboratory, and a non-profit research institute. A publication in the journal *Science* identified a gene likely to determine susceptibility to breast and ovarian cancer. There were forty-five co-authors drawn from a biotech firm, a US medical school, a Canadian medical school, a pharmaceutical company, and a government research laboratory. Both publications reflect the common phenomenon of scientific research communities that evolve around common research interests.

Moreover, these kinds of communities do not principally stem from any contractual arrangements among the employer organizations involved. Any inter-organizational agreements are "the tip of the iceberg" and exclude "dozens of handshake deals and informal collaborations" through which individual scientists identify and collaborate with one another. Rather, research is driven by scientific communities, whose joint enterprise is to locate a particular gene, or isolate a particular virus, even as their members move across different employment settings.

The knowledge generated by these scientific communities goes back to their individual members. This has profound implications for the biotech firm, whose opportunity for innovation is less defined by the people it employs than by the company those employees keep.

The biotech example is about a joint enterprise within a particular industry. However, in other cases we can expect joint enterprise to revolve around shared interests in an occupation, an organization, an alumni group, a religious or political ideology, a hobby, an extended family, or any group intended to provide psychological support for its members.[12] We can expect people to belong to several communities at any one time, and for community attachments to change as time and circumstances unfold.[13] Another feature of the above example is that it involves different member subsets in different locations. With the ubiquity of the World Wide Web, this kind of community – with links across both physical and virtual space – has become commonplace.

The community and the individual

Communities need to begin somehow, and they frequently do so through the extraordinary efforts of one individual. An illustrative story that combines the efforts of one individual and the opportunity of the web is that of Linus Torvalds and the "virtual community" that developed around the Linux operating system.

Linus Torvalds and Linux

On January 2, 1991, University of Helsinki undergraduate student Linus Torvalds determined he would combine his Christmas and twenty-first birthday money to purchase a personal computer. It would be a "no-name, white box" IBM PC-compatible computer with a cut-down version of the basic Disk Operating System (DOS), an Intel 386 chip and as much memory and power as a budget of $3,500 would allow.

Torvalds had become interested at the University of Helsinki in the large-computer operating system Unix, to his mind a "clean and beautiful" system where you could build "any amount of complexity from the interactions of simple things." He envisioned having a version of Unix on his own PC. He used sections from, but later became disenchanted with, an existing "open-source" program (one freely available over the Internet) intended to achieve similar results. He persisted in writing sections of his own program code, becoming more ambitious as he made small gains from early efforts. After a number of mis-steps, Torvalds's code "grew legs" and, with the encouragement of a University of Helsinki teaching assistant, was assigned the name "Linux."[14]

In the same spirit of open-source programming in which he had borrowed other people's work, Torvalds posted a web message about his system in August, 1991. This was quickly followed by the first version of the Linux system in September, 1991, and several further releases over the next few months. Only ten people downloaded Torvalds's first publicly available operating system, of whom five sent back code improvements. However, by the end of 1991 more than 100 people worldwide had joined the Linux newsgroup. By the end of 1992, the number was 1,000, increasing to 20,000, 100,000 and 500,000 over the next three years. Moreover, the operating system continued to gain stature as a vast "virtual community" of software enthusiasts gave thousands of hours of free time to make Linux better.[15]

By 2004, the market for Linux devices and software had reached US$11 billion, predicted to reach $36 billion by 2008. Torvalds had been hired by the Oregon-based Open Source Development Labs (OSDL), set up by computing giants IBM, Intel and others to accelerate Linux adoption. High-technology companies had committed thousands of programmers to support the Linux effort, and the operating system was to be found in such things as Motorola cell phones, Mitsubishi robots and NASA space shuttle simula-tions. Many of the early independent "aces" of the Linux community were in key jobs with collaborator organizations. The aces were valued not only for their individual knowledge and skills, but also for their standing and access to information within the Linux community they had helped to build.[16]

The Linux story is in part a straightforward one, reflecting how many communities get started. One person's enthusiasm for a cause attracts other people to a joint enterprise, such as the foundation of a new char-ity, the development of a new professional interest, the promotion of a new product, the creation of a new support group for parents of young children, and so on. The nature of the enterprise gives rise to both the shared repertoire that members come to utilize, and the mutual engagement through which those members interact. The Linux story also introduces the topic of open-source practices in knowledge work, to which we will return in later chapters.

KEEPING THE COMMUNITY IN VIEW

The story so far is one of communities participating in the knowledge diamond as highlighted in Figure 3.2. Communities engage in two-way communications with all four of: (1) other communities, (2) organizations, (3) host industries and (4) individuals. Communities invest in these com-munications on behalf of their members' espoused joint enterprise, and in the process generate and transfer knowledge that flows not only to the members themselves but also to organizations and their industries. It may be emphasized that individuals and communities frequently begin new processes of knowledge generation that subsequently benefit both the organizations and industries – and through them host national and global economies – that employ the knowledge in question.

As is the case for individuals, the web has become a key factor in both the scope and the scale of community attachments. Long-standing face-to-face and (since the invention of the telephone) voice-to-voice com-munity work is frequently supplemented or even largely replaced by the web. As the Linux story graphically reveals, the web gives communities

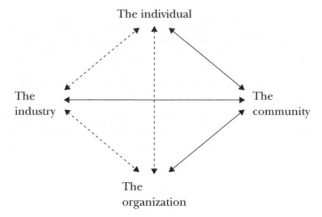

Figure 3.2   The community and the knowledge diamond

a capacity for self-organizing that was not previously available, and will continue to change the economic landscape.

OTHER MEANINGS OF COMMUNITY

The knowledge-based communities of interest to this book are communities that come together around a specialized practice, and can be understood in terms of Wenger's three dimensions introduced earlier. However, an influential book by Robert Putnam describes the "civic" communities he found in certain geographical regions of Italy as follows:

> Some regions of Italy have many choral societies and soccer teams and bird-watching clubs and Rotary clubs. Most citizens in those regions read eagerly about community affairs in the daily press. They are engaged by public issues, but not by personalistic or patron–client politics. Inhabitants trust one another to act fairly and to obey the law . . . Social and political networks are organized horizontally not hierarchically. The community values solidarity, civic engagement, cooperation and honesty.[17]

Putnam's use of the term "community" raises a question. Do the citizens of a geographic region meet the criteria for a knowledge-based community relevant to this book? If they do, it is in a limited sense where their practice concerns how they engage in political affairs. In that limited sense the community's knowledge work involves: joint enterprise to retain the political system in which everyone takes pride; shared repertoire reflecting how the citizenry work through the political system; and mutual engagement in collaborating to make the system work. Along other criteria – such as involvement in the choral societies, soccer teams, bird-watching clubs and Rotary clubs that Putnam mentions – we can more selectively see the citizens belonging to separate communities, and involved in separate practices.

In contrast to Putnam's regional citizens, the forensic accountants described earlier built their regional community around shared occupational investments. In contrast too, the virtual Linux community evolved without geographic constraint, but also focused on shared occupational investments. Hobbyists, churchgoers, volunteers, families and various kinds of alumni groups can all invest in a common practice that nurtures community involvement.[18] However, these examples are distinct from seeing a community as all of a geographic region's citizens, which lies outside the meaning adopted in this book. Situations where people use the term "community" in a prescriptive sense, claiming "We are all one community here!" – as preachers, politicians or corporate leaders sometimes do – also lie outside the scope of this book.

ORGANIZATIONAL COMMUNITIES

A widespread response to the emerging work on communities of practice has been to seek to identify them, or to encourage their development, inside organizations. An example is the initiative of the Clarica insurance company, described here.

An agents' community at Clarica

Clarica is a division of Sun Life Financial providing retail insurance products to Canadian clients. The sales force consists of 3,000 agents, under contract to exclusively represent Clarica products. The company recognized the close relationships that agents frequently build with their customers and the opportunity for inter-agent knowledge exchange. It determined to launch a company-sponsored community of practice among the agents to help them develop their individual and collective capabilities.

A Clarica steering committee determined the intended community objective:

> To develop and share our [the agents'] personal, professional and technical expertise, leading to innovative strategies and growth for our business.

The steering committee also sought to improve computer literacy among the agents, both to support the company's shift toward a paperless approach and to allow knowledge sharing across geographically distant locations. However, Clarica management would not have access to community discussions. This would be a community run "by agents, for agents."

Clarica purchased specialized software to facilitate online community interactions, and dedicated three full-time employees – a "knowledge architect," a project manager and a facilitator – to the project. A pilot scheme was launched with 150 volunteer agents, to be run by a steering group consisting of eight people: two agents, two sales department staff, the dedicated knowledge architect, a second knowledge architect, and the project manager and the facilitator that the group subsequently recruited.

The results of the pilot scheme appeared encouraging. The community quickly claimed responsibility for the content and direction of the conversation, and embarked on case-based learning. For example, one agent was working with a young couple who had received cash from their parents, and the community helped the agent provide useful advice. Test cases around agent–company trust and the company's support in providing expert resources appeared to get successfully resolved. Moreover, it quickly became a challenge to help the community organize and archive its conversations to retain the utility of the rapidly growing database.

At the end of the pilot scheme, 95% of respondents to a follow-up survey reported that they thought the community of practice ought to be continued, with 54% saying it was "very important." However, some of the original 150 volunteer agents had withdrawn from the project, citing problems of time, other priorities or lack of technological familiarity. Some of these agents reported that they already had other ways to network with one another. It remained to be seen how much the pilot scheme community could be expanded to the larger agent workforce.

The Clarica agents' community appears consistent with the three dimensions of community knowledge work, that is of joint enterprise (to become more successful agents), shared repertoire (selling the Clarica range of retail insurance products) and mutual engagement (collaborating with other community members). It is representative of a larger set of initiatives involving an organization's direct funding and support for communities of practice in anticipation of favorable learning outcomes. However, the approach risks departing from the self-organizing aspect of communities of practice which early observers thought to be fundamental.[19] It also risks restricting the community's knowledge to that available within the organization, regardless of the relative merits of knowledge that may be attainable outside.

OCCUPATIONAL COMMUNITIES

An alternative stimulus for community development can come from occupational and professional associations. Increasingly, professional associations are initiating or at least facilitating community knowledge work around shared specialist practices. The example of the forensic accountants given earlier is a typical example. There are also many examples of communities forming among users of a particular product or group of products, such as those among information technology workers around a wide range of specialized software products, or those among pharmaceutical scientists around particular research topics.[20]

The promotion and support of knowledge-based occupational communities suggest a new trend, as national chapters of occupational associations seek to promote their members' interests in the national economies in which those associations exist. An example is Professions Australia, an umbrella association of professional associations representing a variety of occupations, and seeking to deliver value by coordinating knowledge-based services through its website (Table 3.1). The association seeks to promote the emergence of communities focused on occupational practice both within and across its separate member associations.

Table 3.1 Knowledge work initiatives at Professions Australia

---

Professions Australia[21]

Professions Australia (PA) seeks to deliver value to its membership through four mechanisms:

- *Information*: providing *alerts* on government developments that affect PA members, distributing *newsletters*, providing commentary, analysis and updates on matters of interest, and maintaining a *knowledge base* of useful links to other resources available over the web.
- *Interaction*: promoting *knowledge talk* on the association's website through online exchanges, building networks both over the website and through face-to-face meetings, and passing on new ideas that are presently being tested in member associations.
- *Internet*: providing robust online facilities that are "part of the armory of any professional association" and a *knowledge people* portal for links to other knowledgeable professionals based on their areas of expertise.
- *Influence*: to use PA as a recognized media presence for the benefit of member associations, and to complement the actions of individual associations through strong coalitions on matters of broad interest.

Both the Linux and Professions Australia examples point to the rapid emergence of the web as a medium for community knowledge work activities. We will return to this subject in more detail in Chapter 7.

COMMUNITY SOCIAL CAPITAL

In Chapter 2 we referred to social capital as "the advantage created by a person's location in a structure of relationships." We extend this here to "the advantage created by a person's *or a group's* location in a structure of relationships." The term *group* refers to a collection of people, and is used to cover a range of possibilities. In particular, a group can reflect any one of three kinds of knowledge diamond participant: the members of a community, the members of an organization, or the members of an industry. A group can also be a project team, a standing committee or any other collection of people brought together for some common purpose.[22] Let us examine the case for communities, and generalize it later for other kinds of groups.

As we have seen, communities can benefit from their members' bridging activities with other knowledge diamond participants. For example, the story on forensic accountants at the start of this chapter suggested that the accountants gained benefits from relationships with outside individuals (influential leaders in the accounting profession), communities (forensic lawyers), organizations (law firms) and the larger legal industry in which their work was valued. Communities can also benefit from their members' bonding activities with one another. For example, the Linux community story suggested that the members benefited from staying closely connected in pursuit of their joint enterprise.

Sociologist Ronald Burt refers to the two kinds of contribution to social capital described above in terms of brokerage and closure. *Brokerage* involves the development of a community's ties with outsiders through which knowledge can be usefully gained or traded. An example is a software development community's ties with prospective product users. *Closure* refers to the ties that exist among a community's members (occurring through the members' mutual engagement with one another). An example is a software development community's ties among its own members. The opportunity to maximize community social capital occurs when there are high levels of both brokerage and closure. To continue the example, this would involve a software development community having effective external relationships with potential product users, and close internal relationships among its own members. Alternative combinations of high and low brokerage and closure are shown in Figure 3.3.

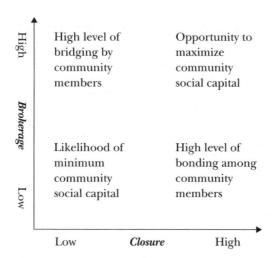

Figure 3.3 Brokerage and closure in community social capital[23]

The conversion of high levels of individual bridging and interpersonal bonding into community brokerage and closure may not be straightforward. Community members may be all talking to the same source, or to different but uninformed sources, and thereby limiting the range of knowledge to which they have access. Community members may also be bonding around issues, such as pay levels or employment conditions, having little bearing on the community's distinctive knowledge base. However, Figure 3.3 does provide a template against which to examine how community social capital may be accumulated.

The conception of group social capital as involving components of both brokerage and closure is the one adopted throughout this book. As previously noted, this uses the term "group" broadly, to include people's membership in any or all of a community, an organization, and an industry. A number of other writers take the same approach.[24] However, some writers view social capital as concerned principally or solely with what Burt calls closure.[25] Those writers need to be understood on their own terms.

THE RETURNS ON COMMUNITY SOCIAL CAPITAL

An example of how communities gain returns on their social capital leads on from the Homebrew Computer Club example introduced in Chapter 2. This time our story concerns a broader comparison between the growth of California's Silicon Valley and Massachusetts's Route 128.

Silicon Valley and Route 128, 1975–90[26]

In 1975, the US West Coast and East Coast high-technology districts commonly referred to as "Silicon Valley" and "Route 128" respectively employed workforces of roughly the same size. Fifteen years later, Silicon Valley had generated a net of 150,000 new technology jobs, around three times as many as Route 128. Silicon Valley had also grown to produce electronic products exports amounting to more than $11 billion, compared to $4.6 billion for Route 128. Silicon Valley further became home to thirty-nine of the 100 fastest-growing electronics companies in the US, compared to only four for Route 128. Why the difference in relative rates of growth?

Part of the answer can be found in the kind of knowledge-based communities that the two regions spawned. The Homebrew Computer Club (described in Chapter 2) was typical of a range of Silicon Valley communities where people would gather their separate areas of scientific interest. As one informant put it: "Around every technological subject, or every engineering concern," groups would meet "to foster new ideas and innovate." There was high employment mobility, but professional loyalties and friendships often remained intact. Silicon Valley engineers maintained greater loyalty to their respective crafts, and to others practicing those crafts, than they did to their employer companies.[27]

By contrast, Route 128 was characterized as "a collection of autonomous enterprises, lacking social or commercial interdependencies." When high-technology workers did meet outside the workplace "it was usually with spouses for a game of bridge, a dinner party, or a tennis match, and the discussion rarely turned to work." Professional socialization was largely subordinated to what was seen as a self-sufficient firm, and there was little interaction beyond the boundaries of each firm. A popular book on Route 128 innovation – Tracy Kidder's *The Soul of a New Machine* – focused only on events within one such firm, and made no mention of any broader technological community.[28]

There are many reasons why the Silicon Valley and Route 128 high-technology regions produced contrasting results over the period described. One may have been that Route 128 companies could insist on non-compete agreements, illegal in Silicon Valley, to restrict knowledge flows to other companies.[29] However, the preceding story suggests that a substantial reason for Silicon Valley's relative success was the distinctive nature of its knowledge worker communities. First, they allowed for greater brokerage of new ideas and information through their members' wide range of contacts. Second, closure tended to occur around shared technological challenges rather than around the situation inside any particular firm.[30]

COMMUNITY AND INTER-COMMUNITY KNOWLEDGE WORK

A final topic for this chapter concerns the distinction between knowledge work within a community and knowledge work between communities. Let us return to the film-making example with which we began this book. Picture a group of performing actors that has been brought together to make a film. Picture in contrast the separate groups of workers, not only of actors but also of production staff, camera operators, set designers, special effects teams, stunt performers and so on, needed to make a film. For the sake of illustration, let us assume that each member of the film crew maintains a long-term affiliation with a community of similar specialists, so that not only do the actors maintain their own community, but so too do the camera operators, set designers and so on.[31]

A community of film actors is likely to engage in knowledge work differently on their own than if they are involved with a more diverse film-making crew. The basis for knowledge sharing within a community of actors will be the similarity across what the actors already know. The actors' purpose in exchanging knowledge will emphasize their joint enterprise to promote the acting profession. They will seek to retain knowledge by adding to the shared repertoire about acting they already possess. The basis for individual learning will emphasize mutual engagement with other members of the acting community. The actors' approach to generating new knowledge will be based on the existing assumptions, or paradigms, that guide the acting profession. The predominant approach to social capital formation will be one of closure, talking inside community boundaries.

In contrast, the basis for knowledge sharing among a crew of actors and other film-making specialists is likely to emphasize the connectedness between different knowledge bases – that is between what actors know about acting, camera workers know about camera work, and so on. The purpose in exchanging knowledge will emphasize task completion – in this case to successfully finish the film. They will seek to retain knowledge by adding to the competencies of individual crew members. The basis for individual learning will emphasize problem-solving, in response to challenges faced in making the film. The approach to generating new knowledge will emphasize market circumstances, such as the budget or intended audience of the film. Their predominant approach to social capital formation will be one of brokerage, talking across community boundaries. These differences between intra-community and inter-community knowledge work are summarized in Table 3.2.

Table 3.2 Characteristics of intra-community knowledge work versus inter-community knowledge work[32]

Characteristic	Intra-community knowledge work	Inter-community knowledge work
Basis for knowledge integration	Similarity across individual knowledge bases	Connections between individual knowledge bases
Purpose of knowledge exchange	Joint enterprise	Task completion
Method of knowledge retention	Shared repertoire	Individual competencies
Basis for individual learning	Mutual engagement	Problem-solving
Knowledge generation process	Paradigm driven – based on shared understanding	Market driven – responding to inter-community goals
Social capital formation	Closure	Brokerage

Another way of seeing the contrast between intra-community and inter-community knowledge work is to see each reflecting contrasting maxims. For single communities, the maxim "we know more than we can tell" depicts communities as bearers of tacit knowledge. For an inter-community group, the maxim "we know less than we can tell" depicts the limits to understanding caused by separate specializations. The persistent challenge in community-based knowledge work is to get the balance right. This means seeking to optimize the extent to which community members can both learn on their own (through closure) and interact with other communities (through brokerage) in their work.

TOOLS FOR COMMUNITIES

Tools for knowledge work communities fall into two main groups. The first group involves guidelines for establishing and developing communities that rely on traditional face-to-face interaction. These tools include a variety of checklists – principles for effective community design, stages of community development, tradeoffs in community functioning, etc. – that can help community leaders or their facilitators help everyone navigate their way toward more effective collaboration and learning.[33] Other tools can provide basic training in the execution and interdependence of roles within a community setting.[34]

A second, more recent set of tools involves IT-based programs and services to either (1) help face-to-face communities do their work or (2) support virtual communities through web-based support services. A variety of software products are available to help the community document its conversations, archive its materials, retain emergent best practices, and brainstorm over fresh challenges and opportunities. Some tools for virtual communities go further, including opportunities for online teleconferencing and video conferencing to better compensate for geographic separation. Other tools seek to combine accepted principles for effective community participation with the capacity for online interaction over the web.[35]

An emerging tool for community collaboration is the *wiki* (named after the Hawaiian word for "quick"), a group of web pages that allows users to add and edit content.[36] The underlying software allows community members to openly edit each other's postings on a website, while at the same time providing quality assurance and feedback on each member's posting and the resulting edited content.[37] The most widely known application of wikis is Wikipedia, an online encyclopedia written and edited by a global community of thousands of individual contributors.[38] IT-based tools continue to evolve as the web continues to provide faster and more economical services than were previously available.

All of these tools come with a strong caution. It is that the communities under consideration throughout this chapter usually evolve and sustain themselves under their members' own initiative. Tools have their place, but there is a persistent risk of means–ends inversion where the tools interfere with or seek to go beyond the natural community-shaping inclinations of current or potential community members. From the community's standpoint, the role of tools is to complement rather than interfere with the natural self-organizing qualities that communities can possess.[39]

SUMMARY

Communities, as viewed in this book, consist of members demonstrating high levels of joint enterprise, shared repertoire and mutual engagement in their work. These three dimensions also provide links to individual members' three ways of knowing described in Chapter 2. The community assumes a distinct place in the knowledge diamond,

involved as it is with other communities (for example forensic accountants and forensic lawyers), organizations (for example pub managers
and property-owning breweries), the host industry (for example scientific
communities in the biotechnology industry) and individuals (for example
between the Linux community and Linus Torvalds). The work-related
communities examined here are distinct from regional communities of
citizens, which lie beyond the scope of this book.

Both organizations and occupations can give rise to communities of
practice, as can groups based on joint hobby, church, volunteer, family
and alumni memberships. Communities possess group social capital,
which ideally involves both brokerage beyond and closure among a
community's members. Intra-community knowledge work – based largely
on similarities in what people know – has different characteristics than
inter-community knowledge work – based largely on differences in what
people know. A number of tools exist to support communities in their
knowledge work activities, with IT-based tools becoming increasingly relevant as the web continues to evolve.

QUESTIONS FOR REFLECTION

1   Select any one community you are a member of, or know closely.
    How would you describe (a) the joint enterprise on which the
    community is working; (b) the shared repertoire the community
    brings to its work; and (c) the mutual engagement that the com-
    munity experiences?
2   For the same community you have selected in question 1, can you
    provide examples of interdependence among the joint enterprise,
    shared repertoire and mutual engagement you have described?
3   Assume your place as a community representative in the knowledge
    diamond. How do your community's knowledge investments relate
    to those of (a) other communities, (b) organizations, (c) the industry
    and (d) yourself and other individuals?
4   What community experiences have you had that (a) have been
    restricted to a single organization, and (b) have gone beyond any
    such organization? How did you identify with those communities and
    how did things work out?
5   What has been your own experience of inter-community brokerage
    and closure activities? Where would you locate your experiences on
    Figure 3.3? Could the community have gained more social capital,
    and if so how?

6 Can you think of an example where you were a community member within a larger inter-community knowledge work activity? Does that example conform with the characteristics in Table 3.2? If so how, and how did things work out?

7 What tools have you used in your own community experiences? How did they help or hinder the community's work?

NOTES

1 Wenger, E. (1998) *Communities of Practice: Learning, Meaning, and Identity*, Cambridge, Cambridge University Press, p. 6.

2 Ibid., p. 7.

3 The principal source for the case study is Lawrence, Thomas B. (1998) "Examining resources in an occupational community: reputation in Canadian forensic accounting," *Human Relations*, 51 (9), 1103–31.

4 Wenger, *Communities of Practice*.

5 Mirvis, P.H. (1997) "'Soul work' in organizations," *Organization Science*, 8 (2), 193–206.

6 Lawrence, "Examining resources."

7 For example Hislop, D. (2003) "The complex relations between communities of practice and the implementation of technological innovations," *International Journal of Innovation Management*, 7 (2), 163–88.

8 Mutch, A. (2003) "Communities of practice and habitus: a critique," *Organization Science*, 24 (3), 383–401.

9 Ibid., p. 386.

10 In Britain this kind of user community is reflected in the idea of a "local," namely a pub that appeals to the tastes and preferences of the group of local residents that form the pub's customer base.

11 Powell, W.W. and Koput, K.W. (1996) "Interorganizational collaboration and the locus of innovation: networks of learning in biotechnology," *Administrative Science Quarterly*, 41, 116–45.

12 Parker, P., Arthur, M.B. and Inkson, K. (2004) "Career communities: a preliminary exploration of member-defined career support structures," *Journal of Organizational Behavior*, 25, 489–514.

13 Wenger, *Communities of Practice*, p. 6.

14 Torvals, L. and Diamond, D. (2001) *Just for Fun: The Story of an Accidental Revolutionary*, New York, HarperBusiness.

15 McHugh, J. (1998) "For the love of hacking," *Forbes*, August 10, 1–12, www.forbes.com/forbes/98/0810/6203094a.htm; DeFillippi, R.J. and Arthur, M.B. (2002) "Career creativity to industry influence: a blueprint for the knowledge economy?," in M.A. Peiperl, M.B. Arthur and N. Anand (eds), *Career Creativity: Explorations in the Remaking of Work*, Oxford, Oxford University Press.

16 Hamm, S. (2005) "Linux Inc.," *Business Week*, January 31, 60–8.

17 Putnam, R.D. (1993) *Making Democracy Work*, Princeton, NJ, Princeton University Press, p. 115.
18 Parker et al., "Career communities."
19 For example Wenger, *Communities of Practice.*
20 For example, the American Association of Pharmaceutical Scientists: see http://www.aaps.org.
21 Table derived from Professions Australia website, http://www.professions.com.au.
22 Burt, R.S. (2005) *Brokerage and Closure: An Introduction to Social Capital*, Oxford, Oxford University Press. On usage of the term "group" see especially Chapter 3, pp. 126–48.
23 Adapted from Burt, *Brokerage and Closure*, p. 139.
24 Again see Burt, *Brokerage and Closure;* see also Cook, S.D.N. and Brown, J.S. (1999) "Bridging epistemologies: the generative dance between organizational knowledge and organizational knowing," *Organization Science*, 10 (4), 381–400.
25 See for example Dess, G.G., Lumpkin, G.T. and Taylor, M.L. (2005) *Strategic Management*, 2nd edn, New York, McGraw-Hill, pp. 133–7.
26 Saxenian, A. (1994) *Regional Advantage*, Cambridge, MA, Harvard University Press; Saxenian, A. (1996) "Beyond boundaries: open labor markets and learning in Silicon Valley," in M.B. Arthur and D.M. Rousseau (eds), *The Boundaryless Career*, New York, Oxford University Press, pp. 23–39.
27 Saxenian, *Regional Advantage*, Chapter 2, quote from p. 34.
28 Saxenian, *Regional Advantage*, Chapter 3, quotes from pp. 59, 61. The popular book was Kidder, T. (1981) *The Soul of a New Machine*, Boston, Little Brown.
29 Kirsner, S. (2005) "What's cost of pact not to compete?," *The Boston Globe*, September 19, E5.
30 Burt, *Brokerage and Closure*, pp. 142–5.
31 This section draws heavily on Lindkvist, L. (2005) "Knowledge communities and knowledge collectivities: a typology of knowledge work in groups," *Journal of Management Studies*, 42, 1189–210.
32 Derived from ibid.
33 Wenger, E., McDermott, R. and Snyder, W.M. (2002) *Cultivating Communities of Practice*, Boston, Harvard Business School Press.
34 For example Senge, P.M., Kleiner, A., Roberts, C., Ross, R.B. and Smith, B.J. (1994) *The Fifth Discipline Fieldbook: Strategies and Tools for Building a Learning Organization*, New York, Doubleday.
35 For a useful review see Rao, M. (ed.) (2005) *Knowledge Management Tools and Techniques*, Oxford, Elsevier.
36 The definition is based on that found in Wikipedia, http://en.wikipedia.org.
37 Dalkir, K. (2005) *Knowledge Management in Theory and Practice*, Oxford, Elsevier Butterworth-Heinemann.
38 Ibid.
39 Wenger, *Communities of Practice.*

CHAPTER 4

ORGANIZATIONAL KNOWLEDGE AT WORK

A core competence represents the sum of learning across the individual skill sets and individual organizational units. Thus, a core competence is unlikely to reside in its entirety in a single individual or small team.

Gary Hamel and C.K. Prahalad[1]

Organizations develop core competencies that reflect knowledge already gained and also serve as platforms for future learning. As the opening quotation implies, these competencies draw on the organization's collective knowing and learning investments. An organization's core competencies influence and are influenced by other knowledge diamond participants. For example, important organization-to-organization relationships include supplier network relationships and various kinds of strategic alliance relationships. Organizations also interact directly with their host industries, with employees and contract workers (and those workers' learning agendas), and with a variety of relevant occupational communities.

Organizations engage in both the exploitation of existing knowledge and the exploration of new knowledge. The organization's emphasis on each of these has further consequences for the organization's overall strategic investments in knowledge work. Organizational approaches toward innovation are influenced by changing industry practices, reflecting a shift from closed toward more open innovation principles. Organizational knowledge work can be aided by a variety of information technology tools.

Let us consider the example of Intel Corporation.

Intel

Intel has enjoyed an enviable position as one of the world's largest semiconductor manufacturers.[2] It has been remarkable for its ability to regularly announce new generations of chips to power faster and more powerful computers with "Intel inside." Yet it may be more remarkable for its approach to knowledge work.

Intel's approach originated with the prior experience of its founders, Gordon Moore and Robert Noyce, and third core member, Andy Grove. All had worked for companies such as AT&T (at that time the owner of Bell Laboratories) and Fairchild Semiconductor, which had invested heavily in central research laboratories and subsequently struggled to bring innovative ideas to the marketplace. Part of the problem was that the research laboratories were physically and organizationally isolated from the manufacturing plants that converted design innovations into commercial products.[3] However, even when the latest research advances were incorporated, there was a tendency for the manufacturing operations to lock into a technology path that precluded the company from adapting to further innovation. As a result, knowledge competencies often became knowledge *rigidities* that turned an initial advantage into a liability.[4]

By contrast, Moore, Noyce and Grove designed their company without a central research laboratory. Instead, they created a distributed model of three specialized laboratories focused on computer architectures, microprocessor architectures and semiconductor technologies respectively. Each laboratory was co-located near manufacturing operations related to the laboratory's area of specialization and the physical and organizational distance between research and manufacturing was kept to a minimum. Moreover, all three laboratories were organized to keep manufacturing outcomes in mind. A guideline of "Minimum Information" sought to leverage existing manufacturing knowledge wherever possible, and further insisted on research stemming from close observation of current manufacturing practice.[5] A "Copy Exactly" program prescribed how to replicate successful process innovations originating in one manufacturing plant for use elsewhere in the company. At the same time, this program helped Intel's production outsourcing activities by providing an internal benchmark against which to compare external production partners.

However, Intel was aware that a decentralized, manufacturing-friendly approach to research was not enough. It therefore sponsored research by university science and engineering students working in relevant technological areas. It participated in the Semiconductor Research Corporation and Sematech, two US government sanctioned research and development consortia intended to foster collaboration on pre-commercial research. It also complemented its three major research laboratories with a series of smaller "lablets," whose sole purpose was to promote cooperative knowledge sharing and exchange with major research universities doing relevant work. Each lablet was led by a university faculty member on leave, and explicitly not by a permanent employee of Intel.

Intel also fostered collaborative linkages between external scientific communities and its own research laboratories. It hosted technology forums and seminars at which non-Intel researchers were invited to share findings with Intel researchers. It published the *Intel Technical Journal* to provide a publication outlet for both Intel and external research participants.[6] It complemented these with internal technology conferences where researchers from its separate internal labs came together to share experiences. The overall effect was to leverage a relatively small base of in-house research staff, while at the same time encouraging this staff to seek out external sources of relevant scientific and technological knowledge.

Intel also sought access to new knowledge through Intel Capital, the company's venture capital investment unit. Intel Capital funded new ventures that commercialized technologies compatible with Intel's own offerings and promised to offer complementary hardware, software and services for use with "Intel inside." In this way, Intel provided seed capital, technical assistance and co-marketing to those complementary technologies that added value to Intel's own product and service offerings and expanded the overall market for Intel compatible complements. Moreover, Intel Capital strategically invested outside the USA with an eye toward those ventures that could further Intel's strategy of globalization and expansion into new international markets.[7]

The Intel case illustrates a variety of practices organizations can use to participate in knowledge work. These involve the use of existing knowledge and the creation of new knowledge, using sources both internal and external to the organization. The case also shows how Intel engages in both knowing and learning, much as we saw in our previous chapters' stories of Mary and the forensic accountants. The case further suggests that both of these internal and external sources can be beneficiaries of new learning from Intel's knowledge work investments.

THE ORGANIZATION'S CORE COMPETENCIES

The focus of this chapter is on how organizations – private and public companies, non-profit institutions and government agencies – participate in knowledge work.

Let us look again at the Intel story. This time we will use it to suggest that organizations invest in three core competencies that influence how an organization engages in knowledge work.[8]

Organizational culture

The first core competency involves an organization's culture, which engages with the shared beliefs and values of its members and their overall investment in its mission.[9] An organization's culture informs its sense of purpose and shapes the way employees relate to that purpose. From a knowledge management standpoint Intel's culture suggests something of a paradox. On the one hand, the company clearly valued the existing knowledge available from its local manufacturing operations. On the other hand, the company sought new knowledge from a variety of external sources. Perhaps the best single statement about Intel's culture is reflected in the title of Andy Grove's bestselling 1996 book: *Only the Paranoid Survive.*[10] Intel remained vigilant in monitoring those knowledge developments that posed either an immediate or a distant threat to its dominating position in the semiconductor industry.

Organizational capabilities

The second core competency involves an organization's overall capabilities, which draw on both the explicit and the tacit knowledge of its members, working alone or collectively, in order to perform the organization's work. These capabilities become embodied in an organization's ability to engage in specific types of work activities, and manifest themselves in the organization's performance of those activities.[11] Intel's research activities were deeply intertwined with those material sciences, multiple technologies and advanced manufacturing arts required to design and manufacture ever faster, more powerful and yet affordable microprocessors for a widening array of applications. These activities drew on learning experiences both internal and external to the company. Intel Capital's work in new venture funding provided further opportunities to learn from pioneering new experiments in knowledge commercialization.

Organizational connections

The third core competency concerns an organization's connections to suppliers, customers and alliance partners, industry contacts and so on.[12]

These connections extend the organization's reach in acquiring new knowledge and in integrating that knowledge with its own knowledge. Intel's connections were wide-ranging in the semiconductor industry, and in complementary industries that contributed to or utilized Intel products and services. These included connections with industry consortia of potential competitors (e.g. Semiconductor Research Corporation, Sematech), academia, and important suppliers and customers. With respect to the discussion on brokerage in Chapter 3, Intel performs a critical broker role in connecting a wide range of industries whose component technologies, products and services are compatible with its own evolving activities.

Intel's culture, capabilities, and connections thus provide an integrative perspective on its approach to knowledge work. The perspective parallels the way that Mary's knowing-why, knowing-how, and knowing-whom investments (in Chapter 2) and the forensic accountants' joint enterprise, shared repertoire, and mutual engagement (in Chapter 3) characterized individual and community perspectives on putting knowledge to work.

INTERDEPENDENCIES AMONG THE CORE COMPETENCIES

As was also the case with Mary and with the forensic accountants, we cannot fully understand and characterize Intel's approach to knowledge work without appreciating interdependence – this time among the three sets of core competencies: culture, capabilities and connections. Each of these is mutually reinforcing of and interdependent with the other two. Let us again use Intel for illustration.

Culture and capabilities

Intel's culture placed a high value on existing knowledge from its local manufacturing operations through the co-location of its research labs near those operations. Its principle of "Minimum Information" reinforced the value of existing manufacturing knowledge, and its "Copy Exactly" program reflected a cultural commitment to the identification and subsequent replication of best practices. In turn, the successes of these approaches to knowledge management reinforced the culture from which they originated.

Culture and connections

The "paranoid" element in Intel's culture underlay the company's relent-less investments in the avoidance of surprise. Joint research with dominant players in each segment of the semiconductor industry provided assurances that the company was among the first to know about scientific or technology developments that may have long-term consequences for its current and future products. At the same time, Intel's apparent success in learning from these collaborations provided further support for its underlying culture.

Capabilities and connections

Intel's research capabilities, organized through its distributed system of research labs and supporting lablets, were purposefully connected to a wide array of external knowledge sources. All three major labs connected Intel to both its ongoing manufacturing operations and relevant develop-ments in the semiconductor industry. Intel's lablets further connected the company to advanced research laboratories at the frontiers of relev-ant new science and technology. Intel's knowledge-based capabilities were heavily intertwined with their investments in network relations with external knowledge sources.

The three core competencies and the links among them are shown in Figure 4.1.

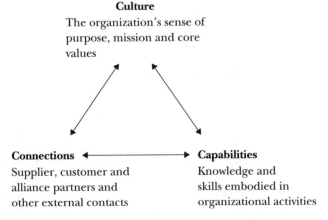

Figure 4.1   A framework of organizational competencies

THE ORGANIZATION AND THE KNOWLEDGE DIAMOND

As was shown previously for individuals and communities, we next examine how organizational knowledge work is related to the other three participants in the knowledge diamond. This involves links between organizations as well as links to all three of individuals, communities and the host industry or industries.

One organization and another

Organizations such as Intel work closely with other organizations in a variety of joint ventures, strategic alliances, research partnerships and subcontracting relations to both exploit existing knowledge and create new knowledge. Various reasons exist for organizations to cooperate with one another in knowledge work activities. A prominent reason is that cooperating organizations can make complementary knowledge contributions. Another reason is to share the risks of exploring and creating new knowledge. Research can be expensive and cooperative research lowers the expense and associated financial risk for each participant.[13]

Yet another reason for organizations to cooperate in knowledge work is because each organization would like to learn something about the capabilities of its partner. However, the desire by one organization to learn more about a second organization's core competencies may be seen by the second organization as threatening to its competitive standing. As a result, close cooperation in knowledge-creating projects by direct rivals in the same industry is rare. Collaborations are more common between companies that enjoy a supplier–customer or subcontractor–producer relationship. In these circumstances one participant, or primary contractor, typically enjoys significant bargaining leverage in setting the conditions for the collaboration and assuring that the flow of knowledge between the parties does not work to its disadvantage. Some companies have created knowledge-sharing networks among their entire family of suppliers. A pre-eminent example is the Japanese automobile manufacturer, Toyota.

Knowledge sharing in the Toyota supplier network[14]

Toyota enjoys an enviable reputation for designing and manufacturing high-quality cars. An important element of Toyota's approach to quality management has been its way of fostering knowledge sharing and learning within its network of suppliers. Six institutionalized practices have facilitated this knowledge sharing, each of them mutually supportive of the others.

The Toyota Supplier Association promotes "mutual friendship" and the "exchange of technical information" between Toyota and its parts suppliers. The association highlights a new theme each year (for example, eliminating supplier design defects) and shares knowledge about that particular theme. The association also offers basic training courses and sponsors tours to best practice plants both inside and outside the automobile industry.

The Operations Management Consulting Division (OMCD) maintains a group of internal consultants to help solve operational problems inside both Toyota and its suppliers. OMCD does not charge fees, but insists that Toyota may bring other suppliers to see the operational improvement. Client suppliers benefit directly from OMCD's intervention, while other suppliers are also able to learn from it.

Voluntary learning teams consist of teams of suppliers using similar production processes who assist each other with productivity and quality improvements. OMCD meets with these teams to establish new projects each year. OMCD periodically visits the teams to appraise their progress, offer assistance, and report back to Toyota on the lessons learned.

Problem-solving teams are teams formed to solve emergent problems within the supplier network. These teams also identify when the quality of one supplier is inferior to that of other suppliers for the same component, and help to transfer information and arrange site visits to the benefit of the inferior supplier.

Inter-firm employee transfers provide another mechanism for transferring knowledge amongst Toyota's suppliers. These transfers can be temporary assignments of Toyota or supplier company personnel to another facility. The transfers provide a means to transfer what is frequently tacit knowledge to a new setting, as well as to expose the transferred person to a new set of circumstances.

Performance feedback and monitoring processes monitor whether or not suppliers implement new knowledge or improved processes. Toyota regularly conducts quality audits of all its suppliers and provides both evaluative feedback and consulting assistance. In return, performance improvements are expected as part of Toyota's mission of continuous improvement among its suppliers.

Toyota reinforces its supplier learning and continuous improvement activities (capabilities) through a broadly understood mission of continuous improvement and a shared approach (culture) toward intellectual property within the Toyota supplier community. Moreover, Toyota's extensive knowledge-sharing capabilities are supported by dense networks of interaction (connections) among supplier network members and Toyota representatives. The interdependencies among culture, capabilities and connections reinforce Toyota's distinctive approach to knowledge work.

The organization and the individual

The complexity and rate of change in a knowledge-based economy calls for adaptive learning from incumbent members of the workforce. A challenge for organizations is to foster this kind of learning. A related challenge is to encourage the workforce to look beyond the boundaries of their own organization to learn about best practices and ideas. A further challenge is to encourage employees to share their knowledge with each other and to put that knowledge to work in new and improved products, services and operational processes. A prominent example of an organization seeking to respond to these challenges is General Electric (GE).

GE's learning culture

GE became among the most diversified corporations in the world, and was widely cited for its ability to put innovative business and management ideas into practice. During the 1980s and 1990s GE's image as a leading generator of management ideas and innovative practices was closely associated with its then Chief Executive Officer, Jack Welch. Despite the cult of personality that surrounds successful CEOs, Welch himself was quick to point out that it was General Electric's "learning culture" that had been responsible for GE's remarkable performance as a company innovator.

Welch has described the GE learning culture in terms of three components:[15]

1   *Dialogue*: idea sharing and best practice sharing are encouraged from anyone to anyone within the company.
2   *Boundarylessness*: breaking down physical boundaries (between locations) and psychological boundaries (between functional specializations) is encouraged to maximize the use of individual and collective intellect both within and outside the company. Ideas and best practices are sought from multiple internal and external sources.

3 *Trust and responsibility:* are guiding principles to create the conditions to encourage GE employees to learn effectively from each other (trust based) and to create the incentive for employees to put shared ideas and best practices to work in their own workplace activities (responsibility).

Moreover, GE has empowered individual idea champions throughout the company and created the office of the Chief Learning Officer, whose first incumbent, Steven Kerr, described his job thus: "Part of my job as CLO was to break down boundaries, and penetrate the [GE's] walls with new ideas."[16] Kerr emphasized the importance of transferring knowledge into *deep action*, that is, into commitments to activity that produce visible operational results within the company.

GE further supports its cultural commitment to employer learning through its world-renowned employee and management training programs. Employees are widely trained in the latest management practices (e.g. demand flow manufacturing, quick service/quick response, and Six Sigma quality) and are expected to use these newly learned tools in their business units. Indeed, company performance evaluations for learning participants and their business units are adjusted to reflect the expected benefits from use of these new tools.[17]

Learning at GE has been driven by its underlying culture, capabilities and connections. At the same time these GE organizational learning investments only succeed because they tap into individual employees' knowing-why motivation to learn, knowing-how basis for learning and knowing-whom relationships through which that learning can be nourished.

The organization and the community

As already discussed in Chapter 3, organizations interact with various external communities that are sources of knowledge or related resources that can serve the organization. Some communities are targets of organizational public relations departments, whose primary focus is on maintaining goodwill with groups possessing the potential to create positive or negative publicity. Other communities contribute more directly to an organization's knowledge-based activities.

Virtual communities – communities largely sustained over the World Wide Web – have become an important resource for organization knowledge and learning. A prominent example occurs in the software industry, where web-based relationships frequently drive, or at least supplement, an organization's knowledge work. Let us pick up again the case of the Linux software community, introduced in Chapter 3.

Red Hat and its Linux
community interactions

The company Red Hat grew to become a major distributor of shrink-wrapped versions of Linux, and a publisher of Linux books, open-source tools and technical support. Red Hat commercializes knowledge created by the Linux open software community, and in so doing has to conform to distinctive intellectual property rules about putting Linux-based knowledge to work.

The Linux community provides a platform for companies like Red Hat to utilize the operating system for commercial applications. However, Linux-based companies do not own the Linux software on which their businesses depend. Anyone can use the "open-source" Linux software or make changes to it without restriction of traditional copyright. Organizations seeking to make a commercial business out of Linux-based software must depend on improvements in the software arising from the virtual community of Linux software programmers who regularly post software patches or improvements onto a shared website. The best of these are incorporated into the next generation of the Linux software kernel by Linux founder Linus Torvalds and an inner core of informal Linux community leaders.

Red Hat was one of the first commercial organizations to invest in the Linux community. For example, Red Hat funded software development work by Linux community "inner circle" member Alan Cox, although he did not directly work for Red Hat. Red Hat also provided an attractive employment setting for Linux community members to continue their involvement in the software's development. Linux community members who were employees of Red Hat benefited further from their increased visibility to and recognition from computer system manufacturers, corporate customers, and distributors.[18]

As Red Hat's Chief Operating Officer, Tim Buckley, put it:

> The last thing we want to do is start getting isolated from the [Linux] community, which we are accused of a bit, but only because we are getting bigger and have a reputation . . . [It] makes us want to double our efforts. We . . . give everything back to the community. [We] have three or four of the top [Linux] kernel developers on our payroll and they're not developing Red Hat stuff – that's just another sign that we're trying to make sure the community and the kernel development remains solid.[19]

The Red Hat story illustrates how an organization's culture, capabilities and connections can together capitalize on existing knowledge and also attract new knowledge from a relevant community – in this case the Linux software community. Moreover, Red Hat appears determined to give back to that community by supporting the joint enterprise, shared repertoire and mutual engagement through which that community does its own work.

The organization and the industry

Our opening example of Intel has suggested how a company may orient its knowledge work culture, capabilities and connections to influence the trajectory of technology, product and service developments throughout an industry. Intel has managed to influence the development of next generation semiconductor materials, chip designs and manufacturing processes, and operating and application software development based on Intel specifications. Also, many of the industry technical and testing standards employed within the semiconductor industry have "Intel inside."

Intel's influence over the semiconductor industry has been paralleled by that of Microsoft in the software industry. The dominance of these two companies has produced a situation in which each generation of Intel chip designs and Microsoft software releases has favored the other, producing the so-called "Wintel" (Windows and Intel) industry standard for computing hardware and software. Other examples of dominant organizations shaping the evolution of knowledge investments in their industry include Wal-Mart's influence on retailing, Procter and Gamble's influence on consumer household goods, and Sony's influence on consumer electronics and electronic entertainment. In each of these cases the firm has not only leveraged its own knowledge capabilities but also influenced the learning and innovation agenda of other industry participants. However, sometimes an organization's attempt to dominate industry development can produce a counter-reaction, such as that from open software developers toward Microsoft, as will be described in Chapter 8.

KEEPING THE ORGANIZATION IN VIEW

As with previous chapters, let us review the story so far. The channels through which an organization participates with other participants in the knowledge diamond are highlighted in Figure 4.2. These involve sim-

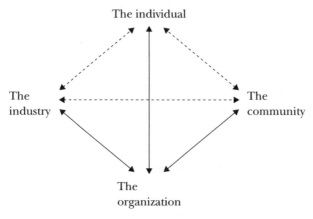

Figure 4.2 The organization and the knowledge diamond

ultaneous, two-way interactions between organizations and all four of: (1) other organizations, (2) individuals, (3) communities, and (4) the host industry. Organizations invest in these interactions for their own advantage, either in applying the knowledge they already possess or in seeking out new knowledge.

We need to be cautious about any traditional assumptions people may bring about an organization's size, or its influence over other knowledge diamond participants. In this regard, Intel's overall approach may be seen as a fundamental rejection of those assumptions. The organization's underlying philosophy is that it cannot control the pace and direction of research. It is better, therefore, to treat key external communities and organizations as collaborators in knowledge work, and to keep the company's strategy persistently open to the new knowledge it accumulates. One avenue for seeking new knowledge is through strategic alliances with other organizations, to which we now turn.

KNOWLEDGE TRANSFER IN STRATEGIC ALLIANCES

A much studied aspect of organizational learning concerns inter-organizational alliances, which commonly involve each organization aspiring to learn from the other as a byproduct of collaborative work. A common theme in studies of strategic alliances is the inherent difficulty of one party replicating the learning capabilities of its partner, particularly when those capabilities are embedded in highly tacit, complex and interdependent processes and activities.[20] More generally, knowledge work collaborations between organizations may entail both competitive and cooperative elements. Some collaborations may be likened to competitive "learning races" where each partner strives to outlearn the other and thus gain advantage in its subsequent exploitation of knowledge acquired from the collaboration.[21] An instructive example is that between Xerox and Fuji Xerox.

Xerox and Fuji Xerox

Fuji Xerox was launched in 1962 as a joint venture between Rank Xerox (itself a Xerox joint venture) and Fuji Photo Films to market xerographic products (copiers) in Japan and other Asian countries. However Fuji Xerox's engineers "reverse engineered" Xerox products as well as those of rival Japanese copier companies and developed new lower-cost copiers. Soon after Fuji Xerox had acquired production facilities from its Fuji Photo Films venture parent, and by the late 1960s it dominated the high-volume segment of the Japanese copier market. Meanwhile, the venture parent Xerox saw its share of revenues in the global copier market decline from 93% in 1971 to 40% in 1985.[22] Xerox CEO David T. Kearns lamented: "We dominated the industry we had created. We had always been successful, and we assumed that we would continue to be successful. Our success was so overwhelming . . . that we became complacent."[23]

As Fuji Xerox's market power increased, the relationship between Fuji Xerox and Xerox evolved. Fuji Xerox enjoyed increasing strategic and operational autonomy from its US parent. While Fuji Xerox continued to depend upon Xerox for basic research, Fuji Xerox increased its own capabilities to design and manufacture low-cost copiers. As a result, Fuji Xerox began to operate as a coequal research partner with Xerox in a growing number of copier-related technologies. In 1990, one Xerox senior manager noted: "It seems that every time Xerox blinks and retracts, Fuji Xerox forges ahead."[24] Yet it was the world-class capabilities of Fuji Xerox in product design manufacturing and management that helped the parent Xerox mount a comeback against both low-end and high-end copier rivals over the 1980s and early 1990s.[25]

During the 1990s, Fuji Xerox's market growth and profitability increasingly outstripped parent Xerox. In 1995, Xerox paid one billion dollars to UK partner Rank Xerox to acquire the needed 20% of stock that would bring Xerox's ownership of Fuji Xerox to 50%. This ownership change did not alter the long-standing autonomy that Fuji Xerox had earned, but Xerox's 50% ownership of Fuji Xerox was short lived. A severe financial crisis in 2000 led Xerox to reduce its ownership stake in Fuji Xerox to

25%. Still, both companies continued their pre-existing technology agreements, ensuring that the two companies retained access to each other's patents, technology and products.[26]

As Fuji Xerox entered its fifth decade, it was clear that technologies and patents were increasingly originating from Fuji Xerox. The relationship between Xerox and Fuji Xerox had been transformed by the asymmetric growth in each partner's skills, market position and financial resources. If this relationship was a learning race, it seemed clear that Fuji Xerox was widening its lead.

In contrast to learning races, other collaborations may be more likened to a cooperative "teaching race" where the knowledge holder (rather than the knowledge seeker) is motivated to cooperate with its partners to accelerate the diffusion of knowledge.[27] Such teaching races are most common when one party is attempting to develop a *de facto* industry standard. A notable example of a teaching race is IBM's investment in alliances to promote open-source web architectures that in fact will grow the world market for IBM software and services.[28] Other cooperative teaching races may arise when governmental and non-profit organizations encourage widespread sharing of knowledge in order to create public good benefits from such knowledge. For example, the World Health Organization has sponsored collaborations between large pharmaceutical companies and firms in the Third World to speed the development of low-cost drug therapies for diseases that afflict low-income countries.[29]

Finally, collaborations may involve less of a race to acquire knowledge than an attempt by each organization to be more effective in utilizing knowledge from both internal and external sources.[30] The term "outsourcing" used to refer principally to business process outsourcing (BPO), where the focus was on routine processes, such as those in a customer call-in center. However, outsourcing now more frequently involves knowledge process outsourcing (KPO) – activities that demand advanced information search, analytical interpretation, technical skills and decision-making. Examples of KPO include intellectual property or patent research, research and development in pharmaceuticals and biotechnology, data mining and database creation, and analytical services such as equity research, competitive intelligence, and financial modeling. Typical users of KPO services include market research firms, investment banks, industry associations, publishing and database firms, and corporate planning departments of large *Fortune 500* companies.[31]

Organizational collaborations, like personal or communal networks, are complex relationships and have multiple determinants and elements that maintain them. We next examine organizational activities premised on two distinct ways of putting knowledge to work.

EXPLOITATION VERSUS EXPLORATION

The essential distinction between knowledge exploration and exploitation is broadly suggested by James G. March: "Exploitation includes such things as refinement, choice, production, efficiency, selection, implementation, execution." Exploitation may be seen as the organizational counterpart to the earlier discussion in Chapter 1 about knowing – that is, putting current knowledge to work. Exploration includes things captured by terms such as "search, variation, risk taking, experimentation, play, flexibility, discovery, innovation."[32] In contrast exploration may be seen as the organizational counterpart to the earlier discussion in Chapter 1 about learning – that is, acquiring or creating new knowledge. Robert Grant has provided a useful elaboration of organizational knowledge work practices, in which both exploration and exploitation are integral to the knowledge work activity of any organization.[33]

Knowledge *exploitation* includes activities related to reusing existing knowledge. One category of knowledge exploitation involves *replication* of knowledge. The preceding example of Intel's "Copy Exactly" program for transferring "best practice" process innovations among its manufacturing operations illustrates replication. A second category involves knowledge *storage*. The creation of specialized databases accessible through knowledge portals and intranets is a routine occurrence in many contemporary organizations. A third category is knowledge *measurement*. This involves applying metrics to the organization's stock of knowledge (intellectual capital) and seeking to transform intangible knowledge into a tangible and tradable commodity. Companies in a variety of industries (e.g. high technology, pharmaceuticals, and entertainment and media) have made significant investments in measuring the economic value of their intellectual property (e.g. patent and copyright portfolios) and in licensing or selling outright their intellectual property to others, a topic to be further examined in Chapter 9.

Knowledge *exploration* includes activities related to the acquisition or generation of knowledge that is new to the organization. One category of knowledge exploration is that of knowledge *creation*. Many business, governmental and non-profit scientific organizations depend upon in-house research and development (R&D) facilities as primary sources of knowledge creation. These kinds of facilities were illustrated in the Intel example, and are found in major corporations everywhere. A second category is knowledge *acquisition*. People, companies and even industries expand their knowledge base by benchmarking activities outside their personal, company or industry boundaries and applying either the knowledge gained or the general principles behind it to their own sphere of practice.[34] Business organizations have increasingly utilized external recruitment activities to expand their workforces' aggregate breadth or depth of knowledge.[35] The common denominator in knowledge acquisition activities is the importation of knowledge from external sources.

Several factors are influencing current practices of knowledge exploitation and exploration. Knowledge exploitation and its supporting activities, including knowledge measurement, storage and replication, assume that knowledge is primarily a commodity that can be easily collected, stored and transferred. However, neither the possession of knowledge nor its retrieval through computer systems guarantees that either individuals or organizations will engage in processes that act on the knowledge, or bring about the creation or utilization of new knowledge.[36] Examples of such learning failures will be illustrated in Chapter 6. Similarly, knowledge creation through company research is made more challenging today by the increasing diversity of knowledge sources available and their global dispersion. The implications of this global knowledge explosion will be more fully explored in Chapters 7 and 8 as we examine how both multinational firms and their geographically dispersed collaborators create and combine knowledge.

In practice, organizations need both explicit and tacit knowledge and they need to invest in both knowledge exploitation and exploration. However, not all companies engage in exploitation and exploration to the same degree. We now turn to consider two contrasting strategies through which organizations can engage in knowledge work.

CODIFICATION VERSUS PERSONALIZATION

The previous discussions of explicit versus tacit knowledge and of knowledge exploitation versus exploration provide a basis for identifying two general strategies which organizations use in their knowledge work. A *codification strategy* emphasizes explicit knowledge and its exploitation on a repeatable basis. Organizations employing this strategy emphasize processes for capturing knowledge and storing it in databases for ease of retrieval. By contrast, a *personalization strategy* is characterized by an organization's emphasis on tacit or exploratory knowledge.[37] These organizations emphasize knowledge acquisition and transfer through people-to-people communication. An example comes from the health care industry.

Codification versus personalization in health care[38]

Access Health, a call-in medical center, heavily relies on information technology to capture, store and reuse knowledge on health care symptoms and their correlation with various health conditions and recommended therapies. Its knowledge repository contains software algorithms of the symptoms of more than 500 illnesses. When someone calls the center, a registered nurse uses the company's clinical database system to rule out possible conditions and to recommend a home remedy, a doctor's visit, or emergency room urgent care. One benefit from the company's knowledge repository is the lower prices it charges its call-in customers.

One insurer further reported that usage of Access Health's call-in services resulted in a 15% drop in expensive emergency room visits and an 11% drop in physician office visits by the insurers' clientele. Beyond the initial costs of database construction and periodic update, office costs are relatively modest, due to a small staff of registered nurses who have been trained to use the knowledge repository to screen symptoms. Access Health thus offers a low-cost means to screen relatively common and non-life-threatening health symptoms for home health treatment.

In contrast, Memorial Sloan–Kettering Cancer Center in New York City provides the highest quality of customized diagnostic and therapeutic services to its clientele. A wide range of experts consult with individual patients, and subsequently deliberate within seventeen highly specialized, disease-specific, cancer treatment teams. For example the breast cancer team has forty specialists who frequently discuss the latest scientific advances and clinical findings that might have a bearing on patient care. A major emphasis in the team-based meetings is to insure that knowledge is transferred between cancer researchers and cancer treatment providers, and shared among specialized care providers to provide the optimum response to the unique challenges presented by each Sloan–Kettering cancer patient.

Top cancer clinicians and researchers seek appointments to staff at Sloan–Kettering, which provides access to state-of-the-art technology and the opportunity to work with world-class research and clinical staff. The costs of providing such premium cancer services are high, and are borne by a combination of private insurance coverage and government funding. Access to the services of Sloan–Kettering is generally reserved for relatively unique and life-threatening forms of cancer that demand the advanced diagnostic and treatment knowledge that the Center can provide.

The codification strategy of Access Health emphasizes the reuse of previously learned skills and organizational routines for further exploitation. Codification strategies stress the provision of standardized, modularized services – in this case health screening services – that can be replicated for different customers. These strategies are likely to be common in organizations where the unit of service or production is a relatively standardized offering. In these cases the organization's culture, competencies and connections (and through these its reputation) emphasize being a relatively low-cost but reliable provider of products or services to price-sensitive buyers.

In contrast, the personalization strategy of Memorial Sloan–Kettering Cancer Center emphasizes new knowledge acquisition. Personalization strategies stress the provision of innovative and customized products and services – in this case sophisticated cancer diagnosis and treatment – at a premium price. These strategies are likely to be common in organizations, such as specialized consulting firms or research centers, that persistently address new problems. In these cases the organization's culture, competencies, and connections (and so its reputation) emphasize being at the forefront of knowledge within the organization's sphere of practice.

The options of codification and personalization represent ideal cases of a more complex reality. Many organizations represent hybrid knowledge strategies, with some businesses or subunits (e.g. R&D) emphasizing a personalization strategy and other businesses or functional subunits (e.g. operations or information technology) emphasizing more codification-based knowledge strategies. However, the contrasting strategies provide a diagnostic approach to (1) better understanding the underlying knowledge strategy an organization employs and (2) examining how the organization goes about integrating diverse knowledge inputs.

CLOSED VERSUS OPEN INNOVATION

For much of the twentieth century, large, hierarchical corporations such as AT&T, DuPont, IBM and many others operated according to largely "closed" assumptions on innovation. That is, they functioned based on assumptions that the knowledge needed for innovation existed or could be generated inside the organization.[39] However, Intel's approach to knowledge work described at the start of this chapter differs sharply from approaches that rely largely on internally generated knowledge. Intel and many other firms emphasize alternative "open" innovation assumptions that at least some of the knowledge needed lay outside the

Table 4.1 Differences between principles of closed and open innovation systems[40]

Closed innovation	Open innovation
The smart people work for us	Not all the smart people work for us
Research and development, and follow-up through product development and launch, are all internal activities	External research and development can complement internal efforts
Profits arise from internal discovery	Profits can be generated from external discovery
Get to market first	Build a better business model
Create the most and best ideas in the industry	Make the best use of both internal and external ideas in the industry
Protect intellectual property from competitors	Trade intellectual property with competitors

organization. Innovation expert Henry Chesbrough has drawn a series of contrasts – about employment, profit realization, time to market, etc. – that distinguish between the two approaches. These contrasts are summarized in Table 4.1.

Chesbrough argues that at least four factors worked to undermine the assumptions of closed innovation. First, the increasing availability and mobility of knowledge workers made it increasingly risky for firms to invest all their knowledge capabilities in their own workforce. An example is firms contracting out much or all of the work previously performed by internal information technology departments. Second, the faster pace of new product development and the shorter life cycles of new products and services made it imperative that new knowledge be quickly put to work. An example is the widespread pattern of licensing patents to other firms for faster commercialization.

A third factor was that the growth of the venture capital industry allowed knowledge workers to exit closed innovation companies and start their own companies. A classic example is the "Fairchild family tree" of high-technology companies – including Intel, AMD and National Semiconductor – that were founded by former employees of Fairchild Semiconductors Inc.[41] A fourth factor was the proliferation of advanced research laboratories within universities. This, along with the growth of companies specializing in contract research, produced a new landscape of more abundant but simultaneously more fragmented knowledge. For example, knowledge process outsourcing (KPO) services are used by investment banks and financial services institutions for data mining, and a range of analytical services such as equity research and financial modeling.[42]

Open innovation has many affinities with the knowledge diamond underlying this book, and in particular with the fundamental assertion that every knowledge work participant – individual, community, organization or host industry – needs to be open to the influence of other knowledge work participants. Moreover, Chesbrough's research suggests that an increasing number of industries – such as automobiles, biotechnology, computing, packaged goods, financial services, health care, insurance and pharmaceuticals – are transitioning from closed systems to open systems of innovation.[43] However, a major challenge lies in determining the mechanisms for knowledge sharing, given the former dominance of closed approaches and their tight control over intellectual property in patent, copyright and trade secrecy legal protections. We will return to this topic in Chapter 9.

TOOLS FOR ORGANIZATIONS

The Access Health versus Memorial Sloan–Kettering comparative case illustrated several types of IT tools for organizations to put accumulated knowledge to work. The knowledge repository for illnesses used at Access Health is an example of a content-based knowledge management tool. It includes such features as a query system for soliciting relevant customer input data, a taxonomy for classifying illness symptoms, a document management system for entering symptoms, and an expert system for matching visitor report symptoms to illness profiles and related diagnostic and treatment protocols. These types of content-based knowledge management tools may be found in many other industries where there are repetitive customer interactions regarding a relatively standardized set of customer relationship situations, such as may be found in call centers.[44] The advantage of content-based IT systems is to provide a software-based expert system for recognizing discrete patterns of customer interaction. These systems support speed of response and efficient service provision by human operators who access the systems on behalf of their clientele.

By contrast, the use of team-based specialist consultations at Sloan–Kettering is an example of a behavioral practice that is less reliant on IT than on the tacit knowledge of the specialist team members. The Sloan–Kettering specialists' use of tools was not explicitly discussed, but these include collaboration tools to foster collective knowledge sharing and record keeping. Examples of such tools in health care include electronic medical record transcription systems that update patient records without the need for paper documentation.[45] Similar tools are available in other industries to foster the collection of real-time data from mobile sales force and service personnel.[46] The common element in these IT applications is to make it easier for knowledge workers to share their knowledge with other workers. Chapter 7 of this book will further examine the IT tools that are available to workers involved in virtual teams.

Many organizations now utilize more comprehensive knowledge management infrastructures that incorporate a wide range of IT and behavioral tools and related practices. These infrastructures seek to link pre-existing and discrete organizational knowledge management subsystems, including enterprise resource planning (ERP) systems to track inventories, customer relationship management (CRM) systems to track customer interactions, and human resource management (HRM) systems to track worker deployment and benefits. These separate knowledge-based systems are often integrated in what are being called enterprise knowledge portals.[47]

Enterprise knowledge portals are increasingly made available to an organization's employees, managers, suppliers and customers. These portals provide an integrated system for managing the technologies associated with the tracking and application of both internal and external knowledge. Companies with well-regarded track records in using knowledge portals include IBM, Eli Lilly, and Accenture.[48]

SUMMARY

Organizations – private and public companies, non-profit institutions and government agencies – inevitably engage in knowledge work. Organizations have three core competencies (culture, capabilities and connections) that support knowledge work and which serve an analogous role to the trinity of attributes separately described for individuals (knowing-why, knowing-how and knowing-whom) and communities (joint enterprise, shared repertoire and mutual engagement). The Intel case provided an examination of these three organizational knowledge core competencies at work and their interdependencies.

The Toyota case illustrated how a business organization can collaborate with other supplier organizations. The GE case then illustrated how an organization's learning culture and supporting capabilities and connections can positively influence individual learning. The Red Hat case provided an illustration of the power of online communities as sources of knowledge to software commercial organizations. Xerox's alliance experiences with Fuji Xerox illustrated the challenges of learning races and their implications for knowledge sharing between alliance partners. Finally, the cases of Access Health and Sloan–Kettering demonstrated the contrast between codification and personalization knowledge strategies. A dominant theme in this chapter was the importance of organizations being open to sources of knowledge beyond their boundaries – that is to other participants in the knowledge diamond.

QUESTIONS FOR REFLECTION

1   Select an organization that interests you. Can you describe how the culture, capabilities and connections emphasized within that organization influence its approach toward putting knowledge to work?

2   For the same organization you selected in question 1, can you provide examples of how its culture, capabilities and connections are interdependent with one another?

3   Assume your place as an organizational representative in the knowledge diamond. How do your organization's knowledge investments relate to those of (a) other organizations, (b) the industry, (c) yourself and other individuals and (d) communities?

4   Does your organization enable people to effectively use their knowledge, and to continue to learn? What would you like to see your organization (or a future employer) emphasize to better meet your requirements as a knowledge worker?

5   What strategic alliances are you familiar with? How well do they work?

6   What examples have you seen of exploitation versus exploration, codification versus personalization, or closed versus open approaches to innovation?

7   What kinds of organizational IT or behavioral tools have you experienced? Were those tools effective? How did they influence you, or other knowledge work and knowledge workers?

NOTES

1   Hamel, C. and Prahalad, C.K. (1994) *Competing for the Future*, Boston, Harvard Business School Press, quote p. 203.

2   Intel's 2001 revenues were $26.5 billion, and employees numbered over 83,000 worldwide. In the same year, Intel's microprocessors led all world markets and constituted over 81% of the company's revenues. Data quoted from Chesbrough, Henry (2003) *Open Innovation*, Boston, Harvard Business School Press, p. 113.

3   Moore, G. (1996) "Some personal perspectives on research in the semi-conductor industry," in R.S. Rosenbloom and W.J. Spencer (eds), *Engines of Innovation*, Boston, Harvard Business School Press, pp. 165–74.

4   Leonard-Barton, D. (1992) "Core competencies and core rigidities: a paradox in managing new product development," *Strategic Management Journal*, 13, 111–25.

5   Chesbrough, *Open Innovation*, p. 116.

6   Ibid., p. 122.

7   Ibid., pp. 126–30.

8   Prahalad, C.K. and Hamel, G. (1990) "The core competence of the corporation," *Harvard Business Review*, 68 (3), 79–91; Hall, R. (1992) "The strategic analysis of intangible resources," *Strategic Management Journal*, 13, 136–9.

9   Barney, J. (1986) "Organizational culture: can it be a source of sustained competitive advantage?," *Academy of Management Review*, 11, 656–65.

10 Grove, A.S. (1996) *Only the Paranoid Survive*, New York, Doubleday.

11 Grant, R. (1996) "Toward a knowledge-based theory of the firm," *Strategic Management Journal*, winter special issue, 17, 109–22. See Nelson, R.R. and Winter, S.G. (1982) *An Evolutionary Theory of Economic Change*, Cambridge, MA, Harvard University Press, for an elaboration of how accumulated skills and knowledge are codified into organizational routines or standard operating processes for the skillful performance of organizational activities.

12 Powell, W., Koput, K.W. and Smith-Doerr, L. (1996) "Inter-organizational collaboration and the locus of innovation: networks of learning in biotechnology," *Administrative Science Quarterly*, 41, 116–45.

13 Child, J. (2001) "Learning through strategic alliances," in M. Dierkes, A.B. Antal, J. Child and I. Nonaka (eds), *Handbook of Organizational Learning and Knowledge*, Oxford, Oxford University Press, pp. 657–80.

14 Dyer, J.H. and Nobeoka, K. (2000) "Creating and managing a high performance knowledge-sharing network: the Toyota case," *Strategic Management Journal*, 21, 345–67.

15 Davenport, T. and Prusak, L. (2003) *What's the Big Idea?*, Boston, Harvard Business School Press, p. 199.

16 Ibid., p. 209.

17 Lucier, C. and Torsilieri, J. (2001) "Can knowledge management drive bottom-line results?," in I. Nonaka and D. Teece (eds), *Managing Industrial Knowledge*, Thousand Oaks, CA, Sage, pp. 231–43.

18 Tapscott, D., Ticoll, D., and Lowy, A. (2000) *Digital Economy: Harnessing the Power of Business Webs*, Boston, Harvard Business School Press, p. 123.

19 MacCormak, A. and Herman, K. (1999) *Red Hat and the Linux Revolution*, Case 9-600-009, Boston, Harvard Business School, p. 11.

20 Reed, R. and DeFillippi, R.J. (1990) "Causal ambiguity, barriers to imitation and sustainable competitive advantage," *Academy of Management Review*, 15, 88–102.

21 Khanna, T., Gulati, R. and Hotria, N. (1998) "The dynamics of learning alliances: competition, cooperation and relative scope," *Strategic Management Journal*, 19 (3), 193–210.

22 McQuade, K. and Gomes-Casseres, B. (1992) *Xerox and Fuji Xerox*, Case 9-391-156, Boston, Harvard Business School.

23 Kearns, D.T. (1990) "Leadership through quality," *Academy of Management Executive*, 4, 86–9.

24 McQuade and Gomes-Casseres, *Xerox and Fuji Xerox*, p. 15.

25 Gomes-Casseres, B. and Spar, D. (2002) *Xerox and Fuji Xerox: Update 2002*, Case 9-703-009, Boston, Harvard Business School.

26 Ibid.

27 Salk, J.E. and Simonin, B.L. (2003) "Beyond alliances: towards a meta-theory of collaborative learning," in M. Easterby-Smith and M.A. Lyles (eds), *The Blackwell Handbook of Organizational Learning and Knowledge Management*, Malden, Blackwell, pp. 253–77.

28 Capek, P.G., Frank, S.P., Gerdt, S. and Shields, D. (2005) "A history of IBM's open-source involvement and strategy," *IBM Systems Journal*, 44 (2), 249–57.

29 Salk and Simonin, "Beyond alliances," p. 255.

30 Grant, R.M. and Baden-Fuller, C. (2004) "A knowledge accessing theory of strategic alliances," *Journal of Management Studies*, 41 (1), 61–84.

31 "From BPO to KPO," *The Hindu*, October 25, 2004, http://www.thehindu.com/thehindu/biz/2004/10/25/stories/2004102500541600.htm, accessed November 5, 2005.

32 March, J.G. (1991) "Exploration and exploitation in organizational learning," *Organization Science*, 2 (1), 71–87.

33 Grant, R. (2002) *Contemporary Strategy Analysis*, Malden, MA, Blackwell.

34 Coers, M., Gardner, C., Higgins, L. and Raybourn, L. (2001) *Benchmarking: A Guide for Your Journey to Best-Practice Processes*, Houston, TX, American Productivity and Quality Center.

35 Orlikowski, W. (2002) "Knowing in practice: enacting a collective capability in distributed organizing," *Organization Science*, 13 (3), 249–73.

36 Newell, S., Robertson, M., Scarbrough, H. and Swan, J. (2002) *Managing Knowledge Work*, New York, Palgrave, p. 108.

37 Hansen, M.T., Nohira, N. and Tierney, T. (1999) "What's your strategy for managing knowledge?," *Harvard Business Review*, March–April, 106–16.

38 Ibid.

39 Chandler, A.D. (1990) *Scale and Scope: The Dynamics of Industrial Capitalism*, Cambridge, MA, Harvard University Press.

40   Table derived from Chesbrough, H.W. (2003) "The era of open innovation," *MIT Sloan Management Review*, 44 (3), 38.
41   "Fairchild Semiconductor Company pedigree," *The Antique Chip Collectors Page*, http://www.antiquetech.com/companies/fairchild.htm, accessed November 5, 2005.
42   "Knowledge process offshoring (KPO) opportunity to be worth USD 17 by 2010," press release of Evalueserve by eMediaWire, July 17, 2004, http://www.emediawire.com/releases/2004/7/emw141793.htm, accessed November 5, 2005.
43   Chesbrough, *Open Innovation*, pp. xxvi–xxviii.
44   Schwenk, H. (2002) "Real-time CRM analytics: the future of BI?," *KM World*, 11 (2).
45   See an example of Electronic Medical Records Software services at http://www.omnimd.com, accessed November 5, 2005.
46   Favreau, M. (2005) *The Future of Portable Computer and Communication Devices*, Norwalk, CT, Business Communications Company, Inc., http://www.bccresearch.com/comm/G185.html.
47   Collins, H. (2003) *Enterprise Knowledge Portals: Next-Generation Portal Solutions for Dynamic Information Access, Better Decision Making, and Maximum Results*, New York, AMACON; Sullivan, D. (2004) *Proven Portals: Best Practices for Planning, Designing, and Developing Enterprise Portals*, Boston, Addison Wesley.
48   Rao, M. (2005) *Knowledge Management Tools and Techniques*, Oxford, Elsevier, pp. 12–13.

CHAPTER 5

INDUSTRY KNOWLEDGE AT WORK

> In a network-based industrial system like that in Silicon Valley, the region – if not all the firms in the region – is organized to adapt continuously to fast-changing markets and technologies.
>
> *Anna Lee Saxenian*[1]

Silicon Valley may be the best-known example of a regional industry system, but neither was it first, nor is it alone. Industries, and in particular industry regions, participate in knowledge work on their own terms, sometimes reflecting collective organizational interests in a manner similar to that in which communities reflect individual interests. However, industries cannot be understood simply as interactions between participating organizations. Industries also engage with other industries (as, for example, between the pharmaceutical and biotechnology industries), with individuals (especially those making industry-centered career investments), and with communities (such as software development or scientific communities with particular expertise to offer).

Industry regions provide for the co-location of participating organizations, communities and individuals. These regions often give rise to particular "industry ecologies" that can lead to superior performance benefiting all of a region's knowledge work participants. However, established ecologies can also have an inhibiting effect as their traditions can interfere with the introduction of new work practices. Knowledge transfer between industries is an increasingly important phenomenon. So too is knowledge transfer between participating organizations, in some cases encouraged by one relatively dominant firm, in other cases stemming from a shared understanding of the collective benefits that can accrue. New communications tools are simultaneously challenging a traditional view of industry "regional advantage" while accelerating communications between regions.

Let us now move to our opening case example.

The UK advertising industry[2]

The London advertising industry has its center of gravity in Soho, in an area of around one square mile colloquially known as "adland." Soho's creative agencies suggest a so-called "second wave" of advertising, in contrast to the "first wave" associated with large US organizations. Soho has pioneered significant innovations in the industry, particularly in the organization of the work around relationships and projects. Personal ties, local professional communities and corporate networks are key sources of the information sharing and creative endeavor within the industry.

London advertising agencies were among the first to introduce the role of account planning. This role was at first somewhat controversial, but became accepted in the UK as an indispensable part of an agency's work. As a result, this work revolves around the collaborative efforts among three main roles: account management, account planning and creative, where the last comprises both copy writers and art directors.

The account manager is a key individual, providing business logic and liaising with the client through all stages of an advertising project. Even though projects with clients are often short term, client–agency relationships are often long lasting, based on the ties that develop between the individual account manager and the client organization's marketing manager. These relationships can be so strong that account managers frequently take "their" clients with them when they move to another agency.[3] Similarly, when a marketing manager changes companies, he or she often retains established relationships with an agency account manager.

At the other end of an advertising project are the needs and perceptions of the client's customers – the consumers. This is where the role of the account planner comes in, providing an analytical or scientific logic to the project. Drawing on the skills of particular individuals, the planning role provides analysis and knowledge of consumer perceptions to the production process inside the agency. Account planners also test out the creative concepts of the agency and gather feedback and information from activities like surveys and focus groups.

At the heart of the agency is the creative process that provides the artistic logic to advertising projects. Here, two key players or "creatives" are involved: the copy writer, who provides script, and the artistic director, who provides the visual art. Acting as creative complements, their careers are "rather the career of a particular partnership than of separate individuals."[4] They build their reputations together, and, if they move on to other agencies, tend to do so as a partnership. Creatives rely strongly on personal networks for links with communities that provide specialized services outside their agency, such as photographers, graphic designers, and TV commercial directors. The relative ease of communication between different communities, all within the Soho district, facilitates free exchange of knowledge and ideas as project collaborators "hang out" with one another.

With three distinctive agency roles converging around the creative process, tensions frequently arise. However, these are kept in check by the relatively short-term duration of most advertising projects. Tension is seen as "creative tension," stemming from and at the same time reinforcing the rapid pace at which work gets done. Also, the boundaries of individual advertising agencies in Soho are somewhat blurred. The district has been described as an "ideas village" like "a university without the academic side."[5] Interactions across the industry, particularly at the personal level, mean that agencies not only contribute to, but also benefit from, the pool of industry knowledge and ideas.

Agencies also interact with one another through projects that are increasingly embedded in international and global corporate networks. In 2001, it was reported that three global groups, Interpublic, Omnicom, and WPP, each operated in over 100 countries and together accounted for some 40% of the gross income of the world's top 100 advertising organizations. This concentration is driven largely by the changing demands of client companies, which, although global, increasingly require local input into their advertising campaigns. Personal networks, again, play a vital role in linking accounts, agencies and expertise across countries, and Soho is seen as a vital node in a wider global network of talent and corporate organization.

In this chapter, we focus on the final participant in the knowledge diamond, the industry. The opening story of the Soho advertising industry suggests that all four of the knowledge diamond's participants are at work as knowledge gets created, transferred and utilized within advertising projects. Creativity in the advertising industry appears fueled by strong personal ties and informal networks, tapping into rich repositories of ideas, knowledge and experiences. As in many other industries, knowledge exploration activity in advertising is steeped in tacit knowledge, in this case acquired through the creatives' interactions with their own and other professional communities.

The advertising industry has also developed new products, improved its technologies and designs, and understood its clients' and customers' requirements better, as it has combined knowledge and learning. Much of this occurs at the interstices between industry participants and frequently goes beyond what would be possible within single firms.[6] The co-location of the industry's many players within the small geographic area of Soho heightens the opportunities for inter-firm communication.

THREE ATTRIBUTES OF INDUSTRY ACTIVITY

As this chapter proceeds, we will see how knowledge is generated and travels within an industry, and how this is facilitated by a complex set of relationships among knowledge diamond participants. Once more, we will work with a framework of three interdependent dimensions, this time involving what may be called industry milieu, industry recipes, and the industry system.[7]

Industry milieu

The milieu of the host industry involves the platform of beliefs, values and shared sense of mission on which interactions among an industry's participants are based. This milieu is heavily shaped by the unique history, structure and cultural influences – frequently involving distinctive regional cultures – on which the industry is based. The resulting milieu can influence important aspects of the knowledge work of industry participants, including the propensity of individuals, communities and firms to interact and share knowledge. In the advertising industry example, the shared sense of professionalism and eagerness of creatives to be recognized and accepted by their peers are strong motivators for informal interaction. Similarly, account managers and their marketing manager counterparts in client organizations tend to share a common creative purpose that forms the basis for lasting relationships.

Industry recipes

Over time, accumulated know-how, repertoires and organizational capabilities in an industry develop into largely accepted ways of doing things – an industry's recipes.[8] Industry recipes provide repositories for past industry learning that reflect shared industry knowledge, and guide the emerging process through which new knowledge is accumulated. In the advertising industry, each advertising campaign, TV commercial, or billboard is an embodiment of the accumulated learning on the part of the producing agency and its network connections. Each new advertising project builds on the know-how of individuals, the shared repertoire of collaborating communities, and the capabilities of the companies involved. It is often creative rivalry among individuals or companies, and tensions around the challenges to established practice, that drive learning in the industry.

Industry system

The industry system refers to the shifting pattern of system of interconnections among industry participants. This system incorporates established patterns of collaboration (or non-collaboration) that have evolved over time. Sometimes, these patterns are established by professional associations that establish professional industry standards. In Soho, interpersonal ties, community links and corporate networks all contribute to the complex, interrelated system that reflects the unique character of the advertising industry. The links among participants provide an important catalyst in the generation, transfer and utilization of knowledge and new ideas. These interconnections, and the learning that accrues from them, are also important in helping the creative staff of advertising agencies gain legitimacy and credibility in their profession.

INTERDEPENDENCE AMONG INDUSTRY ATTRIBUTES

As was the case for individuals, communities and organizations, the three dimensions of industry knowledge work are closely linked. Industry milieu, recipes and system interact not only in the application of existing knowledge, but in the learning that leads to the generation of new knowledge. Let us look at these interdependencies in more detail.

Industry milieu and industry recipes

An industry's unique milieu provides the context in which existing industry recipes are understood and developed. In the Soho advertising example, the "village-like" milieu shapes the way that interdependencies between participants are played out, old industry recipes are shared and new learning is developed. Like all industries, the advertising industry needs to continually adapt to the changing needs of its customers or clients. In particular, this involves changing agency–client relationships, as multinational clients require Soho contacts to work across diverse regional markets. The industry milieu is thus increasingly open to geographically distant participants, and industry recipes are subject to change to accommodate the trend toward globalization.

Industry milieu and industry system

The industry milieu strongly influences the interconnections that develop within it. In the Soho example, we see that an advertising milieu supportive of collaboration and knowledge sharing encourages the development of interpersonal links, informal communities and inter-firm networks. These interactions also promote the exchange of tacit knowledge across and between creative projects in the industry. Industry milieux based on learning through collaboration, and also rivalry, may attract other participants whose relationship building activities may enrich the industry systems already in place. In more rigid industries, such as the chemical or oil industries, the links between the industry milieu and industry system may be less open to outside forces, and to fresh connections being made.

Industry recipes and industry system

The industry's recipes and its system of interconnections are likely to be similarly intertwined. Creatives in advertising agencies rely strongly on their social networks and personal ties to gain industry knowledge and apply new learning. The long-lasting relationships between account managers and client marketing managers contribute to the subtle, tacit and mutual understanding of each other's worlds. Trust, an essential ingredient of both interpersonal and inter-organizational learning, develops through socialization across the boundaries of advertising agencies and communities within the industry. Trust in turn facilitates a greater degree of knowledge sharing than would otherwise be the case.

These illustrations from the advertising industry show how industry knowledge and learning are vested in the interplay between an industry's

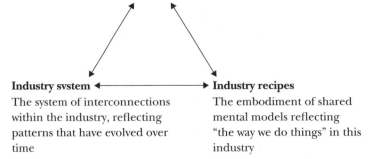

Industry milieu
The collective beliefs and values related to the industry's unique history, structure and culture

Industry system
The system of interconnections within the industry, reflecting patterns that have evolved over time

Industry recipes
The embodiment of shared mental models reflecting "the way we do things" in this industry

Figure 5.1   Three dimensions of industry activity

overall milieu, its recipes and its system of interconnections. The industry milieu can support the propensity of participants in the industry to individually or collectively share knowledge and to learn. As learning spreads among the industry participants it contributes to the development of distinctive recipes that in turn perpetuate the learning process. The dynamic nature of this learning is ensured by an industry system of interconnections, involving both interpersonal and community-centered social capital investments. The overall picture is summarized in Figure 5.1.

Both the application of existing knowledge and the development of new learning are underpinned by the collective involvement of knowledge diamond participants. We now turn to discuss the involvement of each of these participants in more detail.

THE INDUSTRY AND THE KNOWLEDGE DIAMOND

Knowledge work and learning in an industry do not occur in isolation from other industries, or from other knowledge diamond participants. Individuals participate in industry development through their affiliations with communities or companies, and sometimes directly through individual innovations. Communities and companies can determine the success or failure of industries as they help shape the competitive landscape through brokerage activities. These may include brokerage with other industries, sometimes foreshadowing the interdependence or fusion between industries to follow. Next, we offer a series of minicases to illustrate how an industry interacts with other industries and with individuals, communities and companies.

One industry and another

Industries evolve along different trajectories. Sometimes, interactions between industries can result in new technologies that would not otherwise have arisen. At other times, industries diverge as a result of new technologies, or new industries arise that take over part of the work of an existing industry, resulting in new interdependencies. The following case is an example of the latter situation, where the emerging field of biotechnology has influenced the traditional structure of the pharmaceutical industry.

The biotechnology and pharmaceutical industries[9]

Knowledge work in the pharmaceutical industry traditionally emphasized two major areas: one in drug research and development, which is largely skills and know-how based; and one in sales and marketing, which is largely relationship based. New drug development in the pharmaceutical industry drew on research in organic chemistry, which is why many large pharmaceutical companies evolved from chemical company conglomerates. The cost of producing a medicine in this way is extremely high, requiring years of patent protection to recoup the costs of getting new drugs to market.

The biotechnology industry has its roots in very different scientific disciplines, involving molecular biology and genetics.[10] The two industries also differ significantly in their structure. The biotechnology industry is characterized by a strong ethos of cooperation within communities and across many formal and informal alliance arrangements. Over 1,400 biotechnology companies operate in the US industry alone, the vast majority being small.[11] By contrast, the pharmaceutical industry has responded to cost pressures through further consolidation, creating a small number of huge conglomerates with global market coverage. However, it is the pharmaceutical industry that holds most of the accumulated expertise in drug approval processes, and in sales and marketing.

Before the biotechnology industry was invented, pharmaceutical companies did almost all their R&D in-house and had few, if any, alliances with small R&D firms. However, the dynamic has changed significantly.

While some pharmaceutical companies have been developing internal biotechnology capability, they continue to rely heavily on the biotechnology industry for R&D. Since 1995, the pharmaceutical industry has had more R&D alliances with firms in the biotechnology industry than ever before.[12]

The interdependencies between the two industries have strengthened over time. On the one hand, over the period 1988 to 1995, it is estimated that approximately 70% of new biotech medicines released in the US were developed by specialist biotechnology firms. On the other hand, a similar percentage of the biotechnology industry's new drugs was commercialized by pharmaceutical firms.[13] The biotechnology industry is likely to continue to be the source of most new drugs in the future, and the pharmaceutical industry is likely to play the dominant role in commercialization.

The case shows us that, as the biotechnology industry has evolved, it has outperformed the traditional methods of the pharmaceutical industry in research and development. However, the knowledge work revolving around gaining approval for marketing and selling medicines has remained solidly within the pharmaceutical industry, drawing on the sheer scale and scope of its companies' global operations. Similar divisions of knowledge activities across industries have occurred in other areas. For example, many firms have outsourced customer service activities, so that knowledge practices once associated with a diverse range of industries have converged into the practices of call-center operations, to the extent that a new call-center industry has emerged.

The industry and the individual

Industries change, evolve and sometimes spawn new industries. In many cases, developments are driven by the influence of a particular individual or entrepreneur. The host industry provides a learning platform from which new ideas and motivations can arise, and where entrepreneurs can initiate changes at the industry level. The following case illustrates this point.

Richard Branson and the airline industry[14]

Few people have rewritten the rules of business across as many industries as Richard Branson, and few have had the lasting success that he has enjoyed. The Virgin brand includes over 200 companies in industries as diverse as bridal wear, soft drinks (cola), condoms, cinemas, insurance, pensions, trains, books, music, and, of course, airlines. The brand and the Branson personality appear deeply intertwined, so that some would say that Virgin has the personality of its founder.

Branson turns business enterprises into moral enterprises, engaging directly with the personal values of industry players (even competitors), and building on strong and lasting relationships. His purpose for entering an industry is never solely to make money. He passionately believes that it is possible to change an industry, and to give people a better deal. His mode of operation is to get to know people well enough to develop mutual trust, shared knowledge and learning – and then to "have fun" making employees and customers happy.

Virgin Atlantic was one of the first airlines to successfully change the structure of the industry, offering budget travel and high levels of service and customer attention not provided by traditional large players. Judged by travelers' associations and journals, Virgin Atlantic has persistently beaten British Airways and other carriers on service standards. Branson's different approach to business, his self-effacement and subtle mockery of the established industry have earned favor among Virgin Atlantic's customers. He won a landmark suit against British Airways, when the court supported Branson's claim that British Airways had misinformed the public about "cancellations" of Virgin flights. This in turn caused public embarrassment for British Airways and the early resignation of its chairman.

Branson's business philosophy has been imitated by rival Singapore Airlines, which embraces a holistic East Asian approach to customer care. A joint venture between the two airlines, with Singapore Airlines purchasing 49% of Virgin Atlantic, has begun to forge a new recipe for the industry. It is a recipe that traces back to the philosophy of one entrepreneur, and his attention to the social side of knowledge work – to learn and have fun.

The story of Richard Branson highlights the potentially powerful relationship between one person and an industry. Other examples come to mind, such as the influence of Microsoft's Bill Gates over the PC software industry, the effect of The Body Shop's Anita Roddick on the established health and beauty products industry, or the upshot of Dell's Michael Dell on the structure of the PC retailing industry.[15] In all these cases, we see strong personal commitment of the individual to creating or facilitating change through the application of new knowledge and ideas, and the ultimate creation of a new industry recipe. The influence of this so-called "maverick ethos" is not restricted to highly visible corporate leaders, but those leaders provide a convenient point of illustration.[16]

The industry and the community

As industries are often shaped by their interactions with key individuals, so too are industries' interactions with communities able to effect change. Communities of practice have become increasingly important in industries dependent on learning, flexibility and innovation for survival and growth. The following case illustrates how communities of practice play a key role in both the formation and the development of an industry, in particular, in a high-performing industry cluster.[17]

The New Zealand boat building cluster[18]

Shortly after its second America's Cup victory in 2000, commentators claimed that New Zealand was poised to become the yachting center of the world.[19] This acclaim arose from a long history of successful international yacht racing. New Zealand's two successive America's Cup victories, and even its later failure to defend the Cup, had placed the local boat building industry on the world map.

The marine industry employs approximately 8,000 people in New Zealand in over 1,300 companies, most of them within or around Auckland, the "City of Sails." The cluster includes specialist providers of clothing, cabinet making, communications, engines, sales and spars, as well as core boat building firms. All of these industry sectors have developed a high degree of specialization and sophistication, necessary to meet the needs of the marine industry's niche markets – in racing yachts, superyachts, leisure boats and trailer boats.

Many of the managers and employees of the industry's leading companies were, and still are, passionate "boaties." In earlier stages of cluster development, they sailed and raced together, building interpersonal bonds and developing mutual commitments to the boating industry. This reflected an emerging community of practice, drawing on a compelling individual sense of knowing-why tied to a communal spirit of joint enterprise. Those boaties have become the "keen, determined visionaries" at the heart of the current industry.[20]

The informal community attracted a diverse range of specialist skills associated with boating and boat building. The original community of boaties has given rise to a number of specialist communities. Critical for the flow of knowledge inside and outside the cluster, these communities represent research institutions, and offshore as well as local designers, manufacturers, suppliers, customers, yacht racing organizations, and yachting journalists.

The relative geographic isolation of New Zealand meant that the cluster had to build offshore links. Many of these developed from existing personal relationships. Reflecting on an international yacht design symposium hosted by the New Zealand industry, an overseas participant commented: "It gave me a fantastic opportunity to touch base with many people I had not seen for some time, as well as meeting contemporaries who I have eagerly awaited meeting." The flip side to the development of these links has been the international exposure of the New Zealand industry to important and lucrative new markets.

The New Zealand boat building case describes a particular industry arrangement, the cluster. The case highlights the important interactions between host industry and communities of practice. Communities of practice are often important in the early development or evolution of an industry, acting as seedbeds of learning and new company formation.[21] In turn, knowledge practices become routinized and legitimized around emerging industry norms, and the making of the industry milieu and its associated recipes begins. We will further examine the knowledge attributes of industry clusters in a later section of this chapter, when we consider industry regions and regional advantage.

The industry and the organization

Industries evolve and change. These changes may be driven by environmental factors, such as globalization, or by changes initiated by firms themselves. Changes may result from structural transformations, as for instance when old firms leave or new firms join the industry, or from the development of new organizational forms, such as alliances or clusters. The following case is an example of an industry that underwent change as a result of new company entrants with markedly different strategies to those of incumbent firms.

The German television industry[22]

Like many other industries, the TV industry has been affected by the phenomenon of globalization. Historically, two other important drivers of change in the TV industry have been the digitization of its technologies (and the resultant vertical disintegration of the industry), and the privatization of broadcasting. In Germany, privatization drove the TV industry towards a dual system of public and private broadcast sectors. The sectors compete for viewers and advertisers, channels and content.

Private TV broadcasting was established in Germany in the mid 1980s, assisted by deregulation, liberalization and the influence of two media conglomerates entering the private broadcasting sector. For the preceding three decades, TV was run by a decentralized public system fashioned after the British model of the BBC. The emergence of private TV broadcasting coincided with changes in the way that content was produced. In the public system, the two dominant public broadcasters were vertically integrated, and content production was largely in-house. The private broadcasters, on the other hand, followed a different model, sourcing content from outside independent producers.

The independent producers drew on the flexibility of project networks to provide content that met the ever-changing demands of broadcasters. These project networks were populated by independent contributors to the production of TV content, including authors, cameramen, actors, designers, and others. In Germany, this network form of temporary collaboration has evolved in a similar way to the US film industry.

By virtue of their access to content from the newly emerging independent producers, the private broadcasters gained significant advantage over their public broadcasting rivals in both reduced costs and greater programming flexibility. Within a short space of time, the public broadcasters began to adopt the new model for content production. Independent production companies had proliferated to around 1,500.

What can we learn about knowledge work and industry learning from the German TV case? Clearly, the entry and strategies of private broadcasters had a significant role. The simultaneous emergence of independent content producers created a considerably more diverse learning environment than before, enabling new knowledge flows among a greater number of connected players. Knowledge work changed from bureaucratically controlled to socially linked flexible practices, with different specializations organizing around collaborative project arrangements.

The reciprocal influence of the host industry on its member companies is also evident – the changing milieu, resulting from deregulation, new technology (notably digitization technology), and the increasingly linked system of supplier companies. All of these contrived to create a learning environment in which new private broadcasters could thrive. Similar industry–organization changes can be identified in other industries. For example, the miniaturization of components led to Sony and other manufacturers setting the recorded music industry on a new trajectory with products like the Walkman.[23]

KEEPING THE INDUSTRY IN VIEW

These cases illustrate the interactions between a host industry and the other three knowledge diamond participants, as in Figure 5.2. We see that all four participants are necessary for knowledge to flow and industry learning to take place. In turn, industry learning influences the knowledge work and practices of the other participants, in a recursive process that facilitates ongoing industry and knowledge evolution.

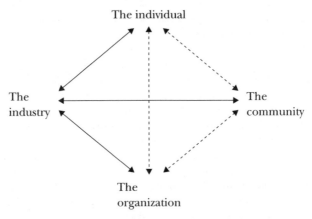

Figure 5.2   The industry and the knowledge diamond

The incorporation of virtual communications and electronic commerce into industry recipes has led to further transformation. For example, the call-center, web-trading, and travel industries have come to operate almost exclusively in virtual space. How the three dimensions of industry milieu, recipe and systems operate in this kind of environment is further explored in Chapter 7. However, many industries continue to benefit from physical co-location of people and firms in the same geographic area, as discussed in the following.

INDUSTRY REGIONS AND
REGIONAL ADVANTAGE

Ten percent of the world's leather shoes are produced in the Sinos Valley in southern Brazil. Twenty percent of the world's stainless steel surgical instruments are made in Sialkot, a small town in Pakistan.[24] Many otherwise little known regions in the world have been dominating production in particular industries for centuries. Why so? In the 1990s, Michael Porter popularized the notion of industry clusters.[25] However, earlier work, particularly in the field of economic geography, identified what have become known as "industrial districts" as long ago as the late 1800s, and associated with the pioneering work of Alfred Marshall.[26] Various other terms have been used to describe these geographically concentrated areas of industrial activity that we will refer to here as industry regions.

The central question is why industries concentrate around particular locations, and why those that do concentrate generally perform better than those that do not. Many researchers believe that the answer is to be found in the knowledge processes and knowledge interactions among people and firms within the region. Companies in industry regions often specialize in producing specific component parts of a product or service in a way that is complementary to other firms in the region. In the New Zealand boat building cluster, for example, we find companies dedicated to the production of a key part of the finished boat, such as sails or winches. A knowledge-based view of clusters sees companies co-locating in order to share knowledge and bring complementary skills together.[27] Companies can also benefit from regional competition, driving up skills and stimulating innovation through local rivalry.[28] Knowledge creation and transfer play key roles in both complementary and competitive clusters of companies located in specific geographic regions.

Over time, as the industry's milieu, recipes and system become more embedded in the local environment, regional advantages become more ingrained. An "industry ecology" of interacting locational factors evolves to support industry activities.[29] For example, even though disadvantaged by limited access to the supply of raw timber, the Danish furniture-making industry succeeds by virtue of the endowment of favorable characteristics, institutions and infrastructure associated with its location. In contrast, the Finnish timber industry, with plentiful raw timber supply, has not been able to support the successful development of a furniture-making industry because the regional characteristics traditionally supported large-scale pulp and paper production.[30] Regional advantages are so intimately entwined with the industry that success cannot be easily transferred to other regions.

While there are compelling arguments and considerable evidence supporting the importance of organizational proximity and regional advantage for industry success, their validity is now being challenged by new communication technologies. Chapter 7 considers this issue as it deals with the characteristics of virtual knowledge work.

REGIONAL CLOSURE
VERSUS BROKERAGE

In some industry regions, participants appear to operate in relative isolation. In other regions participants appear to communicate exceptionally well. The pattern appears to affect the whole industry milieu, and its accompanying recipes and system of interconnections, in a manner that directly affects the region's economic prosperity. An interesting example comes from two sets of electronics industry clusters operating in neighboring countries.

Malaysian and Singaporean electronics industries[31]

Between 1970 and 1995, the rate of growth of Malaysian electronics exports was over 25% per year. By the end of the period, the industry accounted for 25% of the country's manufacturing labor force and 50% of the country's total exports. Over the same period, the electronics industry in adjacent Singapore also grew to account for 25% of the manufacturing workforce. However, Malaysian per capita income was only one-sixth of that for Singapore. Why the difference?

Both countries began with a heavy reliance on multinational corporations as a means to build manufacturing capabilities that matched emerging market opportunities. The Malaysian industry developed around three regional clusters – Penang, the Klang Valley and Johor – all of which capitalized on the low-wage resources that were abundant in the 1970s and early 1980s. However, these clusters have continued to largely emphasize manufacturing, limiting per capita income and exposing the clusters to lower-wage competition able to imitate their production capabilities.

By contrast the Singaporean electronics cluster appeared to realize the likely erosion of early cost advantages. Drawing on a highly responsive education system, and a more active industrial policy, the cluster was able to attract higher value-adding activities from its relationships with the multinationals. Singapore became particularly active in attracting outside technological and scientific talent to supplement its local talent pool.[32] Relatively highly developed entrepreneurial and technological capabilities brought about a shift from low-cost manufacturing to the deployment of "packaging and integration" capabilities. Singapore came to be regarded as a regional headquarters for manufacturing services, responsible for matching demand and supply at local, regional and global levels.

Malaysia continued to have considerable production capabilities in electronics, but the industry lacked effective integration between production systems, skill formation, and an integrated (cluster-based) business model. Little attention was paid to the integration of cluster-based advantages, such as technology, know-how, research and development, and local institutional support. In sharp contrast to Singapore, the country was relatively unsuccessful in attracting higher-value activities from its multinational corporation investors. Moreover, Malaysia's long-standing national policy of *bumiputra* ("sons of the soil") to favor native Malays over non-Malays in education, employment and government service has resulted in a brain drain of Chinese and Indian professionals and scientific and technical knowledge workers, whose skills and knowledge are readily employed by other countries and locales, including Singapore.[33]

The contrasting Malaysian and Singaporean electronics industry clusters reflect the contrast between group closure and brokerage introduced in Chapter 3. The Singaporean cluster, encourage by a more fertile milieu for knowledge sharing and capability development, has become more open to adding further innovation and value creation in response to the multinationals' needs.[34] Over the same time period, the Malaysian cluster has remained focused on the advantage of low labor costs, and relatively closed to broader collaboration with the multinationals with which it was involved.

The electronics clusters example points to a much larger question about the influence of national policies on the development of industry regions, and on the overall prosperity of nations. It has been strongly suggested that the comparison between the Malaysian and Singaporean electronics clusters reflects a pattern of differences in national policy, covering larger issues of openness to foreign workers, education systems, and technology policy.[35] Another kind of comparison to be made is between successive industry policies in the same nation, such as the comparison between India's relatively closed approach before 1990 and the much more open approach adopted since that time. As has been widely reported, the new approach has promoted a whole new pattern of brokerage between Indian industry clusters – most obviously in but not restricted to the software industry – and global customers and collaborators.[36]

KNOWLEDGE TRANSFER BETWEEN INDUSTRIES

To focus primarily on any single industry can mean the neglect of knowledge transfer between industries. The role of Chicago-based Baxter

International provides an interesting extension to the story of the pharmaceutical and biotechnology industries begun earlier in this chapter.

Baxter International and biotechnology[37]

Between 1979 and 1996, the biotechnology industry emerged to become a central player in the knowledge economy. Alumni from the pharmaceutical company Baxter were included in core management teams of almost 25% of all US biotechnology start-ups that went public over the same period. Ninety-three former Baxter employees accounted for 1.9 alumni for every 1,000 employees, compared to only 1.4 alumni per 1,000 employees for Baxter's principal competitors. The trend was especially marked for new CEOs, who were recruited more frequently from Baxter than from any of its principal competitors.

The exodus of Baxter alumni out of pharmaceuticals into biotechnology does not conform to traditional industry logic. These were people who changed industry, rather than going to other pharmaceutical firms. Moreover, the exodus could not be explained by any commonality of geographic region. Baxter's headquarters were in the American Midwest near Chicago, Illinois, whereas major biotechnology centers around Boston, Massachusetts, and San Francisco, California, were respectively 1,000 and 2,000 miles away. Instead, the relocation of these Baxter alumni came about through the influence of the venture capitalists behind the new biotechnology start-ups.

Baxter people were attractive to venture capitalists for the distinctive career experiences that they brought. An entrepreneurial and results-driven organization culture, a decentralized (and therefore empowering) structure, and an emphasis on learning-by-doing prepared people as future general managers. By contrast, comparable experiences at Baxter's pharmaceutical rivals left their managers more specialized in science (Merck), functional specialization (Abbot) or some combination of the two (Johnson & Johnson). A distinctive "career imprint," stemming from the culture, capabilities and connections of Baxter, was carried forward to a different (although related) industry in a new geographic location.

Network connections initiated through prior Baxter employment were sustained in later employment situations. Alumni stayed in contact with their former Baxter colleagues, as well as building strong attachments among themselves through alumni reunions and other less formal events. Baxter itself encouraged continued interaction between present and former employees in order to seek out and capitalize on future business opportunities. At his eightieth birthday party in 1999, former Baxter CEO Bill Graham spoke proudly of there being "forty-three CEOs" together at the event.

Career imprinting – the diffusion of similar career experiences from one organization to other organizations – provides for the transfer of knowledge within or between industries. It has also been noted, for example, in the early evolution of Silicon Valley firms ("Fairchildren") from their leaders' previous employment at Fairchild Semiconductors, in the proliferation of exemplary customer relations capabilities out of IBM, or in the spread of "Six Sigma" quality control systems out of General Electric.[38] Career imprinting involves the initial transfer of knowledge through physical relocation of the people involved, rather than through learning by people already in place. However, we can anticipate that once new leaders are in place further communication of the transferred knowledge will follow, with predictably larger consequences for the industries involved.

As noted above, Baxter International chose to make a virtue of its growing alumni group. The entrepreneurial culture that it fostered meant that managers developed career appetites for new opportunities (knowing-why) which Baxter could not always satisfy. Moreover, the alumni were seen as opening further possibilities for Baxter to develop new business-to-business relationships. Monica Higgins, who conducted the described study of Baxter, has argued that Baxter adopted an "ecosystem perspective" that relationships kept intact could benefit the firm, as they indeed did in the growth of its alliances with biotechnology ventures. Chapter 4's opening case of Intel provides another example of how one particular firm can influence the development and knowledge work of an array of industry participants.

BUSINESS ECOSYSTEMS

If Baxter did indeed adopt an ecological perspective, it was pioneering what has become a popular view of how knowledge work unfolds both within and between industries. The idea of business ecosystems draws on a biological metaphor to highlight the shifting pattern of connections among industry participants. It draws inspiration from the concept of "coevolution," defined by anthropologist Gregory Bateson as a process in which interdependent species evolve in an endless reciprocal cycle.[39] The fundamental assumption of business ecosystems is that members of an ecosystem influence each other's future development due to their interdependencies.

James Moore, an early proponent of ecological metaphors to understand industry systems, first described business ecosystems as occurring where industries and the companies within them "co-evolve capabilities around innovation and work cooperatively and competitively to support new products, satisfy customer needs, and incorporate the next round of innovation."[40] Moore included within the ecosystem not only business firms but also government agencies, regulators, associations, standards bodies, and representatives of the host community. He noted that key organizations – such as Apple, IBM, Wal-Mart and others – had played leading roles in influencing rival firms, suppliers, and distribution organizations within their respective industries. A similar argument has been proposed by Marco Iansiti and colleagues who argue that "keystone" firms, such as Microsoft, integrate and add value to other participants in the ecosystem. These firms seek to provide tools, standards, and protocols that facilitate collaboration between different members of their ecosystems.[41]

By contrast, the European Commission has sponsored a series of initiatives based on a distinctly different vision of business ecosystems.[42] Their vision entails the creation of an ecosystem based on open-source principles, and supported by digital technology. The role of the open-source ecosystem is to provide a platform for small and medium firms to self-organize and coevolve for mutual benefit. Large keystone firms, such as those illustrated by Moore and Iansiti, are not anticipated as dominating this kind of ecosystem. Rather, the European Commission has made it a point to characterize business ecosystems led by large corporations as incompatible with its vision of productive small firm collaboration.[43] The Soho advertising industry, with its intricate web of firms, communities and attendant knowledge flows, comes closer to the European point of view. Whatever the emphasis, the common insight of all business ecosystems accounts is of a shared fate for the ecosystem's participating industries and organizations.

Many valuable technologies have been created through the fusion of technologies already existing in two or more industries.[44] A good example is the optical electronics industry, responsible, among other things, for fiber-optic communications. This evolved from the bringing together of optical technology and electronics to form a new knowledge base and in turn a new industry with which we are now familiar. In this and other cases, we see knowledge and learning being shared across traditional industry boundaries, and new capabilities and technologies being born. As the new knowledge becomes exploited, new industries are created. The original arena for knowledge sharing is thus extended, allowing further opportunities for new knowledge combinations – and so it goes on. Whether any one firm can indefinitely maintain leadership in this kind of ecological milieu remains an open question.

TOOLS FOR INDUSTRY

What tools can industries use to share knowledge and facilitate learning through the knowledge diamond? A number of generic tools and techniques are evident, including the adoption of best practice through industry benchmarking, often seen in prominent industries such as airlines, computers, and telecommunications. The Australian Office of the Information Economy (NOIE) uses case studies of effective practice and application to promote interorganizational collaboration and spur innovation in key knowledge economy industries.[45] Many industries generate learning through knowledge sharing in industry associations, and from customer user groups, as happens in the New Zealand boat building industry. Still others utilize Internet-based tools, such as web portals, industry forums, and sub-sequently blogs and RSS (rich site summary) techniques to share industry ideas and knowledge among industry participants, including customers.[46]

As this chapter has indicated, industry clusters or regions can play a key role in industry learning, and much attention has been paid to the development of tools and techniques to facilitate this kind of learning. One such approach, cluster mapping, seeks to map the actors in a cluster, and evaluate the linkages and learning contributions of these to the cluster. This kind of tool provides information about the locational effects on value creation. Mapping of the Calgary wireless cluster, for example, shows that firms have clustered around a "pond of talent," which provides critical knowledge and capability to the cluster as a whole.[47] Mapping of biotechnology clusters similarly shows them frequently situated around current or former pharmaceutical industry strongholds. From cluster mapping and use of network analysis procedures, it is possible for interventions to be made to facilitate effective knowledge flows and learning through the cluster.

Regarding an ecological perspective, a number of leading firms have developed tools to enhance the benefits of their network structures. For example, Wal-Mart has a unique information system, called Retail Link, that connects thousands of suppliers, including manufacturing giants like Procter and Gamble, Gillette, and Tyson Foods. Microsoft has created a similar information-sharing mechanism through the computing industry, linking downstream firms and end-users.[48] The European Commission has developed a set of industry-wide open-source tools available to a range of business ecosystem members. Their focus is on enabling technologies that will support small and medium enterprises

(SMEs) to share business knowledge and infrastructure. Examples of ecosystems-supportive knowledge tools include the creation of basic software protocols and open-source tools for knowledge sharing, community building, e-learning and e-training.[49] An underlying driver for these open-source tools is to reduce the digital divide between large and small firms and between rich and poor regions that participate in the digital business ecosystem.

SUMMARY

The host industry is one of the four participants of the knowledge diamond. Knowledge practices that emerge from the interplay between all four participants characterize the work and learning that the industry undertakes. The accumulated knowledge attributes of individuals, communities and organizations combine to create the milieu, recipes and communications system unique to a particular industry. These, in turn, influence the interactions between the industry and other participants.

Interactions between the host and other industries results in new industry formation, evolving industry interdependencies (illustrated in the biotechnology and pharmaceutical industries case), and new technological applications, all reflecting the creation and exploitation of knowledge. Individuals can help to shape the structure, dynamics and destiny of their host industry as was illustrated in the case of Richard Branson and the airline industry. The New Zealand boat building cluster showed the key role that communities of practice can play through the generation of a rich web of social connections and shared capability necessary for industry learning. The powerful influence of resident or new entrant companies on the host industry was seen in the German TV industry case, where a new model built around independent content producers significantly changed the basis for competition.

The illustrations provided across this chapter show a persistent theme. Success in the knowledge economy appears to favor industries that are flexible and fluid, with informal collaboration and often temporary organizational arrangements, such as projects, within and outside the industry. These open structures facilitate linkages and interactions between the knowledge diamond participants, and support the process of industry learning described through the first five chapters of this book.

QUESTIONS FOR REFLECTION

1 Consider an industry with which you are familiar. How does each of the milieu, recipes and communications system within that industry affect the way that knowledge work gets done?

2 For the same industry you discussed in question 1, can you give examples of how the three attributes of industry milieu, recipes and communication system are interdependent with one another?

3 Assume your place as an industry representative in the knowledge diamond. How do your industry's knowledge investments relate to those of (a) other industries, (b) yourself and other individuals, (c) communities and (d) organizations?

4 What industries do you know that seem to support or contradict the idea of regional advantage – and in what way do those industries do so?

5 What industries are you familiar with that illustrate the ideas of regional closure versus brokerage, or knowledge transfer between industries?

6 With what business ecosystems are you familiar, either as a worker or as a customer? How may these ecosystems change in the future?

7 What kinds of industry tools have you seen or experienced? How have they influenced you, or other knowledge workers in the industry?

NOTES

1 Saxenian, A.L. (1994) *Regional Advantage,* Cambridge, MA, Harvard University Press, p. 9.

2 Adapted from Grabher, G. (2002) "The project ecology of advertising: tasks, talents and teams," *Regional Studies,* special issue, 36 (3), 245–62.

3 Gosh, B.C. and Taylor, D. (1999) "Switching advertising agency: a cross-country analysis," *Marketing Intelligence and Planning,* 17 (3), 140–6, p. 144.

4 Grabher, "The project ecology," p. 251.

5 Ibid., p. 254.

6 Powell, W.W., Koput, K.W. and Smith-Doerr, L. (1996) "Interorganizational collaboration and the locus of innovation: networks of learning in biotechnology," *Administrative Science Quarterly,* 41, 116–45.

7 Arthur, M.B., DeFillippi, R.J. and Lindsay, V.J. (2001) "Careers, communities, and industry evolution: links to complexity theory," *International Journal of Innovation Management,* 5 (2), 239–55.

8 Industry recipes embody industry causal beliefs, shared mental models and common industry knowledge, which "experienced managers take uncritically

as professional common sense:" Spender, J.-C. (1989) *Industry Recipes: An Enquiry into the Nature and Sources of Managerial Judgment,* Oxford, Blackwell, p. 6.

9   Case adapted from Powell et al., "Interorganizational collaboration."

10 Biotechnology has three main divisions – human, animal and industrial. For the purposes of this case, the focus is on the human biotechnology division – specifically drug research.

11 *The Economist,* "Biotechnology: on the mend," May 13, 2004.

12 Han, Y. (2004) "A transaction cost perspective on motives for R&D alliances: evidence from the biotechnology industry," *Journal of the American Academy of Business,* 5 (1/2), 110–15.

13 Han, "A transaction cost perspective."

14 Adapted from Trompenaars, F. and Hampden-Turner, C. (2002) *21 Leaders for the 21st Century,* New York, McGraw-Hill, pp. 75–99.

15 On Bill Gates, see Gates, B. (1999) *Business @ The Speed of Thought,* Chatham, Penguin. On Anita Roddick, see Hamel, C. and Prahalad, C.K. (1994) *Competing for the Future,* Boston, Harvard Business School Press, p. 98. On Michael Dell, see Trompenaars and Hampden-Turner, *21 Leaders,* pp. 239–57.

16 Personal communication, G. Grabher, May 2005.

17 A cluster is a "geographic concentration of interconnected companies and institutions in a particular field:" Porter, M.E. (1998) "Clusters and the new economics of competition," *Harvard Business Review,* 76, 77–90, p. 78.

18 Adapted from Lindsay, V.J. (2005) "The development of international industry clusters: a complexity theory approach," *Journal of International Entrepreneurship,* 3, 71–97.

19 *Export News,* 2000, Headliner, Christchurch, New Zealand.

20 *New Zealand Business,* 1999, p. 34.

21 Wenger, E. (1998) *Communities of Practice: Learning, Meaning and Identity,* Cambridge, Cambridge University Press; Leonard-Barton, D. (1995) *Wellsprings of Knowledge,* Boston, Harvard Business School Press.

22 Adapted from Windeler, A. and Sydow, J. (2001) "Project networks and changing industry practices: collaborative content production in the German television industry," *Organization Studies,* 22 (6), 1035–60.

23 Sony was particularly renowned for its practice of "expeditionary marketing" in the development and marketing of new products: Hamel and Prahalad, *Competing.*

24 Both of these regions have over 300 manufacturing companies involved in their respective products, supported by well over 1,000 specialist supplier companies. While a few manufacturers have grown into large integrated companies, the vast majority of organizations involved in these regions are small to medium enterprises. See Schmidt, H. (1999) "From ascribed to earned trust in exporting clusters," *Journal of International Economics,* 48, 139–50.

25 Porter, M.E. (1990) *The Competitive Advantage of Nations,* New York, Free; Porter, M.E. (1998) "Clusters and the new economics of competition," *Harvard Business Review,* 76, 77–90.

26   Marshall, A. (1890) *Principles of Economics*, London, Macmillan.
27   Maskell, P. (2001) "Towards a knowledge-based theory of the geographic cluster," *Industrial and Corporate Change*, 10 (4), 921–43.
28   Richardson, G.B. (1972) "The organization of industry," *Economic Journal*, 82, 883–96, distinguishes between vertical (complementary) and horizontal (competing) clusters.
29   An extension of Grabher's concept of project ecologies seems to have utility in the context of the regional location of an industry as a whole. Key features of an ecology are the interacting locational, social and organizational factors, such as companies, personal ties, communities and company networks, that together constitute "a space of collaborative practices." See Grabher, "The project ecology," p. 245.
30   Maskell, "Towards a knowledge-based theory."
31   Best, M.H. (2001) *The New Competitive Advantage: The Renewal of American Industry*, Oxford, Oxford University Press.
32   Overland, M.A. (2005) "A tale of two countries," *Chronicle of Higher Education*, November 11, 52 (12), A42–A45, 3p, 5c.
33   Overland, M.A. (2005) "Malaysia's stagnation," *Chronicle of Higher Education*, November 11, 52 (12), A43–A45, 3p, 5c.
34   Best, *The New Competitive Advantage*, notes that the best performing Malaysian cluster is in Penang, and that this had started to adopt some of the characteristics of the Singapore model.
35   Overland, "Malaysia's stagnation."
36   Carmel, E. and Tija, P. (2005) *Offshoring Information Technology: Sourcing and Outsourcing to a Global Workforce*, Cambridge, Cambridge University Press.
37   Higgins, M.C. (2005) *Career Imprints: Creating Leaders across an Industry*, San Francisco, Jossey-Bass; Higgins, M.C. (2002) "Careers creating industries: some early evidence from the biotechnology industry," in M.A. Peiperl, M.B. Arthur and N. Anand (eds), *Career Creativity: Explorations in the Remaking of Work*, Oxford, Oxford University Press.
38   On GE and IBM see Higgins, *Career Imprints*, pp. 17, 273. On Fairchild Semiconductor see Saxenian, A.L. (1994) *Regional Advantage*, Cambridge, MA, Harvard University Press, pp. 25–6.
39   Bateson, Gregory (1980) *Mind and Nature: A Necessary Unity*, London, Bantam.
40   Moore, J.E. (1993) "Predators and prey: a new ecology of competition," *Harvard Business Review*, May–June, quote p. 76.
41   Iansiti, M. and Levien, R. (2004) "Strategy as ecology," *Harvard Business Review*, March, 69–78.
42   Nachira, F. (2002) *Toward a Network of Digital Business Ecosystems Fostering the Local Development*, Discussion Paper, Information Society Technology Specific Programme, Brussels, European Commission.
43   Nachira, F. (2005) "The role of business ecosystems in the promotion of research in Europe," in *The Emergence of Novel Organisational Forms in the Globalising Planet: Toward the Business Ecosystem?*, July 6–9, Brindisi, Italy.

44   Kodama, F. (1992) "Technology fusion and the new R&D," *Harvard Business Review*, July–August, 70–8.

45   Rao, M. (ed.) (2005) *Knowledge Management Tools and Techniques*, Oxford, Elsevier, pp. 227–34.

46   Rao, M. (ed.) (2005) *Knowledge Management Tools and Techniques*, Oxford, Elsevier, p. 309.

47   Langford, C.H., Wood, J.R. and Ross, T. (2003) "Origins and structure of the Calgary wireless cluster," in D.A. Wolfe and Meric S. Gertler (eds), *Clusters Old and New*, Montreal, McGill–Queen's University Press, pp. 161–86.

48   Iansiti and Levien, "Strategy as ecology," p. 3.

49   Example protocols are e.g. XML, ebXML: see Nachira, *Toward a Network*.

CHAPTER 6

PROJECTS AND KNOWLEDGE WORK

[F]or many situations, the ultimate innovative organization is a free floating pool of talent that moves into any project at any time based on market-like interactions.

James Brian Quinn[1]

Quinn's ideal of a free floating pool of talent reflects an emerging consensus that knowledge work is often best accomplished through projects. Projects offer a flexible means to bring together unique combinations of knowledge and experience to meet the requirements of the task at hand. Projects also allow for the development of innovative managerial and organizational practices. As a result, project-based organizing of knowledge work has rapidly diffused across a wide range of situations where there is a need to create new products, services or business processes based on novel combinations of expertise. This chapter illustrates how project-based organizing can foster innovative practices and subsequent learning across a variety of industries as projects evolve over time.

However, project work also poses significant challenges for knowledge work and knowledge workers. Sponsoring organizations are often more focused on immediate task accomplishment than on knowledge creation and learning. Projects vary in the degree to which they foster both project performance (being on time, on budget, and on target) and project learning (developing knowledge and capabilities for use in future projects). Project practices may develop that challenge the status quo of sponsoring organizations and their management, who may fail to heed the lessons to be learned. A variety of concepts and tools have been developed to help foster the transfer of learning from one project to another, or from a project to a sponsoring or participating organization.

Let us turn to the example of Ericsson and its use of projects in the European telecommunications industry.

Ericsson and the evolution of outsourcing capabilities[2]

In 1995, Ericsson Telecommunication Limited (ETL), the UK arm of Swedish-based telecommunications manufacturer Ericsson, won a contract to supply a turnkey solution for One-2-One (O2O), the UK mobile phone operator.[3] The contract broke new ground for Ericsson, with O2O outsourcing its previously in-house network design and implementation to ETL. Ericsson's corporate managers recognized that this project created an opportunity to enter into an emerging new market for turnkey solutions within the telecommunications industry.

ETL had previously developed the capabilities to perform two types of projects for mobile phone operators. One type was to make incremental improvements in existing products; the other type was to configure and install standard equipment to meet individual customer requirements. Because the O2O contract did not neatly fit into either type, and because of the unique challenges involved, a Turnkey Projects Group was established. The group was allowed to operate relatively autonomously from the rest of ETL, giving it the room to experiment with new forms of project organizing, management and capabilities. However, given the strategic importance of this project, its progress was monitored closely by top management in Ericsson's Swedish headquarters.

The O2O project began awkwardly. Over the first six months, unforeseen events caused over twenty different changes to be made in the way the project was organized. The project team finally settled on a modified version of Ericsson's traditional "matrix" structure, so that technological challenges and options could be quickly shared and resolved. To carry out the O2O project, ETL had to acquire or develop a number of new capabilities, including cellular systems planning, site acquisition and civil engineering functions. It also had to learn to manage a long-term partnership with its customer and its customer's subcontractors.

After embarking on the O2O project, Ericsson moved quickly to take on other turnkey projects elsewhere in the UK and Europe. The Managing Director of ETL explained: "We were the first within the Ericsson group to move into turnkey solutions in such a big way. Now the know-how we have built up can be exploited in other markets."[4] However, another senior manager cautioned: "The trend towards turnkey contracts will require additional competence in the company, not only in certain areas of cellular networks, but also in project management."[5]

ETL created a new internal unit called "Turnkey Solution Services," with the project managers involved in the first turnkey project as core members. This unit added to the capabilities developed in the initial turnkey project and offered a service that Ericsson's established functional departments did not provide. The new unit was made responsible for supporting turnkey bid preparations and subsequent turnkey projects undertaken by Ericsson's local companies throughout Europe. The unit also enabled ETL to capture and transfer knowledge and experience gained from previous turnkey projects.

Turnkey Solutions Services personnel were assigned to different projects to guarantee that the knowledge and experience gained from previous and concurrent projects could be utilized in subsequent turnkey projects. For example, the unit created standardized procedures to provide support throughout the turnkey project life cycle with an emphasis on separate procedures for front-end bid preparation, project set-up and execution.

While Ericsson's product divisions and local operating companies were launching bottom-up initiatives to meet customer demand for turnkey projects, the company's corporate management team was formulating a far-reaching strategy. In 1996, Ericsson's Corporate Executive Committee determined to reorganize around the delivery of turnkey solutions and services. The strategy would respond to increasing customer demands from operators, like O2O, for mobile networks to be designed, built and managed on a turnkey basis.

In 1999, Ericsson implemented its strategy by bringing together dispersed turnkey and service activities to form Ericsson Services. The reorganization was seen as "strengthening Ericsson's position as complete supplier, system integrator and partner."[6] In 2000, a new division, Ericsson Global Services, was created to support the delivery of turnkey solutions and services throughout Ericsson's global operations. In September 2001, Global Services became one of Ericsson's five business units.

A traditional view of projects saw them as one-shot, time-bound, goal-driven activities directed toward the delivery of a new product or service – like the building of a bridge, or the delivery of a suite of computer programs. In this traditional view projects were punctuations within relatively unchanging work arrangements. A successful project was one that coordinated among the parties involved to finish on time and under budget.[7] If this occurred the project-sponsoring company was satisfied, and the project was considered successful. Many who practice project management still adhere to this view. However, the Ericsson case study challenges this perspective and suggests that projects are as much about generating and utilizing new knowledge as they are about completing specific task assignments.

From a knowledge work perspective, project success depends on both knowledge exploitation and exploration, as previously discussed in Chapter 4. The principal purpose of exploitation is to take near-term advantage of the knowledge already assembled. The principal purpose of exploration is to pursue long-term enhancement of a company's knowledge-based capabilities. Moreover, the Ericsson case teaches us that no single project should be viewed in isolation.[8] Instead, projects are interconnected to each other in an evolutionary sequence involving the successive exploitation of existing knowledge and exploration of new knowledge, thereby contributing to an organization's (or an individual's or a community's or an industry's) long-term position in the marketplace for goods and services.

THE EVOLUTION OF PROJECT-BASED KNOWLEDGE

The Ericsson case suggests that organizations can usefully view projects as unfolding in an evolutionary sequence. The origins of any project lie in the projects that preceded it, and knowledge previously gained can be borrowed or modified to contribute to successive projects, much as Ericsson did as it gained experience in the provision of turnkey solutions. A similar view can be taken of the successive projects undertaken by individuals, communities or whole industries. For example, Mary (Chapter 2) spoke metaphorically about choosing successive roles carefully, aware that each role would craft the layers for her next role. The community of forensic accountants (Chapter 3) built experience through successive client projects and court appearances. The Hollywood filmmaking industry (Chapter 1) and the UK advertising industry (Chapter 5) both unfolded one project at a time.

Projects involve *organizing*, an action verb that is distinct from the term "organization," which we use in this book to mean a legal entity. The term "organizing" emphasizes the dynamic nature of project-based activities. Organizing has been described by management scholar Karl Weick as the assembly of interdependent actions into sequences that generate outcomes, and where both the sequences and outcomes "make sense" to one or more of the actors involved.[9] Weick and various other scholars have also described organizing as occurring through three basic phases of evolution.[10] First, there is a *variation* phase, characterized by a readiness to do something different, such as to form or join a new project team. Second there is a *selection* phase, in which choices get made between alternative ways of working. Finally, there is a *retention* phase, when the results of choices made and work done are retained, and are available for reuse in subsequent organizing activities. Let us reexamine the Ericsson case with these phases in mind.

Variation: the beginnings
of exploration

Ericsson's creation of a new project team for its O2O project, like the creation of any new project team, was an act of variation. However, in the Ericsson case the project-sponsoring company realized it needed to do things differently. Existing in-house project processes were unable to cope with the scale and complexity of the new types of projects demanded by their customers. Although Ericsson sought to apply existing capabilities where it could, it realized it needed to develop new areas of expertise to meet the changing requirements of its customers. It needed to engage with a variety of individual, community, organizational and industry knowledge sources to accomplish its project work.

Ericsson's senior management team in the UK also created a context that allowed project members to question existing institutional norms.[11] The O2O turnkey project was allowed to operate at a distance from the larger organization to encourage experimentation with new approaches and to provide the space to deviate from established routines.[12] In addition, Ericsson's corporate organization in Sweden recognized that the rewards from exploration could only be realized in the longer term. They were willing to accept the short-term risks of cost overruns, delays and other problems associated with conducting unfamiliar projects in anticipation of the potential returns from future projects.

Selection: between exploration
and exploitation

Next, the O2O project got off to an uncertain start, involving no less than twenty variations in the organizing of the project over the next six months. However, the project moved relatively quickly to select new capabilities that lay outside the project team's original area of expertise, for example in site acquisition and civil engineering, which were needed for successful project completion. It was anticipated that these capabilities would be useful to the project-sponsoring company in its later business contracts.

Senior management also sought to extend the selection process, by taking on overlapping projects that provided other opportunities for variation on which the company could draw.[13] This was chosen as an alternative strategy to letting the O2O project conclude before other turnkey projects were attempted. However, rather than simply encouraging proliferation of alternative practices, the company chose what appeared

to be successful new practices and carried them forward into other projects. In the language of Chapter 1, these attempts sought to convert
mainly tacit to more explicit knowledge as the projects moved along.

Retention: the shift to exploitation

Ericsson's O2O project team members were wiser for the experience
they had gained from the project, and this experience became available
for either individual or collective application in further project activities. Previous chapters in this book have suggested that learning from
project activities is likely to accrue to other knowledge diamond participants, that is individuals (Chapter 2), communities (Chapter 3) or
whole industries (Chapter 5). However, Ericsson's senior management appeared mindful of this likelihood. It moved decisively to take
advantage of the knowledge gained by keeping most of the project
team together to help establish subsequent turnkey projects elsewhere
in Europe.

Turnkey Solution Services played a key role in supporting the
growing volume of turnkey projects executed in the UK and elsewhere
in Europe. Along the way, the emphasis switched from exploration
toward exploitation of what had been learned from previous projects. Knowledge gained from bidding on and executing these projects
became part of organizational memory. New company-specific capabilities – new routines, processes and tools – were developed to execute a
growing volume of bids and projects more efficiently and effectively.
However, key members of the early project team had little time to reflect
on their experience before moving to their next project.

As a turnkey project organizer, Ericsson coordinated the contributions
of an array of project participants to provide integrated solutions to the
needs of its turnkey service clients. Ericsson's role as a system integrator
was similar to the "keystone" role previously described in Chapter 5.[14]
A project ecosystem of in-house and outsourced telecommunications component and subsystem manufacturers, system designers, operational service
providers and business consulting and finance specialists was orchestrated
by Ericsson. All of these players coevolved through their mutual interdependence around shared learning from collaborative project work.

In sum the Ericsson case illustrates each of the variation, selection and
retention stages of evolution and their respective knowledge exploration
and exploitation activities. It shows how project-based learning – the accumulation of new knowledge – evolved from exploration to exploitation
over time and how the initial project's exploratory learning provided

a foundation for subsequent project-to-project learning, in this case culminating in organizational learning.[15]

PROJECTS AS EPISODES IN KNOWLEDGE WORK[16]

The preceding discussion of Ericsson makes clear that projects are not only production episodes but also knowledge building opportunities for the sponsors and participants involved. For individuals, in particular, John Kotter has suggested a "new rule" for project selection: "You need to figure out what skills will be relevant in the future and you need to map out projects to develop those skills."[17] Populist author and consultant Tom Peters has added: "In the new economy, all work is project work, and you are your projects."[18] Similar arguments apply to the development of communities, or of host industry clusters. Each knowledge diamond participant may see projects as providing learning opportunities.[19]

The image of knowledge workers involved in company-sponsored projects raises a series of questions about project-based learning. What is the alignment between the learning investments of a project's individual participants and the project's organizational sponsors? What about the learning of particular communities involved in project activities? How much does any learning gained by project participants accrue to the project sponsor? Alternatively, how much and how quickly does learning flow beyond the project sponsor to the host industry as participant workers move on, or share knowledge with others? What about inter-company alliances, where two or more company learning agendas are involved? How does a company learn from freelancers and consultants, who bring their own learning agendas to the project table?

These questions lead us to the model of project-based organizing represented in Figure 6.1. Variation begins with project initiation, with all four kinds of knowledge diamond participant – individuals, communities, one or more organizations and the host industry (or industries) – as prospective contributors to project activities. Selection occurs over the duration of the project, and involves the choices made regarding two kinds of processes, one involving project performance, the other involving project learning. Performance refers to those choices that contribute to having the project conclude on time, under budget, and to the satisfaction of its intended customers. Learning refers to those choices that involve the generation of new knowledge for any project participant.[20] Finally, retention occurs when one or more project participants takes new knowledge and makes it available for future use, which may again involve any or all of the four knowledge diamond participants with which we are now familiar.

Figure 6.1   A model of project-based organizing[21]

Figure 6.1 represents the three phases of variation, selection and reten-tion occurring in linear form. The representation is analytically useful, and provides a convenient framework for examining project activities. However, the reality is that project-based organizing is dynamic, so that attempts at selection can call for new variation (as for example in the assumptions that Ericsson's UK arm first used for organizing its O2O project). Project-based learning also occurs between active projects (as for example when Ericsson sought to learn from its various turnkey projects that were simultaneously under way). Project-based organizing goes beyond any single project and includes the coevolution of related projects at varying stages of variation, selection and retention.

CONTRASTING PROJECT-BASED LEARNING EXPERIENCES[22]

Next, we offer four short case studies to illustrate how project-based know-ledge work can unfold, and what kinds of performance and learning can occur. Each case study involves a project-sponsoring company, and each is written to reconnect with the underlying individual ways of knowing described in Chapter 2, and the company core competencies described in Chapter 4. We will say more about both community and industry outcomes later. Each case study offers a different lesson about the variation, selection and retention sequence, and the different com-binations of company performance and learning that can emerge.

Low performance, low learning

Figure 6.1 suggests that the least satisfactory outcome of a project activity is both low performance and low learning, as suggested in the EastBank case study.

EastBank

EastBank was a large, regional bank in the US Northeast that sought to "reengineer" itself in the interests of improved customer service. The old organization "silos" – departments providing separate functions which customers had to access independently – would be replaced by "one-stop shopping" providing superior customer service. The bank's redesign intentions were encouraged by employee feedback that reflected low (knowing-why) motivation caused by the limitations of the bank's present systems. Employees also complained about being denied access to broader internal systems knowledge (knowing-how) that would help them to provide better customer service, as well as about a lack of wider (knowing-whom) contacts because of the silos surrounding the bank's separate departments.

The bank chose what it believed to be an opportune moment – immediately after the takeover of a significant regional competitor – and engaged the services of an outside consulting company recognized for its expertise in bank reengineering. A team-based structure was set up with a steering committee of senior managers responsible to the bank's board, and specialized process teams each led by a steering committee member. The process teams were kept in "bull pens" away from day-to-day operations, to help them better develop the capabilities needed for the reengineering project's success. Both the teams and the coordination among them were intended to enhance the connections through which the reengineered structure would be implemented.

The project began well, and the process teams were reportedly making good progress in mapping customer needs and perceptions. The teams tested and questioned the efficacy of existing systems, including one scenario that required a customer to read 348 pages, sign in 142 places, fill out seventy-four orders and undertake sixteen agreements to establish eight accounts with fourteen services! The consultants helped process teams build fresh scenarios of how the new integrated customer services might be delivered. However, the bank's financial situation changed, as its stock price fell and an investment in a capital markets firm turned sour. A new emphasis on technology-driven efficiencies was introduced. Budgets intended for the redesign effort were cut back, and redesign initiatives were subjected to "reevaluation" based on new financial constraints.

EastBank's initial variation brought in outside expertise and sought to build new bridges between workers from separate departmental silos. However, senior management's response to financial adversity interfered with the selection of sought-after outcomes. Team members' early enthusiasm to join the project, to help improve customer services and to collaborate across departments were all frustrated by management's response. The new competencies sought by the bank were never retained. Both performance and learning outcomes were low. (Shortly after this episode the bank was acquired.)

High performance, low learning

A second potential outcome from Figure 6.1 is when a project leads to an outcome of high performance combined with low learning, as suggested in the GulfBank study presented.

GulfBank

GulfBank was a young retail banking company, with a 60–40 ownership ratio between Middle Eastern investors and a major American banking partner. It was founded to take advantage of the greater demand for international banking services, and to combine its Middle Eastern partners' access to both clients and financial capital with the American bank's expertise across a full range of international banking services. The bank's young officers brought (knowing-why) motivation to participate in the dynamic international banking industry. The officers had shown high potential in their prior education and the recruitment process. However, they typically lacked but were eager to build (knowing-how) capabilities and (knowing-whom) contacts that could become the hallmark of successful banking careers.

The bank saw an opportunity for its highly regarded information technology department to develop a computer-driven knowledge management system. This would log the bank officers' expertise and experiences and make the database available for the officers to share with one another. The bank presumed that the initiative would be welcomed, and that its organizational culture would gain the officers' collaboration. It saw a distinct opportunity to leverage its officers' previous work, and thereby to offset the cost of a fairly high officer turnover rate. The bank also saw an opportunity to build connections through the increased support for its loan officers that the computer system was expected to facilitate.

The system that was developed was technically adequate, and a number of early "hits" were achieved where experienced officers were able to support their less experienced colleagues. However, the overall level of usage of the system turned out to be disappointing. The system was not seen as user-friendly, and the loan officers seemed more concerned with their own industry experience and networks than with contributing to a knowledge management system that asked for a lot and gave little back. These problems, coupled with the continued turnover of officer personnel, led to a gradual degradation of the quality of information that the system provided.

GulfBank's act of variation was to authorize its information technology department to develop the new system. The system was delivered, and selected by bank management for implementation. However, insufficient bridges were built to the loan officers who would use the system, and as a result the new system was not retained. The system's performance was a technical success. However, learning was low, since the system did not bring about any long-term change in the competencies of the bank's loan officer workforce.

Low performance, high learning

A third potential outcome from Figure 6.1 is when a project leads to an outcome of low performance but high learning. This is suggested in the Voicetech case study.

Voicetech

Voicetech was a leading provider of speech and language technologies, including speech recognition. Its expressed mission was to be a global leader in its field by partnering with other technology-driven companies to provide "best solutions" to new product opportunities. Its employees were recruited from around the world for their distinctive (knowing-how) linguistic and engineering capabilities. The employees' shared (knowing-why) identification was to see themselves as technological leaders, with continuing (knowing-whom) links through their work at Voicetech to innovative manufacturing companies. These links complemented the employees' own industry attachments as alumni of prestigious engineering schools and members of related professional associations.

Voicetech took on a new project to provide the voice technology component of a sophisticated "handless" telephone answering machine being developed by ConsCo. The project began when ConsCo invited more than twenty vendors to attend a one-week project launch, and to develop a shared vision of how the product could be designed and manufactured. Voicetech's part would be to conduct voice sampling and vocabulary development that would drive the new machine. To help ConsCo manage overall project costs, Voicetech agreed to give ConsCo six months' exclusive ownership of their product component, after which ownership would be shared. Voicetech also drew prepaid royalties from ConsCo to fund the component's development, while ConsCo retained some claim over Voicetech's future services in the event that the intended product never materialized.

The product did not materialize. An Asian vendor got caught in a regional economic crisis and could not produce its component as it had agreed. No other supplier could be found offering the price and delivery schedule to meet the market opportunity. From a performance standpoint, the project was a clear failure. However, from a learning standpoint both ConsCo and Voicetech reaffirmed their separate cultures as industry innovators, and both accumulated further capabilities and connections from their collaboration in the answering machine venture. ConsCo could afford the venture as part of a larger portfolio of new product initiatives. Voicetech even gained some financial returns, as ConsCo made good on its royalty advances, and Voicetech also earned the opportunity to work with ConsCo again on another innovation cycle.

Voicetech's initial decision on variation – to take part in the answering machine project – allowed its engineers to make new career investments at the cutting edge of their field. This was valuable, even if on this occasion there was no final product. Despite the financial failure of the project, Voicetech was able to select new competencies in voice recognition and keep its engineers at the forefront of their specialized field. Retention occurred through the engineers' willingness to stay with the company for future developmental projects. Performance on the telephone answering machine project was low, but learning was high.

High performance, high learning

An apparently ideal project outcome is one that combines high performance with high learning, as illustrated in the Copyco case study.

Copyco

Copyco was a large printing systems company involved in the manufacture and marketing of high-volume copiers. The market and the opportunities within it were shifting from analog to digital copiers, which were anticipated to account for 95% of new copier sales within five years. However, Copyco's sales force organization was traditional. Most sales representatives had little (knowing-how) awareness of the digital revolution, lacked the (knowing-why) motivation to become more aware, and communicated with conventional (knowing-whom) print customers who were followers rather than leaders of technological innovation. The company and its salespeople were losing touch with the marketplace, as new copier technology and applications began to replace the old.

Copyco made changes before introducing its first digital copier. It recruited a group of "mavericks" familiar with digital technology to complement its existing salespeople. It then embarked on a project to develop digital copier literacy, first among the company's sales managers and later within each regional sales office. This included the playing of a "baseball game" in which teams competed to see which team could show superior digital copying knowledge. The intended outcome of the game was to develop new sales capability through the establishment of a "new language" about digital copying. Supplementary outcomes sought included making the company culture more appreciative of digital copying, and building new connections by giving the sales force the language to better communicate with high-technology professionals.

The project was a considerable success, with sales performance for the new copier going far beyond budgeted expectations. The sales force was also reported to exhibit a fresh collective sense of purpose. Many of the sales made were to new, more technologically advanced customers, whose valuable feedback was relayed by the sales force to product development specialists. Copyco made a successful transition from its traditional role as a supplier of analog copiers to a respected digital copier producer, with the opportunity for further rapid product development in the digital technology arena.

Copyco's act of variation brought in outside expertise, the "maverick" new salespeople, and also found a way to have them bond with existing salespeople. The program of change that was introduced brought about the selection of new sales capabilities and connections around digital copiers. Also, these new company competencies were retained in the behavior of the sales force, as was demonstrated through subsequent sales performance. Performance and learning from the project were both high.

To summarize, each of the four preceding case studies began with a particular variation that launched the project. Each project underwent its own process of selection resulting in a particular combination of low or high performance and learning outcomes for the sponsoring organization.

LEARNING LANDSCAPES
AND THEIR BENEFICIARIES

Another way of seeing the four case studies from the previous section is to see them as representing different *learning landscapes*. These are project environments that provide particular learning opportunities for the participants involved. An international research program across forty-three different organizations in the USA, Europe and Asia identified three principal kinds of learning landscape as described in the following.[23] Moreover, the evidence affirms some of the earlier lessons in this book.

One kind of learning landscape may be termed *exploitative*. It emphasizes both the exploitation and codification of knowledge (described in Chapter 4) by formal means, almost invariably through information technology, and seeks to make that knowledge widely available throughout the project-sponsoring organization. Lessons learned are placed in a centralized repository, the use of which is supported by corresponding hardware and software tools. The previous GulfBank case study reflects this kind of landscape.

A second kind of learning landscape may be termed *explorative*. It emphasizes the exploration and personalization of knowledge (also described in Chapter 4) through one-to-one communications, and encourages the kind of informal interaction through which knowledge sharing can come about. The people involved record lessons learned in dairies or notebooks. This recording may be in electronic form, but there is no expectation for further knowledge sharing by the project-sponsoring organization. The previous Voicetech case study reflects this kind of landscape.

A third kind of learning landscape may be termed *navigational*. It provides for navigation between separate pockets of tacit knowledge to lead to greater and more explicit shared understanding. Much project work is done through team meetings and project reviews, where lessons learned are openly discussed and debated. Lessons learned are recorded in meeting minutes and written project histories. Again, these may be electronic records, but there is only limited circulation to other parties. The previous Copyco case study reflects this kind of landscape.

The above reports are written from the standpoint of the project-sponsoring organization. However, the different landscapes described can give rise to a range of learning outcomes for the other three knowledge diamond participants. Despite the problems for sponsoring organizations, we can point to high learning outcomes for the individual system designers in GulfBank, the engineers in Voicetech, and maybe even the dispirited bankers at EastBank. The same may be said for the occupational communities with which the individual systems designers, engineers and bankers were affiliated, and where they were likely to share their experiences. Finally, host industries have opportunities to learn, for example, about the pitfalls of leaving information technology specialists to lead the development of computer-based knowledge management systems, or about the necessity for greater cost-cutting in the increasingly global banking industry.

ORGANIZATIONS AND PROJECT ORGANIZING

The previous discussion suggests the possibility of managing projects to achieve favorable outcomes in both performance and learning. However, from the standpoint of the organization, there are serious questions about whether every organization seeks to promote new learning, or about how willing the organization is to sacrifice productive efficiency to achieve that learning. Making the trains run on time as an organizational objective may well compete with the idea of slowing the trains down to learn more about them.

The Thurstone and Redby projects[24]

Two company-sponsored construction projects illustrate how projects may differ in both their project organizing requirements and their learning opportunities. The Thurstone project was sponsored by a large UK construction company and involved building a logistics warehouse. Such warehouses were described by one site manager as "bread and butter jobs" typical of projects previously performed by the sponsoring company.[25] The Redby project was sponsored by a water supply and treatment firm and required a unique combination of civil engineering, complex mechanical and electronic skills beyond the firm's current capabilities. Project activities ranged from bridge building, land remediation, and provision of public accessibility, to development of sophisticated software control systems.

In the Thurstone project, the sponsoring company determined it already had the in-house expertise to do the work. Moreover, those specialists – for example architects, site planners, environmental engineers, civil engineers, quantity surveyors, and so on – were all represented in and coordinated from the same head office location. In the Redby project, the sponsoring company determined it lacked the expertise that it needed. It therefore put together a consortium of specialist consultants and subcontractors to jointly accomplish the project.

In each project a similar range of specializations was represented, and in each project there were similar incentives to solve on-site problems to make the project a financial success. However, the learning outcomes from the project organizing approaches were quite different. In the Thurstone case, learning was relatively low, but easy to apply to future projects. In the Redby case, learning was relatively high, but difficult to apply to future projects. What conditions for learning distinguished the two projects from one another, and where would the learning from each project be retained?

The construction case study suggests different approaches to project organizing, involving two distinct learning landscapes. The Thurstone project was organized for knowledge exploitation, and the Redby project was organized for knowledge exploration. What specific conditions, however, led to the emergent learning differences? Harry Scarbrough and his colleagues suggest three key conditions, concerned with project protocol, knowledge boundaries and project autonomy respectively.[26]

Regarding the first condition, *project protocol,* a key distinction is between projects that use established procedures (Thurstone) and projects that lack established procedures (Redby) for integrating team members' specialized knowledge. In the Thurstone project, team members were accustomed to working with each other in a particular way. In the Redby project, the approach to collaboration among contributing specialists needed to be worked out on site. In the language of Chapter 3, there was higher closure among the long-established specialist groups at Thurstone and higher brokerage within the novel combination of specialist groups at Redby. Moreover, the novel combination at Redby thereby required team members to modify existing practices in order to integrate their knowledge.

Turning to the second condition, *knowledge boundaries,* the important distinction is between projects that involve low boundaries to knowledge integration (Thurstone) and projects that involve high boundaries (Redby). A boundary may be simply described as any phenomenon that separates the knowledge of one group of workers from another group. In the Thurstone project, knowledge boundaries were low because of the specialists' established ways of working together. In the Redby project, knowledge boundaries were high because the specialists were relatively unfamiliar with each other's fields of expertise.

Regarding the third condition, *project autonomy*, the key distinction lies between projects that provide low autonomy for their workers (Thurstone) and projects that provide high autonomy (Redby). In the Thurstone project, the team members involved were accustomed to working together in a certain way, and it was assumed they would continue in this way. In the Redby project, the team members had not worked together before, and were relatively free to determine the best way to collaborate to get things done.

The different conditions gave rise to different patterns of organizing and subsequent learning outcomes. Within the project, learning appeared higher in the Redby case because different specialist groups had to reach beyond their separate practices, and overcome the high boundaries that stood in the way of project completion. However, between projects there was a different story. Learning from the Thurstone project was limited, but was easily transferred within the construction company for future projects. In contrast, there was no clear repository for project sponsor learning from the Redby project, as participating specialists each went their separate ways. The alternative forms of organizing largely reflect the distinctions between exploitation and exploration described earlier, and the resultant learning outcomes are summarized in Table 6.1.

The last row in Table 6.1 provides the link from the project-sponsoring organization to other knowledge diamond participants. The extensive exploration-based learning from the Redby project was difficult for the organization to retain. However, the learning was retained by the Redby project workers and their associated occupational communities that contributed to the work, and through them the lessons learned spread to the host industry. In contrast, individual and occupational community learning was blunted by the Thurstone workers' tradition of collaborating within the same company to exploit their accumulated but company-limited knowledge and experience with similar types of projects. As a result, neither the Thurstone workers nor their host industry were as well prepared for the new challenges likely to come from later projects requiring more novel project organizing approaches.

Table 6.1 Contrasting project learning conditions, forms of organizing and associated learning outcomes

Conditions for learning	Organizing for exploitation (Thurstone)	Organizing for exploration (Redby)
Project protocol	Conforms to existing divisions of practice	Challenges existing divisions of specialist practice
Knowledge boundaries	Low boundaries to knowledge translation and integration	High boundaries to knowledge translation and integration
Project autonomy	Low autonomy calls for routine task performance	High autonomy calls for novelty in task performance
Learning outcomes		
Within the project	Learning constrained by staying within knowledge boundaries	Learning generated by overcoming knowledge boundaries
Between projects	Learning limited but straightforward for project-sponsoring company to retain	Learning extensive but difficult for project-sponsoring company to retain

PROJECTS, PRACTICE AND "BOUNDARY OBJECTS"

The previous section introduced the idea of boundaries between separate groups of specialists, or communities, participating in project activities. The suggestion was that knowledge boundaries have to be overcome if both project performance and project learning are to occur. How, though, does this happen? The case study here refers to the coordination of different practices underlying a prototype safety valve.

The on-board vapor recovery valve[27]

The on-board vapor recovery valve project was to develop an automobile valve that offered the functionality of three valves in one. It would be a "rollover" valve to cut the flow of gas in the case of an accident, a "pressure relief" valve to prevent the risk of explosion, and a "vapor recovery valve" to meet new environmental requirements about minimizing vapor losses into the atmosphere. The design of the valve brought together four kinds of specialist.

Ken was in charge of sales, and focused on questions regarding sales volume, specification, costs, etc. for negotiations with the intended customer. Ken's practice led him to think in terms of "getting the numbers right," "closing the deal," and "standing behind" the numbers that would work for the customer.

Vaughn was head design engineer responsible for leading the design team in developing a prototype on time and within the budget that he was allocated. His practice led him to attend to matters of "design review," producing a "functional prototype," and "passing specification."

Mick was a manufacturing specialist who needed to ensure that a machine to manufacture the new valve could be designed and built to do the job. His practice involved "keeping it simple stupid," seeking "a high-volume process" and anticipating the "fine tuning" of that process.

Jim was a production technician whose responsibility was to keep the production line moving. The design of the valve and its manufacture both had to assure reliable delivery. His practice led him to talk about getting "products out the door," controlling the "scrap rate" and keeping "people working" on the production process.

Each of these above specialists used a series of artifacts or "objects" – numbers, blueprints, faxes, parts, tools, and machines – that they applied and manipulated to do their own work. Some of these were used only within a specialist's own practice. However other objects provided common information that needed to be shared across the specialists' different practices.[28]

For example, one of the problems encountered in the development of the on-board vapor recovery valve was that a new CAD system for design drawings had been installed, and the assembly design drawing was out of date. The drawing was satisfactory for Vaughn to prepare a functional prototype, but not for Mick to develop a high-volume production process. Continuing disagreements over the assembly design drawings threatened to adversely affect Ken's ability to meet negotiated customer delivery dates and Jim's ability to assure reliable production.

Boundary objects are any objects – design drawings, critical path diagrams, project management software, product prototypes, service protocols, and so on – that need to be understood across the traditional boundaries that separate the specialist practices that contribute to project activities. Boundary objects provide for the maintenance and building of shared understanding. They play an important part in contributing to project completion, and to the learning that can be achieved along the way. Boundary objects fulfill three critical purposes, as described in the following.

One purpose of boundary objects is to establish a *shared language* through which specialists from different practices can communicate. The assembly drawing for the on-board vapor recovery valve was intended to provide such a shared language – about parts, tolerances and detailed functional requirements – through which all parties involved could communicate. The second purpose is to provide *concreteness*, against which people can form their own interpretations and express their concerns about project challenges. For example, Mick needed the latest version of the assembly drawing of the valve in order to clarify and express to other specialists his concerns about manufacturing reliability. The third purpose is to provide for *knowledge transformation.*[29] The specialists involved in developing the valve needed to learn about the differences in each of their perspectives in order to be able to effectively negotiate with one another, and in turn to modify their practices in response.

These three purposes involve both practical and political considerations. Practical considerations are those that address the functionality of the product or service being developed. Political issues are those that call for changes to long-standing practices, with potentially positive or negative outcomes for the specialists and communities involved. Our previous case comparison of Thurstone and Redby illustrated the challenges to existing practices at Redby when new combinations of specialists were brought together. Boundary objects can be used to promote both practical and political outcomes, with further consequences for what shared languages, concreteness and knowledge transformation come to occur.[30] The uses of communications media as boundary objects for knowledge work between geographically dispersed project teams and organizations will be further examined in Chapter 7.

TOOLS FOR PROJECT WORK

A wide range of behavioral and IT tools exist to support the knowledge work practices of individual project workers, project teams and their sponsors.[31] Project knowledge tools can run the gamut from simple paper documents and reporting systems to IT-enabled project management knowledge repositories that reside on corporate knowledge portals.[32]

A variety of behavioral tools for project work can be used without information technology. For example, brainstorming is a common tool used at the onset of projects to generate and explore a variety of project possibilities.[33] Another behavioral tool involves the redeployment of experts across successive projects.[34] Experts who have contributed to particular types of projects may move to new projects where their expertise is required – a feature of the Ericsson case described at the start of this chapter. Another behavioral tool to foster project learning is the project milestone review, where work accomplished at the end of one step (milestone) of a project is reviewed before moving to the next step.[35] Finally, project post-mortems are reviews of completed projects where participants and sponsors share perspectives on accomplishments, mistakes made and lessons learned.[36]

However, many projects today are supported by a rich array of IT tools that complement the behavioral tools also in use.[37] For example, knowledge generated from project work reviews and post-mortems may be codified into a database of lessons learned, as was the intention in the earlier GulfBank case. Such knowledge is then classified according to a knowledge taxonomy that can subsequently be used to respond to specific queries, using key terms or questions. Data mining processes may be employed to search for specific content residing in databases of project documents and other codified project knowledge stored in a centralized knowledge management information system.[38] Also, expert contributors to past projects may be identified for reuse in an expert locator system accessible online to project sponsors and project organizers.[39]

Some research suggests that IT-based project tools may be ignored or treated dismissively if they are not skillfully integrated with the established practices of individual project participants, project teams and project-sponsoring organizations.[40] Projects pose unique challenges for knowledge work due to their temporary nature and the requirement for fast and flexible responses to changing work requirements. Trust must be built swiftly for new project teams, especially for members who have not worked together before. Team members must rely on each other for expertise that no one else on the project team possesses. The additional challenges of utilizing and managing the expertise of geographically dispersed project members have accelerated the use of IT tools, and the uses and limits of these tools for virtual knowledge work will be examined in Chapter 7.

SUMMARY

Projects provide particular opportunities for the organizing of knowledge work. The opening Ericsson case showed how projects could be seen through an evolutionary lens, with successive knowledge variation, and selection stages leading to emergent knowledge retention. Projects involve all four knowledge diamond participants and provide episodes for both the transfer of existing knowledge and the generation of new knowledge among these participants. Projects can create different patterns of performance and learning outcomes for all four types of participant, as was shown in the contrasting EastBank, GulfBank, Voicetech, and Copyco examples. As a result, projects lead to further consequences for future project episodes. Projects are also influenced by the learning landscape (emphasizing exploration, exploitation, or navigation) in which each project occurs, and – as the Thurstone versus Redby comparison revealed – by what kinds of project protocol, knowledge boundaries, and levels of autonomy are involved.

The question of knowledge boundaries led on to the topic of boundary objects – those artifacts, documents and tools used by project participants across different specialist practices. The example of the on-board vapor recovery valve showed how these objects can bring about a shared language, a concrete basis for communication, and the opportunity for knowledge transformation among the specialists involved. Many of the tools available to support project work serve as boundary objects in some way. These tools range from software reflecting traditional project management ideals of finishing on time and under budget to more sophisticated tools to promote participant learning.

QUESTIONS FOR REFLECTION

1   Consider a project with which you have been involved. Who was the project sponsor, and what *variation* brought the project about? What did the sponsor anticipate would be *selected* as the project unfolded, and *retained* upon project completion?

2   Reflect back on the same project as in question 1. Was each type of knowledge diamond participant involved? What did the separate participants bring to the project? What did each participant contribute to project performance? What did each participant contribute to and take from project learning?

3 Have you ever been involved in a project characterized by any of the combinations of high or low performance and high or low learning? Describe the project briefly and its pattern of performance and learning.

4 For any project you have experienced, reflect back on the project protocol, knowledge boundaries and project autonomy involved. How did these each contribute to the conditions for learning? What were the within-project and between-project outcomes?

5 What is your experience of trying to develop a shared language with other project participants coming from a different practice to your own? What subsequent specification of knowledge differences and facilitation of knowledge transformation took place?

6 Select an organization with which you are familiar. What kinds of tools does it employ to support project work and project-based learning? What type of learning landscape is suggested by those tools?

NOTES

1 Quinn, J.B., Baruch, J.J. and Zien, K.A. (1997) *Innovation Explosion*, New York, Free.

2 Brady, T. and Davies, A. (2004) "Building project capabilities: from exploratory to exploitative learning," *Organization Studies*, 25 (9), 1601–21.

3 "Turnkey" has been defined to refer to "a system or software package that has been built, installed or supplied by the manufacturer complete and ready to operate:" http://isp.webopedia.com.

4 Brian Barry, quoted in *Linx* (1997), ETL internal newsletter, issue 28.

5 Richard Whittaker, quoted in ibid.

6 Ericsson 1999 Annual Report, p. 7.

7 Wheelwright, S.C. and Clark, K.B. (1992) *Revolutionizing Product Development*, New York, Free.

8 Engwall, M. (2003) "No project is an island: linking projects to history and context," *Research Policy*, 32, 789–808.

9 Weick, K. (1979) *The Social Psychology of Organizing*, New York, McGraw-Hill, p. 3.

10 Campbell, D. (1969) "Variation and selective retention in sociocultural evolution," *General Systems*, 16, 69–85; Weick, *The Social Psychology of Organizing*; Robinson, D. and Miner, A. (1996) "Careers change as organizations learn," in M.B. Arthur and D.M. Rousseau (eds), *The Boundaryless Career*, New York, Oxford University Press, pp. 76–94.

11 Ayas, K. and Zeniuk, N. (2001) "Project-based learning: building communities of reflective practitioners," *Management Learning*, 32 (1), 61–76.

12 Senge, P.M. (1990) *The Fifth Discipline*, New York, Doubleday.
13 Keegan, A. and Turner, R.J. (2001) "Quantity versus quality in project-based learning practices," *Management Learning*, 32 (1), 77–98.
14 Prencipe, A., Davies, A. and Hobday, M. (2003) *The Business of Systems Integration*, Oxford, Oxford University Press.
15 Brady and Davies, "Building project capabilities." Also see Davies, A. and Hobday, M. (2005) *The Business of Projects*, Cambridge, Cambridge University Press, for a comprehensive integration of project-based organizing and innovation research relevant to the perspectives of this chapter.
16 This section is derived from Arthur, M., DeFillippi, R. and Jones, C. (2001) "Project-based learning as the interplay of career and company non-financial capital," *Management Learning*, 32 (1), 99–117.
17 Kotter, J. (1997) *The New Rules*, New York, Free.
18 Peters, T. (1999) "The Wow Project," *Fast Company*, May, 116–28.
19 DeFillippi, R.J. and Arthur, M.B. (1998) "Paradox in project-based enterprise: the case of film making," *California Management Review*, 40 (2), 1–15; DeFillippi, R. (2001) "Project-based learning, reflective practices and learning outcomes," *Management Learning*, 32 (1), 5–10; Sydow, J., Lindkvist, L. and DeFillippi, R. (2004) "Project-based organizations, embeddedness and repositories of knowledge," *Organization Studies*, 25 (9), 1475–90.
20 The distinction between performance and learning relates closely to Levitt and March's (1993) ideas on the distinction between a company's established competence – or core competencies as we use the term in this book – and new learning. See Levitt, B. and March, J.G. (1988) "Organizational learning," *Annual Review of Sociology*, 14, 19–40.
21 Arthur et al., "Project-based learning."
22 Arthur et al., "Project-based learning." To respect the confidentiality with which information was provided, all company names in the text have been disguised.
23 Prencipe, A. and Tell, F. (2001) "Inter-project learning: processes and outcomes of knowledge codification in project-based firms," *Research Policy*, 30, 1373–94. See also Brady, T., Marshall, N., Prencipe, A. and Tell, F. (2002) "Making sense of learning landscapes in project-based organizations," in P. Love, P.S.W. Fong and Z. Irani (eds), *Management of Knowledge in Project Environments*, Oxford, Elsevier Butterworth-Heinemann, pp. 197–217.
24 Scarbrough, H., Swan, J., Laurent, S., Bresnen, M., Edelman, L. and Newell, S. (2005) "Project-based learning and the role of learning boundaries," *Organization Studies*, 25 (9), 1579–600.
25 Ibid., quote pp. 1586–7.
26 Ibid. We use the term "protocol" instead of the term "practices" used in the original article to avoid ambiguity with the ways the latter is used elsewhere in this book.
27 Carlile, P.R. (2002) "A pragmatic view of knowledge and boundaries: boundary objects in new product development," *Organization Science*, 13 (4), 442–55.

28 Ibid.
29 Ibid.
30 Ibid.
31 Wankel, C. and DeFillippi, R. (2005) *Educating Managers through Real-World Projects*, Greenwich, CT, Information Age.
32 Prencipe and Tell, "Inter-project learning."
33 Rickards, T. (1999) *Creativity and the Management of Change*, Oxford, Blackwell.
34 Wheelwright and Clark, *Revolutionizing Product Development.*
35 Ibid.
36 Prencipe and Tell, "Inter-project learning."
37 Becerra-Fernandez, I., Gonzalez, A. and Sabherwat, R. (2004) *Knowledge Management*, Upper Saddle River, NJ, Pearson Prentice Hall.
38 Awad, E.M. and Ghaziri, H.M. (2004) *Knowledge Management*, Upper Saddle River, NJ, Pearson Prentice Hall.
39 Qu, L. and Pao, S. (2005) "Tools for tapping expertise in large organizations," in M. Rao (ed.), *Knowledge Management Tools and Techniques*, Burlington, MA, Elsevier Butterworth-Heinemann, pp. 365–77.
40 Bresnen, M., Goussevskaia, A. and Swan, J. (2005) "Embedding new management knowledge in project-based organizations," *Organization Studies*, 25 (9), 1535–55.

CHAPTER 7

VIRTUAL KNOWLEDGE WORK

> Clearly, it is now possible for more people than ever to col-
> laborate and compete in real time with more other people
> on more different kinds of work from more different corners
> of the planet and on a more equal footing than at any previous
> time in the history of the world.
>
> *Thomas L. Friedman*[1]

Dramatic improvements in information and communications technology enable knowledge workers to rapidly search, collect, evaluate and
transmit enormous amounts and varieties of data and to engage in complex, collaborative work activities with anyone, anyplace, anytime. As a
result, much knowledge work today arises within virtually distributed teams
or networks of participants. However, the presence of virtual communications and information technologies does not in itself resolve the
challenges of conducting knowledge work virtually. Geographically distant knowledge workers may also differ in their specialized knowledge,
cultural and organizational practices. Hence, it is often necessary to bridge
these differences through the development of suitable knowledge work
collaborative and communication practices.

Moreover, virtual knowledge work is rapidly expanding its sphere of
participants to include third-party knowledge suppliers, geographically distant company subsidiaries, and online communities of users of
knowledge work products and services. Virtual collaborations now link
multiple individuals, organizations and communities in diverse industries
and locales. All these participants are now collaborating on real-time and
customized product and service offerings that are designed, developed,
tested and distributed online. These products and services span every
industry and include the provision of business, governmental and
humanitarian services. Such services are limited more by people's

imagination and resistance to change than by any inherent limitations of virtual technologies or virtual knowledge work practices.

Now let us turn to the example of Teltech.

Teltech[2]

Founded in 1984 by entrepreneur Joe Shuster, Teltech, a small Minneapolis-based company with 160 employees and $17 million in annual revenues, sports an unusual organizational arrangement. Drawing on the success of an earlier business venture, Shuster recognized the value in being able to access a broad range of expertise from outside the company to satisfy a variety of customer needs. These experts are typically academics, recent retirees from industry or consultants.

Teltech's business is essentially accessing, managing and maintaining a network of thousands of experts in a range of technical fields. In many respects, Teltech acts as a knowledge broker, matching clients seeking particular technical solutions with its pool of technical experts. The types of issues for which the technical expert network is called upon to provide expertise vary widely. Some examples are advice on electronic buoys, thermal blankets for jet engines, antibacterial activity of wood oils, and patents for engine heaters.

In addition to maintaining its network of available experts, Teltech offers clients access to over 1,600 online databases. Teltech's in-house knowledge analysts, who account for most of its head office employees, link clients to needed expertise. Typically, the knowledge analysts explore client information needs over the telephone, and then access the appropriate databases. One database carries the names and areas of specialization of Teltech's technical experts, so that the knowledge analyst can provide one or more of the experts' names to prospective clients. If the client then calls and has a discussion with the expert, Teltech bills the client and pays the expert at a predetermined rate.

The "Knowledge Scope" database includes a thesaurus of over 30,000 technical terms. Several full-time "knowledge engineers," who add 500 to 1,200 new concepts per month and remove outdated ones as well, maintain the database. Each technical term has a preferred usage and several possible synonyms. Teltech's goal is for this database to carry all terms that are used by their clients. Teltech has also developed sophisticated software to enable its in-house knowledge analyst to "take over" the client's computer screen and help the client navigate the database and search options, while talking with the client over the telephone.

Teltech sources suggest that most technical experts participate not only for the money, but also for the professional connections and learning opportunities they receive. These experts have pledged to respect the client's proprietary interests by keeping its information confidential. They have also agreed not to use the Teltech referral as an opportunity to sell their own consulting services (although clients sometimes do ask experts to consult, which increases the attractiveness of serving as a Teltech expert). Teltech works on the premise that its experts are an important repository of knowledge, and that this knowledge cannot be captured in any computer database. As a VP of technology at an aerospace firm stated, "There is nothing like talking to someone who has spent their entire life working on a problem."

Teltech is sensitive to the "information behavior" of its clients. This relates to the way that clients seek out, use, share and manage information – in other words, their knowledge practices. For example, Teltech recognizes that it is sometimes important for clients, such as engineers, to feel able to take credit for the information acquired. Similarly, the vast majority of clients want to access information on their computer desktops. Teltech aims to understand and help clients improve on their knowledge practices, and in turn to help clients improve their project or business success.

Teltech has developed logical extensions to its core service of information management. These include a Vendor Service and a Technical Alert Service. The Vendor Service is a database and matching service for clients seeking vendors for particular products and services. The Technical Alert Service provides weekly briefings tailored to the critical interests of clients. Both of these services are supported by direct contact from Teltech's knowledge analysts, and thereby add to the company's revenue stream.

Teltech utilizes phone, fax, computer dial-up and Internet media to communicate with its clients, its knowledge experts and its wider networks. Through these media, Teltech is able to provide most of its services in real time, and the proportion of Internet usage is growing rapidly.

Teltech's business has grown through, and come to largely rely on, the World Wide Web, or the web as it is now commonly called. The web allows clients to access Teltech's many databases, and to download specific information that Teltech's experts provide. The web also allows client workers to communicate with remote technical experts to share background information and project specifications, and to collaborate in problem-solving activities. The web is at the heart of Teltech's business, and that of many other contemporary organizations.

It wasn't always so. Until very recently in human history communication among people across different geographic locations was a rarity. It was the work of merchants and diplomats, mediated by letters carried by horse-driven messenger or sailing ship. Things began to change in the late nineteenth century after the arrival of the telegraph and telephone, and travel between locations became easier after the arrival of the steamship, and more recently the jet plane. However, circumstances changed dramatically with the creation of the World Wide Web.

The web grew out of a 1958 US Defense Department initiative that was initially aimed at building technological superiority over the Soviet Union. It was a modest initiative, and the Advanced Research Project Agency network (the ARPANET) remained a minor Defense Department program until the late 1960s. By that time, the Agency had built bridges to a few select computer scientists, so that by 1971 ARPANET linked the mainframe computers of fifteen research centers, most of them in universities. Shortly after, a working group sketched out a basic architecture for a "network of networks."

By 1990, the Defense Department had released ARPANET from any military obligations, and the open software movement (that lent support to Linux, as described in Chapter 3) was under way. A Geneva-based programmer, Tim Berners-Lee, working at the European particle physics laboratory CERN (now the organisation européenne pour la recherche nucléaire), developed an information-sharing program to take advantage of inter-computer networking, in the first instance for the benefit of the globally dispersed high-energy physics research community. Within four years, the first commercial web browser, Netscape Navigator, was released, followed in the next year by Microsoft's Internet Explorer.[3]

The consequences of the above events are everywhere. Since 1995, work in general, and knowledge work in particular, has relied increasingly on the infrastructure that the web provides. Where work once primarily occurred in physical space, with fellow workers able to directly see each other, it now frequently takes place in virtual space, where workers occupy separate locations and rely on telecommunications to bring their efforts together.

VIRTUAL VERSUS PHYSICAL SPACE

In physical space, such as that occupied by Teltech's staff at company headquarters, people can make face-to-face contact with one another. In virtual space, there is no face-to-face contact. Instead, there is the capacity for instantaneous communication and data transfer around the globe. As a result, today's knowledge work collaborations are increasingly accomplished through dispersed project teams, whose participants work in geographically separate locations.[4] Teams of collaborating individuals, communities, organizations and industry participants are required to navigate the virtual space in which their task or project exists.

A number of advantages and disadvantages of virtual space have already been recognized.[5] One advantage is the ability to bring on board people from anywhere in the world at any time. A related advantage is the ability to access the most knowledgeable and competent workers. Time zone differences allow for work to continue up to twenty-four hours a day, as different subteams take over from other subteams. People also seem to respond to the opportunities that working in virtual space can provide. One senior VP reports: "employees like the flexibility that [virtual] work offers for a variety of reasons, such as working during peak performance periods, reducing the commute time and forming project teams based on knowledge versus location."[6] It has also been found that offering the option of "going virtual" is a successful way of attracting and retaining qualified workers. Most respondents to a survey on virtual work arrangements – involving one or more of telecommuting, virtual teams, flexible time and pay plans, and temporary, project-based professionals – spoke positively of those arrangements.[7]

However, twenty-four hours a day, continuous virtual knowledge work assumes a high degree of coordination. Work delays by one dispersed team can adversely affect other virtual team members' task performance. Work situations can frequently demand real-time problem-solving, calling on some virtual team members to confer in the middle of the night with their globally distant collaborators. A key barrier to twenty-four hour virtual work is the timeliness of communications between geographically distant team members, a theme to which we will return shortly. Moreover, the ability to recruit non-local expertise obscures the challenge of being able to evaluate whether virtual team members will effectively cooperate during times of stress or crisis. The challenges of aligning virtual team members become more daunting if those members are located in culturally diverse work settings, where language, values and social practices may also vary.[8]

In sum, working in virtual space brings fresh opportunities and challenges, and the knowledge work participant needs to navigate this space skillfully. How this work unfolds depends in part on the communications media being used.

PROPERTIES OF VIRTUAL COMMUNICATIONS

The communications media available for virtual knowledge work range from commonly available telephone, e-mail, and instant messaging media to more specialized video conferencing, intranets (covering an organization's own employees), extranets (covering others outside the organization) and collaborative software or groupware technologies. These media differ according to two key properties. One is the *timeliness* (or speed) of communication. The other is the *richness* of communication, defined as the ability to communicate multiple cues, convey feelings, use natural language, and provide rapid feedback.[9] The timelier and the richer the communications, the greater is the opportunity to put people's knowledge to work. Looking back once more on the Teltech story, the ability of customers to solve their informational needs is both accelerated (timeliness) and enhanced (richness) by the opportunity to communicate with Teltech's online databases, knowledge analysts and technical experts.

A basic question concerns the relative merits of communications in virtual space versus physical space. As might be expected, evidence from both Europe and the United States suggests that physically co-located work groups share knowledge and communicate better than those where group members are dispersed.[10] Physical space benefits overall communication because it permits intense and ongoing face-to-face interactions, and more timely problem-solving and task completion.[11] In contrast, all of the communications media available to virtual work groups (telephone, e-mail, video conferencing, instant messaging, groupware) are reported to provide less "richness" than face-to-face interaction.[12] However, the tools for communication in virtual space continue to improve, and skilled use of these tools can enhance the likelihood of success.

The various media presently available for virtual knowledge work may be mapped onto a two-dimensional model as shown in Figure 7.1. The vertical dimension reflects the timeliness of the interaction between individuals, running from asynchronous (for example, through package delivery delays) to synchronous (for example, through telephone conference calls). The horizontal dimension reflects the richness of the media through which coordination is pursued, ranging from low richness of contextual knowledge provided by formal documents to the high richness of social context and verbal and non-verbal nuances found in face-to-face interactions.

Each communications medium has different advantages and disadvantages.[13] To generalize, those media that are lower in richness (e.g. documents, letters, facsimile) tend to provide fewer cues about the social context of the communicated content. However, they do allow the receiver to reflect on the content before needing to reply, since they are asynchronous. These forms of communication also need to be precise in order to avoid

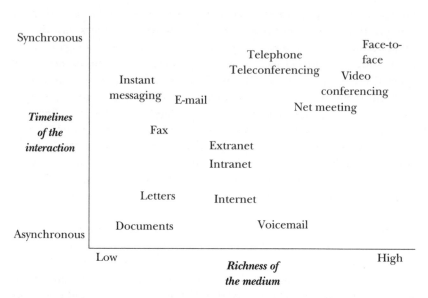

Figure 7.1 Types of media by timeliness and richness

misunderstanding by the recipient, who lacks any immediate means to seek clarification of the message. By contrast, those media that are higher in richness and also synchronous (for example, video conferencing and face-to-face conversation) offer much more subtle and complex messages and also invite immediate response by all participants. We will say more about the choice of media later in the chapter.

BROKERAGE AND CLOSURE IN VIRTUAL WORK

Let us recall the Teltech case, and picture a team of project engineers at a client company location, and a remote technical consultant assigned to help on the engineer's project. The engineers and the consultant have not worked together before. Moreover, the engineers appear to have developed a strong sense of community from working together in previous collaborations. How does the consultant communicate with the engineers to promote productive collaboration?

The technical consultant's solution can be guided by the earlier discussion of intra-community versus inter-community knowledge work presented in Chapter 3. If the consultant's and the engineers' knowledge bases are largely similar it may make sense for the consultant to seek to bond with the engineers, that is to become included in their community. However, if the consultant's and the engineers' knowledge bases are substantially different, it may make sense for the consultant to simply build an effective communications link between the consultant's own and the engineers' potential project contributions. In the language of Chapter 3, the consultant's choice is between closure (getting inside the engineers' community) and brokerage (building a relatively distant but effective working relationship with the engineers). The choice will in turn dictate the extent to which the consultant identifies with the engineers and their established practice, in contrast to adopting a more task-centered and problem-solving approach. A set of parallel considerations applies to the engineers' approach to working with the consultant.

A similar logic prevails when we turn to consider virtual collaboration between two communities. If the communities are engaged in the same practice (as for example two subcommunities working on separate elements of the Linux operating system), members of the two communities may bond with one another. In the language of Chapter 3, the two communities may become comfortable with a shared sense of closure, allowing them to function as one. However, the more usual situation is one of virtual collaboration between communities engaged in substantially different practices. In the language of Chapter 3, this calls for brokerage – that is for a market-driven, problem-solving approach. The intra-community and inter-community contrasts in virtual space are much like those in physical space, with the added challenges of timeliness and richness of virtual communications.

The available research reinforces the importance of brokerage in effective knowledge work.[14] Studies of multidisciplinary teams (such as scientific research or product development teams) suggest that team members serve as knowledge brokers with the specialized technical communities to which the team members belong.[15] The value of multidisciplinary teams lies less in the team members' own knowledge than in the access the members provide to the collective knowledge of external knowledge communities. Rather than seeking tight closure among team members, knowledge work in general and virtual knowledge work in particular needs to promote brokerage among these different communities.

MANAGING VIRTUAL PROJECTS

We turn next to examine how brokerage and closure can work to moderate or amplify the challenges inherent in virtual project activities.

As in Chapter 6, we will focus first on organizationally sponsored project activities, but with an emphasis on virtual collaboration. Also, in contrast to Chapter 6, we examine the community rather than the individual participants in knowledge work. This is because it is often useful to diagnose virtual projects in terms of the separate practices that participating communities bring, and how these might be combined to promote both project performance and learning.

Working with a distant subsidiary

One of the benefits of the World Wide Web is the potential it holds for inexpensive and instantaneous international communications. However, uninformed use of this potential, and misunderstandings about the underlying community and organizational dynamics, can have unfortunate consequences, as the new business case illustrates.

New business venturing from London to India[16]

A multinational telecommunications corporation decided to create a new Internet business (NIB) that would focus on new, online, customer relationships and extend the corporation's brand. The idea was for NIB to function independently from the parent corporation.[17] The NIB project was a geographically dispersed project involving teams from London in the UK and Bombay and New Delhi in India. Initially, everything for the development of the NIB was created in Bombay, because the project's first information technology workers were located there and Bombay was considered the media capital of India. The Bombay team quickly realized they needed to expand their Internet business activities to New Delhi, India's political capital and a center for many of the governmental and regulatory institutions whose support would be essential to the NIB.

The project workers recruited within the London-based corporate headquarters were familiar with emerging changes in telecommunications, but relatively unfamiliar with developing Internet-based businesses. As a result, the Indian project team members were allowed to explore and develop their own ways of doing things. Over time, the Indian project members found themselves developing a sense of community – based on a sense of joint enterprise in the NIB venture, a shared repertoire of Internet-related expertise, and mutual engagement among the workers from the two Indian offices.

The same sense of community was not shared by the headquarters staff. Time zone and cost considerations meant that the headquarters staff communicated primarily over e-mail, supplemented by periodic teleconferencing. However, even when teleconferencing did occur the nuances of face-to-face communication were absent. The lack of both timeliness and richness in London to India communications gave rise to increasing delays. In the words of one of the London participants:

> One of the issues with just teleconferencing is you tend not to pick up the personal. [You are] immediately talking pure, hard and fast business issues . . . Yet the things that actually get in the way sometimes aren't those things at all . . . Accent or dialect [or] language are all blockers when it's a virtual team.

Friction developed between an impatient headquarters staff, accustomed to more traditional project arrangements, and the less predictable practices of the NIB project teams in India. This friction discouraged headquarters workers from continuing in the NIB venture.

> In the beginning everybody wanted to work for NIB . . . You know, people said it's risky, but it's exciting. Now . . . people are saying, no, I don't want to go to NIB. They haven't delivered last year . . . There is a risk for everyone that works in NIB, if you want to be in [the parent corporation] long term.

Two years later, the parent corporation decided to disband the NIB as a separate entity and to reorganize the business under an existing corporate unit. The India e-learning project team, despite having done an "excellent job" in the words of their launch manager, was suspended. Most of the Indian employees are now working for other companies.

The failure of the NIB venture reflects a pattern of low face-to-face interaction, ambiguous lines of authority and low richness in communications media. Part of the problem appears political, since some research on global virtual projects indicates that centrally located participants in virtual projects tend to rely on face-to-face communications with each other. In doing so, they downplay the importance of virtual communications with their geographically distant project partners. The choice of communications media can thus reflect the power relations between centrally located and geographically dispersed and more politically peripheral project participants.[18]

However, there was also an inter-community dynamic at work in the NIB venture. The London and Indian workers were part of the same company, but geographically isolated from each other and involved in largely separate practices. The project team as a whole (including the London- and India-based participants) possessed no overall shared repertoire around which a sense of community might emerge. An appropriate approach in this and other virtually coordinated projects is one of brokerage. This involves making sure that participating communities' separate investments in the project are clearly understood, and promoting a problem-solving, task-centered approach toward project success. This approach can also bring separate community agendas to the surface, and thereby anticipate unnecessary magnification of political differences.

Working on a complex project

Participants in virtual knowledge work projects need to develop the skills to anticipate, initiate and contribute to the maintenance of effective communications. The hockey rink case study invites a series of questions on how these communications can best be established and maintained.

Designing a hockey rink for Seattle, Washington[19]

The project involves the construction of a new ice hockey rink for a National Hockey League team to be located in Seattle, Washington. The client for the project is a wealthy businessman who owns several sports teams. He would like to create a state-of-the-art stadium for his hometown's new team. He has appointed a construction management company to help run the project. They are responsible for delivering the project, but he has told them to work closely with the architect. Both the client and the construction management team are based in Seattle.

The architect responsible for the design is the world-famous Helmut Vanderlay, who has offices in New York, Los Angeles and Berlin. He is enthusiastic about the stadium project and welcomes opportunities to experiment with new technologies, materials and designs. Working full-time on the project is a key junior architect on Vanderlay's staff. He is based in Berlin and is responsible for the day-to-day management of the architectural elements of the project.

The architect and design team were chosen jointly in the early stages of the project. The architect specifically recommended the design services team chosen to work on the project. The design services team involves a multidisciplinary group of mechanical, electrical and structural engineers, responsible for the delivery of the design services. All of the design services team are co-located in London.

The project is a year old and as yet there is still no completed design. Small changes by the architect have forced the design services team to redesign the project several times. The client is increasingly unhappy, but he is unwilling to let go of the architect. His construction management agents are worried about the time and cost of the design process. They have already had to reprogram the project several times in response to delays in the design. They are highly frustrated with the architect.

To date, the European-based project team has held twice-monthly meetings, usually in London. The construction management organization has visited the European team once every four months. E-mail is common on the project, especially between the design team and the architects. The design team has used video conferencing in the past, but found it fairly difficult. Vanderlay is uncomfortable with the lack of personal touch in video conferencing.

This project again reflects an underlying tension between timeliness and richness of communications, but this time across several separate organizations. Once more, inter-community dynamics are behind the problem. It is unrealistic to view the diverse project participants (architects, local client, design services team, construction management team) as a single community with any single shared purpose (joint enterprise), or common methods of work and decision-making (shared repertoire), or close-knit relationships with one another (mutual engagement). These players represent separate communities, but can still come together around a common task and the problem-solving needed to fulfill that task. The more complex the project, the more skilled is the brokerage required.[20]

Selecting communications media

A further challenge in both of the previous case studies concerns the use of communications media. Which media are the most appropriate, and when and for what purpose can they best be used? Evidence from a study of globally dispersed versus co-located project teams across a variety of industries revealed that both kinds of team used high levels of face-to-face communication in searching for new ideas, consulting team members and resolving management problems.[21] Both kinds of team were heavy users of e-mail, but the dispersed teams relied more heavily on telephone conversations and teleconferencing than co-located teams. Video conferencing and extranet were not found to be significantly useful by either the co-located or the dispersed teams. Both kinds of teams gathered simple information through e-mails, faxes and quick one-to-one phone calls, while comprehensive decision-making was more typically accomplished through face-to-face meetings.[22]

Some communications media are more appropriate for certain tasks than for others.[23] Complex and more ambiguous tasks such as unstructured problem-solving, dispute resolution or persuasion call for media in the upper right quadrant of Figure 7.1 (that is, face-to-face or perhaps video conferencing). Tasks that are more routine, factual, and informational in purpose can be done with media in the lower left quadrant of Figure 7.1 (that is, documents). Some communications tools, such as e-mails and instant messaging, use the same media as those used for other documents but anticipate a more timely response. Use of communications media and the timing of face-to-face interaction are also linked to the status and stage of any project. At the beginning of a project, face-to-face communication is likely to help team members search for new ideas and determine their approach. As a project develops, the need for face-to-face communication is likely to decline. However, near the end of a project, when it is time to roll out deliverables for approval, face-to-face communication is likely to become important again.[24]

Although no single pattern of project-based communications can be prescribed for all projects, Table 7.1 illustrates how communications media might be employed to accomplish specific project-based communications tasks across the three stages of an evolving project.[25] For illustrative purposes, Table 7.1 limits the inclusion of a communications task to a single stage of project development. However, some tasks, such as the need to persuade and gain agreement, may arise and may call for informal face-to-face contact at multiple project stages. Other tasks, such as the need for sharing large amounts of data among project members, may call for more formal communication at multiple stages.

We are still relatively inexperienced in the skilled and cost-effective use of the communications media. And as we learn from this experience, the cost of voice and video media continues to decline. As a result, we can expect that virtual communications will play a larger role in geographically dispersed projects and virtual knowledge work in general. However, there are still things that may be better achieved by physical face interaction, or to paraphrase actor Jimmy Stewart (Chapter 2), by "looking them in the eye and telling them the truth." We turn to more specific challenges involving virtual communications among cross-disciplinary teams.

Table 7.1 Matching communications media to communications task by project stages

Communications media	Project launch (variation)	Project development (selection)	Project conclusion (retention)
Formal face-to-face	Searching and scanning for new ideas		
Informal face-to-face	Persuading, motivating and gaining agreement		Determining how to report on project outcomes
Telephone	Verifying and validating information and ideas	Consulting project members on solutions to problems	
Telephone conferencing	Resolving management problems	Consulting project members on solutions to problems	
E-mail		Exchanging routine information	
Video conferencing	Persuading, motivating and gaining agreement		Determining how to report on project outcomes
Extranet		Coordinating work among project members	
Intranet		Coordinating work among project subteams	
Net meeting or similar		Supplementing data sharing with voice communications	
Internet		Sending large amounts of electronic data	Distribution of final project report

FACILITATING CROSS-DISCIPLINARY TEAMS

The rapid pace of scientific and technological discovery continues to drive new research opportunities, many of them transcending the usual disciplines through which science has been organized. One such opportunity is to pursue more effective cure and control of cancer, which is the mission of the National Cancer Institute.

Providing infrastructure for cancer research[26]

The traditional approach to cancer research has been described as a "cottage industry" of small, independent groups working out of medical schools, universities, and research institutes, with occasional *ad hoc* collaborations. However, the emergence of biomedical science challenges the traditional approach. In response, the US National Cancer Institute (NCI) has concluded that multidisciplinary teams will be needed to solve the "big" problems in cancer research – sequencing the human genome, creating the next generation of imaging devices, or discovering and testing target-specific treatments.

The scope of the challenges, and the need for interaction among laboratories, clinics and patient populations, calls for interdisciplinary teamwork. This will involve collaboration among and between biologists, chemists, computer scientists, epidemiologists, imaging scientists, mathematicians, physicians, and physicists across a range of clinical and laboratory settings. The challenges lead beyond any single institution, and instead call for effective virtual collaboration among specialists wherever they happen to be located.

In response, the NCI has established a Consortia and Networks program to coordinate multidisciplinary team activities. One example is the Cancer Genetics Network, dedicated to studying inherited predisposition to cancer. The Network was launched with eight designated centers and an informatics and information technology group, and charged to accelerate the way knowledge about genetic links to cancer is converted into clinical application. Another example is the Diagnostic Imaging Network, concerned with imaging technologies and their potential for early detection, and bridging to both device manufacturers on the one hand and clinical treatment centers on the other hand.

In seeking to facilitate the above kinds of collaborations the NCI has called for a "culture change" toward a more problem-centered, interdisciplinary approach that celebrates the opportunity for broader collaborations. It has also committed to provide the infrastructure and the information technology tools to support those collaborations.

The NCI is largely a sponsor, rather than a direct producer, of cancer research. As such, it is positioning itself as a provider of the technological support that will better facilitate virtual communications across a wide range of professional disciplines. The NCI's positioning also denies any single organization a pre-eminent role. Rather it calls on a diverse range of talented individuals, professional communities, manufacturing and clinical organizations and industry representatives to self-organize around a common goal. The goal is to accelerate both performance improvements and learning outcomes in alternative cancer treatments. As we will see later, the NCI is not the only sponsor of this kind of virtual, cross-disciplinary, activity.

OPEN-SOURCE SOFTWARE COMMUNITIES[27]

Other examples of web-based organizing support more widespread participation and collaboration within and across communities. A particular example involves open-source software (OSS). OSS projects allow interested parties to participate in the development, application and testing of new software by making the source code for the software freely available. These projects usually begin with someone posting a software "kernel" and inviting people to write "hacks" (additional programming code) to add to the kernel's functionality. Others are invited to test the software for defects (bugs) and to offer solutions (patches) back to the online website, which serves as a central clearing house for all volunteer software development activity. OSS projects have become increasingly significant contributors to the software industry as a whole. They stand in contrast to more traditional in-house proprietary software development, and are now employed by a growing number of major computer industry companies, such as Netscape and IBM.

A prominent example involves the OSS community behind the Linux operating system, introduced in Chapter 3. How does this community gain control over partner contributions, and in turn create trust in virtual collaboration? To begin, Linux and other long-standing open-source communities have evolved explicitly defined roles for certain community members. These roles correspond to typical roles in internal company software development projects, but the primary distinction is that the roles are typically voluntary, and subject to neither corporate compensation nor control. The roles are not only functional, but also provide a means for community participants to build trust through web-based exchange and cooperation.

However, OSS virtual communities also succeed through implicit control mechanisms.[28] For example, Linux utilizes a workflow governed by the Linux kernel mailing list, which determines which developers receive which messages. To help neophyte Linux community members participate appropriately, an FAQ document specifies rules of open-source conduct and process and also reiterates the norms and values of the Linux community.[29] Observers suggest that open-source projects depend on both self-control by participants (to preserve one's reputation) and social controls by peers, who can monitor member contributions and sanction inappropriate conduct.[30] Through these controls, community members exercise mutual engagement and contribute to the joint enterprise of collective software development.

Moreover, open-source projects are iterative and each project's performance generates knowledge about what worked and what didn't. This is captured both in the project documentation and in the electronically facilitated e-mail conversations occurring within the community of open-source project participants. These participants share their project experiences, and their stories provide a narrative that provides for further community-level learning.[31] As a result, open-source projects often outperform conventional in-house projects in producing robust and reliable software.[32]

GRID COMPUTING

Advances in information technology and virtual knowledge work tools, in part inspired by the open-source software movement, are driving a transformation in how industries organize both knowledge creation and knowledge utilization activities. Grid computing first emerged in the mid 1990s, as scientists and engineers at leading government, private and university research centers sought a hardware and software infrastructure that would allow dispersed networks of people and organizations to securely share computing power, databases, instruments and other online tools without sacrificing local autonomy.[33] Over time a variety of specialized grids have arisen, including many on the forefront of the physical sciences such as the Grid Physics Network (for physics research) and the Fusion Grid (for fusion research), and networks to foster collaboration between geographically defined participants such as the European Data Grid. Each of these grids uses open-source software tools to facilitate communications and knowledge sharing across different hardware platforms. Membership in each grid is restricted to people who have the requisite specialized knowledge and tools to participate in that grid.

A dramatic example of the power of grid computing is the case study of how Pacific Rim health care communities were mobilized in response to the SARS epidemic.

SARS and community mobilization[34]

When several hospitals in Taiwan were quarantined during the SARS (severe acute respiratory syndrome) epidemic, Taiwanese doctors and other medical professionals were suddenly cut off from the global health community. Quarantined physicians could no longer seek help from specialists at other institutions, and hospital staffs and patients were unable to see their families. On May 13, 2003, the World Health Organization reported that the viral respiratory illness had infected 7,548 people worldwide, killing 573.

Early on May 15, 2003, the head of Taiwan's National Center for High-Performance Computing (NCHC) sent a request for immediate technical assistance to the chair and several other members of the Pacific Rim Application and Grid Middleware Assembly (PRAGMA) steering committee. Soon the message was forwarded to the rest of the PRAGMA members, an international community of researchers whose communications are usually focused on grid computing applications. From there, the request spread to a variety of other communities networked through the grid to PRAGMA.

Almost immediately, offers to assist poured in from around the world, with volunteers ready to provide equipment, expertise, and Chinese-speaking support staff. In less than twelve hours, grid technology was deployed from the US to Taiwan. On the evening of May 17, an emergency video teleconference was held to review the implementation of the grid network within three Taiwanese hospitals. The list was later expanded to seven health care sites, where grid computing would extend standard video and teleconferencing services, and allow physicians to share detailed X-ray images, patient data and other information in online meetings across different sites. The grid also hosted private virtual rooms for patients or hospital staff to visit with family members. These services reached well beyond the capacity of more broadly available web-based applications to provided both life-saving and comfort-providing services.

The SARS story illustrates how grid-computing technology can mobilize globally dispersed health and technical support community resources during a health epidemic crisis. The applications of grid computing and other virtual technologies are rapidly spreading to other areas of health care delivery. The National Cancer Institute example described earlier provides another illustration of a virtual forum available to specialized research communities.[35] It is also an example of a new approach to scientific research that spreads the cost of more expensive research efforts and more complex data around networks of research centers that the grid can now support.

Grid computing has now spread to industry knowledge work. For example, Rolls Royce is part of a collaboration with four research universities and two other firms to demonstrate how grid computing may be used to design and develop systems for engine diagnosis and maintenance. Nearly half of Rolls Royce's revenues are based on its maintenance and servicing of engines in aircraft, ships (naval vessels) and power stations, and grid computing offers the promise of rapid identification of engine deficiencies and improved speed of engine maintenance services.[36] Other industries are likely to follow, as similar opportunities present themselves for the rapid data collection, analysis and application of solutions to a global set of users.

FROM E-BUSINESS TO VIRTUAL PRODUCT TESTING[37]

Virtual coordination of complex projects has emerged to replace an earlier fascination with "e-business" – that is, web-based new business ventures that sought to replace physical assets and physical location with intangible, knowledge-based assets and virtual coordination. Although few companies are now launched as pure e-business ventures, certain underlying business models survive. One model involves a company serving as an "infomediary" or broker to connect producers and customers together, such as Monster.com having job seekers and employers post their requirements and make matches with one another. A second model involves the aggregation of online information to meet market demands, such as Amazon.com's pioneering activity in the online book retailing business. Another model involves the creation of exchanges for the online auctioning of goods and services, most prominently illustrated by the online auction house. (A widely circulated story claims that a software development project team once auctioned its services on eBay.)[38]

Most pure e-business or so-called "pure dotcom" ventures have now perished, as customer demand failed to meet rising costs, and criticism spread of mismanagement and miscommunication of financial and market performance data.[39] Yet what may have changed most, and what continues to change, is the capacity of the web to enhance established approaches. A prominent example lies in applications for virtual prototype development and virtual product testing.[40] Both applications are possible because of recent advances in modeling and simulation tools that enable digital prototypes of physical products to be created and made available over the web. As a result, companies in a variety of industries use virtual prototyping and virtual product testing to speed the process of product development and to lower the costs of development and product testing.

Procter and Gamble uses virtual prototypes to experiment with multiple versions in the design of a product. Virtual prototypes can be designed online, shared with product developers across the company's design centers for critical feedback, and then subjected to computer simulation testing of product performance before any commitment is made to a physical prototype. Procter and Gamble also uses virtual shopping malls to observe how virtual shoppers respond to different product placements. In the residential construction industry, the Japanese company Sekisui House provides "customer experience centers" where customers work with housing designers to virtually assemble their house and take a simulated walk-through of their virtual home. A CD-ROM is provided to allow prospective home shoppers to share their prototype designs with family, friends and neighbors and to then return with revised specifications for their home's construction. However, Sekisui realizes that not all product experiences can be virtual, and also gives shoppers an opportunity to physically inspect and directly experience certain housing features, such as the quality of a shower head's performance.[41]

In the entertainment software sector, video game developers often release prototype (beta) versions of their games to selected users, whose sophistication provides rich sources of feedback to company game designers and marketers. Subsequent evaluations of games by online user communities via online game ratings services or game user blogs are also significant predictors of many games' market success.[42] Some companies have begun to assemble user kits to allow members of their user community to actively modify characters and game features to their customized requirements. These user modifications (called mods) may then become traded amongst game community members, not always without conflicts of interest. For example, one company uses characters (called avatars) similar in style but not identical to popular Marvel comic characters. When some members of the company's game-playing community began customizing their avatars to look exactly like the Marvel characters, the comic publisher's attorney stepped in to protect his company's trademarked and copyrighted characters.[43] Such conflicts over intellectual property rights will be further discussed in Chapter 9.

Virtual prototyping and product testing tools make possible virtual collaboration amongst geographically dispersed communities of product developers and product testers. These communities frequently overlap, with user communities becoming increasingly involved in the co-creation of products and services. Indeed, the proliferation of "user toolkits" in a variety of industries assures that user communities will play an increasingly active role as partners with producers in knowledge creation and knowledge utilization.[44]

TOOLS FOR VIRTUAL KNOWLEDGE WORK

Perhaps the greatest challenge facing knowledge work practitioners is their choice of the optimal blend of virtual and non-virtual communications tool usage. Many knowledge workers appear to show systematic biases toward using some communications tools rather than others. E-mail is widely used even among co-located workers, but e-mail is no cure-all for all virtual knowledge work. At the same time, business organizations and other project sponsors cannot afford the time and expense of continuous face-to-face meetings. Figure 7.1 summarized some research findings on the use of different communications media for different tasks, and Table 7.1 illustrated how to match communications media to different tasks across three successive stages of virtual knowledge work projects.

New virtual communications tools and practices continue to proliferate. One of the more rapidly expanding practices among knowledge workers is the use of web logs or blogs (first mentioned in Chapter 2), whereby individuals can publicly post their presumably expert views on topics and invite anyone with web access to interact with them either in synchronous online chatrooms or in asynchronous "threaded discussions." Many organizations have now recognized the reach and potential richness of blogs, and they are now a common feature of many businesses, government and non-profit organizations.[45]

What does the future hold for the use of virtual knowledge work practices and tools? For a glimpse into the future, it can be instructive to look to the youngest generation. For example, the use of instant messaging among younger people is transforming both writing conventions and the timeliness of synchronous communications. Similarly, the growing popularity of "podcasting" (web-based access to audio files) among young people globally is leading some universities to put their lectures onto websites, to provide their students with free portable digital media players (e.g. iPods), and to permit them to download college lectures for any-time, any-place access.[46] It seems that the future use of virtual tools is primarily limited by the ability of today's knowledge workers and their organizations to adapt their practices to the sensibilities of the next generation of educated and tech-savvy knowledge workers.

SUMMARY

Virtual knowledge work is now widespread. The opening Teltech case illustrated how the World Wide Web has created new possibilities for conducting knowledge work in virtual space. However, the possibilities of virtual space also pose significant challenges of coordination and communication. Communications media vary in their richness and timeliness, and can fulfill different purposes over the three stages (variation, selection, retention) of virtual project development. The NIB and Seattle Hockey Rink cases illustrated some of the communication challenges of virtual work and the complexities of simultaneous brokerage and closure among virtually connected communities.

The National Cancer Institute and SARS cases demonstrated how geographically separate scientific and medical communities can be mobilized with the aid of communications technology such as grid computing. Procter and Gamble, Sekisui House and the video games industry illustrated how shoppers and customers are being asked to play an increasingly active role in testing and improving virtual prototypes. The chapter closed by reviewing uses and abuses of specific communications tools, and the role of a new generation of knowledge workers in developing practices using virtual tools such as blogs, instant messaging and podcasting.

QUESTIONS FOR REFLECTION

1   What types of communications media do you use most often at work (see Table 7.1)? What communications media were used in a recent project, and how did those media compare with the project stages and media uses suggested in Figure 7.1?
2   What do you see as the primary challenges of virtual work interactions among people representing different occupational, functional or organizational communities? How do you cope with these challenges?
3   Can you apply the brokerage and closure concepts to your present relationships with specific communities, and to the types of

communications media you typically employ when interacting with those communities?

4   How do open-source software applications pose either an opportunity or a threat to your company's current software applications?

5   What role do e-business models play in your professional or personal life? How do you participate in such e-business activities (infomediary, online content aggregation, online auctioning)?

6   What role (if any) do blogs, podcasts or instant messages currently play in your virtual communications and virtual interactions with others? How might you incorporate these tools more fully into your own knowledge work contributions?

NOTES

1   Friedman, T.L. (2005) *The World Is Flat*, New York, Farrar, Strauss, and Giroux.

2   Adapted from Davenport, Thomas H., "Teltech: the business of knowledge management case study," http://www.mccombs.utexas.edu/kman/telcase. htm.

3   Castells, M. (2001) *The Internet Galaxy*, Oxford, Oxford University Press; Gribble, C. (2005) *History of the Web Beginning at CERN*, http://www.hitmill.com/internet/web_history.html, accessed November 30, 2005.

4   Gibson, C.B. and Cohen, S.G. (2003) *Virtual Teams that Work*, San Francisco, Jossey-Bass.

5   Ibid.

6   Ceridian Employer Services (1999) "Companies offer boundaryless work arrangements as incentive to attract and retain workers," Ceredian Corporation website, http://www.ceridian.com/myceridian.

7   Ibid.

8   See Smeds, R., Olivari, P. and Corso, M. (2001) "Continuous learning in global product development: a cross-cultural comparison," *International Journal of Technology Management*, 22 (4), 373–91, for an examination of how cultural differences in the national subsidiaries of Ericsson impact the choice of different media for knowledge transfer and communications between the subsidiaries and with corporate headquarters.

9   Daft, R. and Lengel, R.H. (1984) "Information richness: a new approach to managerial behavior and organizational design," in B.M. Staw and L.L. Cummings (eds), *Research in Organizational Behavior*, vol. 6, Greenwich, CT, JAI, pp. 191–233.

10   Sapsed, J. and Salter, A. (2004) "Postcards from the edge: local communities, global programs and boundary objects," *Organization Studies*, 25 (9), 1515–34.

11   DeSanctis, G. and Monge, P. (1999) "Introduction to the special issue," *Organization Science*, special issue on "Communication Processes for Virtual Organizations," 10 (6), 693–703.

12 Daft, R.L. and Lengel, R.H. (1986) "Organizational information require-
    ments, media richness and structural design," *Management Science*, 32 (5),
    554–71; Sproull, L. and Kiesler, S. (1986) "Reducing social context cues:
    electronic mail in organizational communication," *Management Science*,
    32 (11), 1492–1512.

13 Buchel, B. and Raub, S. (2001) "Media choice and organizational learning,"
    in M. Dierkes, B. Antal, J. Child and I. Nonaka (eds), *Handbook of Organiza-
    tional Learning and Knowledge*, Oxford: Oxford University Press.

14 Sapsed, J., Bessant, J., Partington, D., Tranfied, D. and Young, M. (2002) "Team-
    working and knowledge management: a review of converging themes,"
    International Journal of Management Reviews, 4 (1), 71–85.

15 Allen, T. (1984) *Managing the Flow of Technology: Transfer and the Dissemina-
    tion of Technological Information with the R&D Organization*, Cambridge, MA,
    MIT Press; Keller, R.T. (2001) "Cross-functional project groups in research
    and new product development: diversity, communications, job stress, and
    outcomes," *Academy of Management Journal*, 44, 547–55.

16 Case study from Garcia-Lorenzo, Lucia (2004) "From networks to networking:
    implications of a social practice for organizing and knowledge sharing," in
    *Coalitions and Collision: 11th International Conference on Multi-Organizational
    Partnerships, Alliances and Networks*, June 23–26, Tilburg, The Netherlands.

17 Ibid, p. 5.

18 Sapsed and Salter, "Postcards from the edge."

19 The hockey rink scenario was developed in 2003 within Managing Know-
    ledge Spaces, a two-year research project funded by the Engineering and Physical
    Sciences Research Council (Gann, D., Salter, A., Sapsed, J. and Marshall,
    N., 2004, GR/R54132/01). This project was conducted jointly by CENTRIM,
    the Centre for Research in Innovation Management at the University of
    Brighton, and the Innovation Studies Centre, Imperial College London.

20 Burt, R.S. (2005) *Brokerage and Closure: An Introduction to Social Capital*, Oxford,
    Oxford University Press.

21 Managing Knowledge Spaces.

22 Maznevski, M. and Chudoba, K.M. (2000) "Bridging space over time: global
    virtual team dynamics and effectiveness," *Organization Science*, 11 (5), 473–92.

23 Marshall, N. (2004) *Managing Knowledge Spaces: Coordinating across Talent,
    Teams and Territory*, workshop presentation, June 22, Falmer, University of
    Sussex Freeman Innovation Centre.

24 Sapsed, J., Gann, D., Marshall, N. and Salter, A. (2005) "From here to eternity?
    The practice of knowledge transfer in dispersed and co-located project organ-
    isations," *European Planning Studies*, special issue on "Knowledge Management
    and Innovation in Urban and Regional Development," 13 (6), 831–51.

25 Based on Marshall, *Managing Knowledge*.

26 http://2001.cancer.gov/promoting.htm#1.

27 This section draws upon material from DeFillippi, R. (2002) "Information
    technology and organizational models for project collaboration in the new
    economy," *Human Resource Planning*, 25 (4), 7–18.

28   Gallivan, M.J. (2001) "Striking a balance between trust and control in virtual
     organizations: a content analysis of open source software case studies," *Informa-
     tion Systems Journal*, 11, 277–304.
29   Moon, J.Y. and Sproull, L. (2000) "Essence of distributed work: the case
     of the Linux kernel," *First Monday*, http://www.firstmonday.org/issues/
     issue5_11/moon/index.html.
30   Markus, M.L., Manville, B. and Agres, C.E. (2000) "What makes a virtual
     organization work?," *Sloan Management Review*, 42, 13–26.
31   DeFillippi, R. and Arthur, M. (2002) "Career creativity to industry influence:
     a blueprint for the knowledge economy?," in M.A. Peiperl, M.B. Arthur and
     N. Anand (eds), *Career Creativity: Explorations in the Remaking of Work*, Oxford,
     Oxford University Press, pp. 298–313.
32   Raymond, E.S. (1998) *The Cathedral and the Bazaar: Musings on Linux and
     Open Source by an Accidental Revolutionary*, Sebastopol, CA, O'Reilly.
33   The Globus Alliance website, www.globus.org/.
34   Ferguson, C. (2005) "Pacific Rim group evolves into international model of
     collaboration," *National Partnership for Advanced Computational Infrastructure:
     Archives*, http://www.npaci.edu/enVision/v19.3/pragma.html, accessed
     October 23, 2005.
35   National Cancer Institute Research Network (2005) "Infrastructure needed
     for cancer research: NCI's challenges promoting collaboration through cen-
     ters, networks, and consortia," http://2001.cancer.gov/promoting.htm#1.
36   Dodson, M., Gann, D. and Salter, A. (2005) *Think, Play, Do*, Oxford, Oxford
     University Press.
37   This section draws upon material from DeFillippi, "Information technology."
     The e-business models in this section are based on those described in Tapscott,
     D., Ticoll, D. and Lowy, A. (2000) *Digital Capital*, Boston, Harvard Business
     School Press. The material on virtual product testing is derived from
     Dodson et al., *Think, Play, Do*.
38   Tapscott et al., *Digital Capital*.
39   Martin, P. (2001) "The technological evolution," *Financial Times*, December
     24, London Edition, 17.
40   Dodson et al., *Think, Play, Do*.
41   Ibid.
42   DeFillippi, R. (2004) personal communications with anonymous video
     game industry executives.
43   Ibid.
44   Von Hippel, E. (2005) *Democratizing Innovation*, Cambridge, MA, MIT Press.
45   Heires, K. (2005) "The blogosphere beckons: should your company jump
     in?," *Harvard Management Communication Letter*, 2 (4), reprint CO511A.
46   Read, B. (2005) "Lectures on the go," *Chronicle of Higher Education*, October
     28, pp. A39–A42.

CHAPTER 8

GLOBAL KNOWLEDGE
AND LEARNING

In a globalizing world, where information and images are
routinely transmitted across the Globe, we are all regularly in
contact with others who think differently, and live differently,
from ourselves.

Anthony Giddens[1]

Regular contact with others who think and live differently is a part of
many knowledge workers' everyday experience. One way this experience
happens is through the activities of global organizations. These organizations, such as Nokia in the opening story in this chapter, focus on global
knowledge transfer and learning. They represent an evolutionary shift
from multinational organizations, whose primary concern was knowledge
exploitation. There are several ways for organizations to become global,
including harnessing local knowledge, acting locally but thinking globally,
and being "born global." A global organization is involved in parallel knowledge work interactions with key actors in each of its countries of operation. Moreover, evolving standards of country expertise and productivity
are transforming global supply chains and shifting the division of labor
(including knowledge work) between its country-specific participants.

Individuals, communities and industries all contribute to global knowledge work, in each case taking advantage of the emergent capacity of
the World Wide Web. Moreover, all four knowledge diamond actors
participate in the exchange of local and global knowledge. In some cases
this unfolds with heavy encouragement from local governments. Part of
that encouragement includes attracting and retaining key participants
(individuals, organizations and community groups) whose expertise
and reputations make possible network connections with important
players in other global centers of relevant knowledge.

Let us move on to the Nokia story.

Nokia[2]

Nokia, the Finnish company now best known for its mobile telephones, started business in the forestry industry in 1865. By 1967, three companies – Nokia Forest and Power, Finnish Rubber Works, and Finnish Cable Works – had formed the roots of what was to become a remarkable global organization. Although the company had been one of the world's leading mobile phone manufacturers since the 1970s, it was not until the early 1990s that the mass consumer industry took off. In 1994 and 1995, Nokia's handset sales doubled two years in a row. By the start of the twenty-first century, Nokia was a global giant in the industry.

In 1994, the Nokia Board of Directors switched the language of its minutes from Finnish to English. This symbolic switch, coupled with a listing on the New York Stock Exchange, marked the start of a new era for Nokia. The company realized it would need to extend its knowledge base beyond its traditional Nordic markets to be part of the next wave of innovation. It would need to combine its Finnish culture and competencies with research and development capabilities from the UK, advanced technology and market know-how from the US, miniaturization and data applications technologies from Japan, and low-cost manufacturing capability from South East Asia.

In a short space of time, the company identified emerging trends, including customization of mobile phones in Europe, new types of functionality in the US and Japan, the mobile phone as a fashion accessory in the US and Asia, and the substitution of mobile telephony for fixed lines in China and India. The identification of these trends was helped by the dispatch of Finnish managers to key locations around the world, providing bridges between local experts and the global organization. Learning gained from the leading Japanese market, where small phones were already half the size of Nokia's initial design, led to the development of Nokia's 2100 series – a breakthrough product and a global hit.

Nokia led its competitors in recognizing and exploiting the rapidly emerging fashion accessory market for mobile phones in California and Japan. By the mid 1990s chic new Nokia mobile phones and other innovations had catapulted the company to first place in mobile phone sales growth and return on capital employed. As it became more successful, Nokia turned its attention to the development and agreement of international standards. In particular, it helped to craft the 3G (i.e. third-generation) standard that promised greater transmission speeds and capability, including video conferencing and high-speed web browsing. Nokia also established "future watch" groups to identify and analyze technical and market developments occurring at this time.

Having established a leadership position in mobile communications, Nokia turned its attention to Internet-based solutions. The challenge was connecting between wireless and Internet communications while sustaining the company's competencies in both areas. For Nokia, Internet developments were less constrained by quality control and intellectual property issues, so that it turned toward greater collaboration with other companies, including firms like IBM, Motorola, Ericsson, Cable and Wireless, and Lucent Technologies.

Technical innovation also inspired organizational innovation. Under the leadership of CEO Jorma Ollila, the company sought to carefully decentralize authority, while at the same time creating a common, corporate-wide information system and articulating company-wide values. Nokia also recognized that the process of technological knowledge accumulation called for effective extra-organizational connections. In addition to its growing base of alliance partners, the company built strong ties with universities and other research institutions. These included overseas universities, especially those located in countries where Nokia has its larger operations.

Nokia aspired to maintain a clear and straightforward business strategy, consistent execution of that strategy, an inspirational work atmosphere and the persistent recruitment of talented personnel.[3] CEO Ollila described "the Nokia way" as "based on a flat, decentralized organization, with emphasis on efficient teamwork and entrepreneurial spirit." In this kind of organization, flexibility, continuous learning, respect for the individual and the ability to innovate were seen as key factors. The Nokia logo "Connecting People" was coined to encapsulate the company's business philosophy, spanning its products and markets on the one hand and its internal organization and partnerships on the other hand.

The Nokia story represents a departure from traditional ideas about the multinational organization. The traditional multinational emphasized centralized strategy making and research and development, and sought to penetrate global markets through adaptation to local preferences, and balancing competing political pressures.[4] Thus, the knowledge work of the traditional multinational emphasized knowledge exploitation – spreading the advantages learned in their headquarters or key subsidiaries around the rest of the world. Even more recent "transnational" strategies, which emphasize worldwide learning, assume that relevant knowledge already exists in the organization, and they pay less heed to seeking out new knowledge. However, the imperatives of the knowledge economy mean that these strategies no longer assure success.

Organizations operating in the knowledge economy face significantly different problems from their predecessors. Relevant competitive knowledge seldom exists in a single organization, especially in rapidly developing technology-dependent industries. As a result, we see Nokia and similar companies organizing to facilitate knowledge flows and learning from around the world.[5] Subtly, but critically different from previous ideas of worldwide learning, this approach assumes an *absence* of appropriate knowledge within the organization.

THE GLOBAL ORGANIZATION

The Nokia story is even more remarkable given the company's origins. Proud of being Finnish, Nokia had long relied on its Nordic markets for both workforce talent and customers. Its globalization process involved a dramatic extension of its traditional activities, including a widespread search for new knowledge across all three of the world's major trading regions, as well as the emerging market of China. Nokia also came to rely heavily on its alliance partners. Its approach to the synthesis and mobilization of knowledge from these diverse sources was critical in its development of new products, and its penetration into new markets. Nokia explored new knowledge from around the world, and then sought to rapidly exploit this knowledge in the development of new products.

Global organizations are increasingly emerging from diverse origins. For example, the Nordic roots of Nokia and Ericsson, and the Japanese roots of competitor NTT–DoCoMo, are far removed from the high-tech center of California's Silicon Valley. However, these companies extend their research and development into Silicon Valley and other centers of innovation in their search for new knowledge, regardless of the location of their headquarters. In Nokia, specific projects, such as the establishment of the 3G standard, required connections with key players around the world. Sometimes, this involved cooperative partnerships in order to access specialized knowledge and skills for specific projects. Nokia's partnership with Cable & Wireless over its mobile Internet platform project is one example of the company tapping into new knowledge sources.

The following three case studies describe how some companies are achieving this kind of transition toward a more networked, metanational organization.[6] The first two cases describe companies combining the benefits of local and global learning, one by leveraging local knowledge worldwide, the other by leveraging global knowledge within local markets. The third case study illustrates how global learning can be achieved out of successful local entrepreneurship, and encapsulates the increasing tendency of new companies to internationalize quickly after their inception – to become so-called "born global" organizations.

Harnessing and exploiting local knowledge

One path toward the evolution of global organizations lies in the harnessing and exploitation of local knowledge. Consider the story of Taiwan-based Acer Inc. and its US subsidiary Acer America Corporation (ACC).

Acer: advent of the Aspire[7]

Ronald Chwang joined Taiwan-based Acer Inc. in 1986 and took over as CEO of its US division, Acer America (AAC), in 1992. After guiding the money-losing US division to breaking even by 1994, Chwang turned to the consideration of new products. For the most part, new product development occurred at the Taiwanese home base, but Chwang believed this was too far removed from the diverse tastes of consumers around the world. Moreover, a new global philosophy was emerging as Acer founder and CEO Stan Shih pledged to "make Acer an organization that would think and learn."[8]

A three-pronged approach to change encapsulated a new guiding philosophy, a new model of organization and a new business concept. A "Global Brand, Local Touch" philosophy articulated a commitment to strengthen the links between the company and its national markets – to make the company "a truly global organization with deeply planted local roots."[9] A "Client Server" model of organization adopted the metaphor of the computer network, whereby Acer's Taiwan headquarters would act as a "server" supporting "client" business units around the world. These units were encouraged to develop their own ideas, while the role of headquarters was to support and mediate rather than to dictate or control. The "Fast-Food" business concept involved a number of initiatives to increase efficiency, flexibility and control.

It was in this environment of corporate change that Chwang perceived an opportunity. He promoted twenty-nine-year-old engineer and recent MBA graduate Mike Culver to become AAC's Director of Product Management. Alert to unfolding trends in computer design, the Internet, multimedia, and working from home, Culver recognized the potential for an innovative home consumer PC. He assembled a project team to develop the concept, including a key Silicon Valley designer for whom he would require Chwang's approval. That approval, and the commitment to spend $200,000 on a prototype PC, was given in a single twenty-minute hallway discussion.

Culver's team estimated that the new model, named the Aspire PC, could gain a strong foothold in the existing PC market, and planned a global rollout in late 1995. Acer's headquarters, under Shih's leadership, enthused about both the global potential of the product and the process – reflecting both "Global Brand, Local Touch" and "Client Server" prongs of reorganization – through which the product was being developed. Shih, Chwang and others talked with project supporters, project critics, consumers and industry experts, as well as Culver and his project team. The eventual decision to support development and global release of the Aspire was well rewarded.

The Aspire story illustrates how changes in a global company's philosophy can fundamentally change its knowledge practices and, as a result, create significant new business opportunities. Under Acer's former model, company headquarters usually determined project decisions affecting regional units. As a result, opportunities for company-wide learning from regional units were limited. Acer's new three-pronged business model fundamentally changed the company's approach, allowing greater interaction between local markets, and wider access to worldwide learning.

The new approach also helped Acer to overcome the global–local dilemma that faces most global companies. These companies are physically dispersed in different industry milieux populated by different communities and often reflecting markedly different social, political and economic realities.[10] The success of a global company depends on the extent to which its subsidiaries successfully interact with, learn from, and serve these distinct milieu or "external networks." Success also depends on the extent to which the subsidiaries and the headquarters interact with, learn from, and serve each other.[11] AAC's Aspire project team worked innovatively with significant individuals, communities and organizations in its local environment, including customers, designers, and retail stores, in the process of product design and development. At the same time, it drew on the existing knowledge, technology and networks of the parent company.

Acting locally, thinking globally

Another path toward becoming a global organization involves developing a global strategy and then seeking to have local initiatives respond to that strategy. A case in point is ABN AMRO.

ABN AMRO[12]

ABN AMRO Lease Holding (AALH) was a twenty-year-old Netherlands-based company with 5,000 employees and a strong international presence. Its car leasing business earned 72% of the company's profits, and its core brand, Lease Plan, set the standard for the car leasing industry in Europe. The brand involved a new leasing model, the "open calculation concept," allowing for the global management of an entire fleet of company cars. However, ABN AMRO's competitors had largely adopted the concept, and the company was increasingly troubled that its founding principles of business unit entrepreneurship and autonomy were insufficient for future success. Increasing international competition, cross-national harmonization of car leasing policies and pressures for cost reductions were forcing change on the company's global operations.

Driven by an ambitious strategic goal to be among the top three car leasing companies in the world and in each local market where it operated, the company decided on a single global strategy. While still able to make local adaptations – such as CARPLAN, a variation of its leasing model for the French market – all business units would have to cooperate in realizing this strategy. CEO Hugo Levecke, one of twenty-five entrepreneurs that first founded the company, struggled with the prospect of getting business unit managers to cooperate in this different approach. He had previously been a champion of decentralization, and had actively encouraged unit managers to make autonomous decisions. The shift in focus from local problems to global cooperation called for a major transformation of the business, one that required "changing our deeply held beliefs, our daily habits, the way we are used to working."[13]

Levecke did not believe that the new global approach should inhibit the local entrepreneurship that had been central to earlier success. He made the subtle but important distinction between acting locally, using local judgment, skill and autonomy, but *thinking* globally – sharing information and knowledge to promote local effectiveness. To implement this approach and its underlying philosophy, Levecke developed a number of knowledge-sharing initiatives across the company. One of these was a company-wide "scoreboard" recording everyone's autonomous activities and the results from these activities. Levecke explained, "We now know and share what was tried, what succeeded, what failed, and especially *what was learned* from the initiative." In this way, managers did not have to repeat mistakes, and could incorporate wider knowledge into local contexts.

Central to ABN AMRO's approach was to emphasize learning from dispersed local knowledge, and to exploit this knowledge in the global arena. He gained the trust of business unit managers from strong interpersonal bonds he had developed earlier in the company. The business unit managers came to act like a community of practice, exhibiting joint enterprise in pursuing fresh innovation, developing a shared repertoire of past experience, and sustaining mutual engagement in solving the problems that they faced.

ABN AMRO also practiced project-based learning, as project teams drew on the learning from earlier projects, and specialized skills were formed and reformed around new project opportunities. Consistent with the ideas introduced in Chapter 6, performance and learning were jointly emphasized so that local projects became platforms for both the further exploration and exploitation of opportunities around the world.

Born global through international alliances

What has been learned about the advantages of the global corporation means that some corporations are now being founded as global. An example is PixTech.

PixTech[14]

PixTech was founded in France to specialize in field emission display (FED), a technology that provides flat-panel displays in products ranging from laptops to medical devices and high-definition television sets. From a standing start, PixTech became a global company in an industry occupied by established giants in Japan and the United States such as Sharp, Toshiba, IBM and Motorola. Rather than develop its own capabilities, PixTech "cherry-picked" the best capabilities and knowledge from around the world. It did so using a strategy of global partnering through strategic alliances.

PixTech signed its first long-term licensing agreement with one of the research arms of the French Atomic Energy Commission, gaining commercial rights to its accumulated research on FED technology. The company then targeted the world's best pool of venture capital for high-tech start-ups in the US, and became incorporated as a subsidiary of a US corporation. From this base, and drawing on previous industry experience of some of its managers, PixTech was able to develop technology alliance arrangements with key technology developers, including Texas Instruments, Motorola and Raytheon in the US, and Futaba in Japan.

The same alliance partners were also potential customers. Motorola, in particular, saw FEDs as key to developing its capabilities in video technologies and enhancing the display performance of its end products. As a result, it provided key information on the manufacturing processes for FEDs that was essential to successful design. It also planned to invest heavily in manufacturing facilities for FEDs. To complement the pool of technologies needed for FED design, PixTech set up close working relationships with a range of companies around the world; for example, with Rhône-Poulenc in France and Nichia of Japan in the field of phosphors.

Using clean-room facilities leased from IBM, PixTech produced its first defect-free display in 1995. The second phase of global partnerships then began, this time focusing on gaining access to knowledge and facilities associated with high-volume manufacturing of FEDs. Two significant agreements followed: a manufacturing agreement with Unipac of Taiwan in 1996, and a distribution agreement with Sumimoto some time later. PixTech secured contracts for its flat-screen displays in applications for the US army and in portable medical equipment. Both of these contracts required new technology developments, and extended the global partnerships PixTech already had in place.

PixTech utilized strategic alliances to expand its knowledge space and facilitate rapid global entry into the flat-screen industry. Links with key established industry players allowed PixTech to access and combine geographically dispersed technology and knowledge. These were then connected and mobilized in the design and prototyping of PixTech's new FED flat screen. The company's approach to manufacturing illustrates the importance of "learning by doing" in international joint ventures.[15] PixTech management recognized the delicate linkage between manufacturing and research and development, and took advantage of this in the early decision to align with Motorola, a manufacturer of flat-screen displays. PixTech management realized that they could only learn about the limits of a technology by manufacturing. The company's later manufacturing agreement with Unipac enabled those technological limits to be continually tested.

Much of the success of born global companies lies in the prior existence of personal networks and the boundary-spanning roles of managers.[16] Some of PixTech's management team had previous experience in companies such as Motorola and IBM, and were well linked to the global network of key industry players. The informal professional communities common in the industry helped forge the personal relationships underlying the success of the company's international strategic alliances.

KNOWLEDGE FLOWS IN
GLOBAL ORGANIZATIONS

Let us persist with a focus on global organizations. So far, we have seen how global organizations can utilize their subsidiaries and their alliance partners to both explore and exploit knowledge. We have examined how global organizations can evolve from different circumstances. How, though, can we relate those ideas back to earlier chapters?

The Nokia, Acer, ABN AMRO and PixTech stories all provide contrasting examples within a general framework. That framework involves interactions between headquarters and subsidiaries or alliance partners. The headquarters may be seen as representing the company's core competencies – its culture, capabilities and connections. Each subsidiary or partner may be seen as operating in a distinct industry context that has its own industry milieu, recipes and communication systems. The role of each subsidiary or partner is to effectively tap into its own industry context to promote new knowledge for either exploration (product or service innovation) or exploitation (by reaching the national market) and to interact effectively with the parent company. These interactions are shown schematically in Figure 8.1. The headquarters also operates in a distinct industry context, and each subsidiary will also have distinct competencies, but for the sake of simplicity these are not shown. The essential point is that the global organization is seeking to tap into the national industry context of each of its subsidiaries.

In the case of Nokia, a strategic decision in company headquarters led to dramatically different relations with its national subsidiaries. In the case of Acer, an innovation from its US (Silicon Valley) subsidiary connected with headquarters' search for a new approach to global business activity. In the case of ABN AMRO, the challenge was to promote a new company culture to orchestrate the largely separate activities of its national subsidiaries. All three cases fit with the broad framework suggested in Figure 8.1. In the case of PixTech, company headquarters was formed with global links either already in place or under way, but these links were mainly with alliance partners rather than subsidiaries. Figure 8.1 indicates that company headquarters may be connected to either subsidiaries *or* alliance partners in its global activities.

Figure 8.1 offers a framework for examining the knowledge work of a global organization. Where is it making its knowledge investments? What are the characteristics of its relationships with the relevant industry or industries around the regions and nations of the world? What markets do those relationships open? What opportunities do they provide

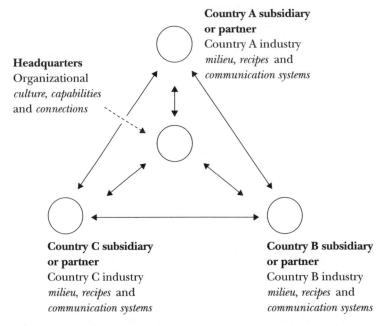

Figure 8.1 Knowledge flows between global headquarters and national subsidiaries

for innovation? These kinds of questions draw us deeper into the industry characteristics behind each subsidiary or alliance partner, and in turn help us better see the opportunities for effective collaboration.

THE INDIVIDUAL'S ROLE IN GLOBAL KNOWLEDGE WORK

In Chapter 2 of this book we highlighted the role of the individual in knowledge work. We emphasized that knowledge and learning involve individuals and interpersonal relationships across broader social arrangements with communities, organizations and industries. A global perspective enlarges the arena in which individuals can contribute to the creation, transmission and utilization of knowledge.

A number of studies have identified the importance of individual motivation in the knowledge transfer process across global companies – specifically those individuals' (knowing-why) disposition (1) to transmit and (2) to receive knowledge from other parts of the globe.[17] We see this played out in many different situations. For example, the success of ABN

AMRO's new strategy emphasizing global communication and knowledge sharing was dependent on the motivation of subsidiary managers to transmit and receive knowledge. Given the high level of autonomy these managers had previously enjoyed, their adjustment was by no means assured. Levecke's own (knowing-why) disposition to change the company culture, and the closeness of his (knowing-whom) relationships with the subsidiaries' senior managers concerned, played an important role in facilitating their acceptance of the change. Professional relationships were reinforced through interactions in project teams, and the company-wide scoreboard provided a shared focus for people's knowledge work investments.

Similar observations may be made about the other three cases presented in this chapter. Nokia's transition from a national to a global company needed the vision and commitment of its base of Finnish employees. Acer America's Taiwanese CEO was persuaded to promote the Aspire in company headquarters and win the support of its senior managers. PixTech's global strategy relied extensively on individuals' motivation to share and receive knowledge – in this case across alliances, and through the different company cultures that those alliance partners represented. In each of these examples, organizational or inter-organizational global knowledge work was dependent on the (knowing-why) motivations of individual workers and the (knowing-whom) relationships they cultivated. Favorable individual investments in each of these leads in turn to the transfer and generation of new (knowing-how) skills and knowledge.

The World Wide Web provides an alternative lens through which to view global knowledge creation and sharing. In Chapter 7, we were introduced to examples of individual programmers contributing to open-source software, providing and sharing knowledge with instant global reach. Companies, user communities and industries subscribing to open-source approaches are able to draw on global knowledge almost at will. We also see organizations connected through the use of grids – also discussed in Chapter 7. Organizations and industries are now using blogs to communicate widely, although the extent to which they provide new knowledge or enhance knowledge work is not yet clear. What is clear is that global knowledge has never been more accessible, and individuals can take advantage of that.

THE COMMUNITY'S ROLE IN GLOBAL KNOWLEDGE WORK

If we were to dig a little deeper in each of the preceding cases we might expect to also find a strong sense of community among certain key players. Nokia's telecommunications engineers were probably an

occupational community in their own right, embarked on the joint enterprise to be innovators in their field. The opportunity to extend that
enterprise to collaborate with other cutting edge engineers around the
world was perhaps a welcome one. The Finnish and other national
occupational communities also reached out to people from leading university and research institutions in the same industry milieu. The engineers in Acer Inc.'s US subsidiary seem to have already been embedded
in a Silicon Valley engineering community that provided a key design
contribution. PixTech's managers built high-trust relationships with
leading researchers in the field. In all of these cases, community building between geographically separate organizations was made easier and
made manifest through the use of the World Wide Web.

A powerful example of the potential of global, largely virtually coordinated, community formation and expansion is that of the Linux community. As already noted in Chapter 3, this began in 1991 when Finnish
graduate student Linus Torvalds posted his operating system to an Internet
software newsgroup. Ten people downloaded Torvalds's first operating
system, and five sent back "fixes" to make the code better. At the end of
the year 100 people had joined a worldwide Linux newsgroup. As the
number of newsgroup members soared into the millions, a small fraction
of them self-organized under Torvalds's leadership to enhance the Linux
code. In the language of Chapter 3, this virtual community participated
in the same joint enterprise, the development of the Linux system; had
a shared repertoire based on their specialized software expertise; and
were linked through mutual engagement in the task that they took on.

INDUSTRY'S ROLE IN
GLOBAL KNOWLEDGE WORK

In the same way that organizations are no longer bound to a single
country location, we see whole industries relying on global dispersion
and integration in order to succeed in the rapidly changing, technologically driven world. In recent times, requirements for industry learning and innovation have forced global supply chains to become dispersed.
Most commonly, supply chains are globally configured to capture low-
labor-cost production capability in particular markets, or to acquire
specialist knowledge in others. The example here shows how this has
occurred in the global apparel industry, as outsourcing of production has become the norm, much of it to manufacturing companies
in China. As industries in China continue to evolve, the survival of
those industries in the countries of earlier origination has been seriously
questioned.

Reconfiguring the apparel industry's global supply chain

Japan was a major exporter of apparel products in the 1960s and 1970s. Since then, it has steadily lost ground as the industry has globalized into a widely dispersed apparel supply network. A similar story can be told for former apparel producing countries, such as the US, the UK, The Netherlands, Germany, France and Belgium, among others. Since the early 1990s, the long-established industry in the US and Europe, in particular, has faced increasing competition from less developed countries.[18]

The traditional producers are focusing their attention on the knowledge-based, high-value components of the industry supply chain. As a result, and to counter the competitive threat, the traditional producers are outsourcing the relatively high-labor, low-value manufacturing activities to countries like China and Vietnam. They are retaining the more specialized and knowledge-intensive elements, such as fabric technology and production, and garment design. Germany and the US are well known for fabric innovation, and France for garment design.

The disaggregation of the supply chain is by no means restricted to the apparel industry. However, it was one of the earliest industries to migrate its manufacturing base to lower-labor-cost countries. Being one of the most labor-intensive industries, apparel manufacturing has a huge labor-cost differential around the world. For example, there is a 1,000% to 3,000% labor-cost difference between Japanese and Chinese manufacturing costs.[19] Fashion apparel is one of the most geographically dispersed industries in the world.[20] However, it is also one of the most integrated, since the key activities of fabric production, design and manufacturing tend to be concentrated in a relatively few countries that have retained and developed specializations in these areas.

How long will the prevailing configuration support the industry globally, or provide competitive opportunities for the companies in the traditional producer countries around the world? There are two possible answers to this question. One answer is that manufacturers in China and other low-cost countries will rapidly absorb production knowledge from the global network of which they are a part. There is already evidence that China is advancing its capabilities in fabric production and garment design, threatening to become a major competitor to companies in the US, Europe and Japan.

However, another answer is that the reciprocal knowledge flows that have enabled China to upgrade its manufacturing process and production capability have also helped the rest of the industry upgrade – the so-called "ratcheting-up" effect.[21] Here, we see apparel manufacturers driving improvements in design and manufacture, as capability in the former extends the scope for innovation in the latter. The global connectedness and mutual dependency in the industry facilitate this by enabling industry-wide knowledge flows. We thus see the shifting of value around the network, as the knowledge and capabilities of the participants in the industry evolve. How these changes will influence the industry in the long term remains to be seen.

Industry learning evolves, as practices in one location inform practices in another, in a virtuous cycle of innovation and improvement – mostly incremental, but sometimes radical. Most industries are globally linked, not only with their own participants in the industry, but also with other industries. As noted in Chapter 5, we often see clusters increasingly interconnected across national boundaries. The New Zealand boat building cluster owes much of its innovation to links with other clusters in Europe and the US. Similarly, multiple interconnected national geographic clusters characterize the optical electronics industry.[22] We now explore how the knowledge diamond participants discussed in earlier chapters interact in a global context, where not only the participants, but also entire nations, gain from the results.

LOCAL VERSUS GLOBAL KNOWLEDGE

The cases earlier in this chapter highlight the importance to organizations and industries of connecting with global, as well as local, knowledge. The idea of the globally integrated multinational corporation has grown from previous conceptions of headquarters–subsidiary relations. The multinational corporation is envisaged as having more of a networked than a hierarchical structure, and having a decentralized rather than a centralized form of governance.[23]

When a company is making foreign market investment decisions, both the company and the target nation seek to optimize their knowledge, and the key for both parties is to link between local and global knowledge. The multinational corporation must tap into the local knowledge in its host nation to compete effectively, and it needs to leverage its access to local and global knowledge, for international success. The nation needs global knowledge to develop its own processes for economic development and to assist its organizations and industries to compete in the global arena. The following example illustrates how mutual knowledge sharing between multinational corporations and the host nation has assisted in the development of the Singaporean biotechnology industry.

Singapore: the "Biopolis of Asia"[24]

Through its success in the semiconductor and electronics industries, Singapore has developed a reputation as the "Silicon Island of the East."[25] However, the Singapore government, drawing on its electronics industry experience, has identified biotechnology as another "pillar" of its economy for the twenty-first century.[26] The idea is to build a world-class regional center of excellence in the biotechnology and biomedical industries. Heavy investments are being made in higher education and research, based on the creation of a "triple-helix" approach – of government, industry and academia – to promote network-driven innovation.[27] Singapore has also coined the term "the Biopolis of Asia" to reflect its claim to regional excellence in this industry.

Through the various triple-helix actors, a number of initiatives have been established in Singapore's quest for pre-eminence. These include the facilitation of strategic alliances among firms, national research centers, statutory boards, academic research groups, and university spin-off firms.[28] A new government organization, called A*STAR (Agency for Science, Technology and Research), was created in 2002, and is charged with fostering "world class scientific talent for a vibrant knowledge-based Singapore."[29] Many other government and industry initiatives and organizations have been established to help fulfill this mission.

How is this ambitious project playing out in practice? Already, clusters have been created in both biomedicine and biotechnology, each with impressive investments from, and links across to, world-class global corporations. For example, most of the world's major pharmaceutical companies are part of, or linked to, the biomedical cluster. A key strategy has also been to attract top researchers from overseas – including Nobel laureates – to foster capability in the industry, and to enhance the educational offerings of local universities.

Researchers have noted distinct elements to Singapore's development of its biotechnology and biomedical industries – elements contributing to what they call a "high-skill ecosystem" derived largely from the activities and interactions of the triple-helix participants. In considering progress to date, the same researchers note that: "While Singapore appears to have put in place some of the elements needed" for a high-skill ecosystem, it remains "too early to judge where an ecosystem will flourish."[30] Already, though, the investments of foreign companies in skilled personnel and capital structures are such that significant progress has been made. To date, a number of start-up small to medium enterprises have arisen from the project, developing a pool of specialized local knowledge already integrated with global knowledge from larger world-renowned players.

Singapore's biotechnology ecosystem is still a work in progress, and there are further challenges to face before any claim can be made to enduring success. However, the ambitious project is already drawing the attention of a global audience, and is likely to provide substantial lessons on how local regions can reserve and retain a place at the global knowledge table.

In the case of the electronics industry discussed in Chapter 5, Singapore's strategy was apparently superior to that of Malaysia. In contrast to Singapore, Malaysia focused solely on its local competence in low-cost labor production and did not seek to develop or integrate global knowledge, even though it had similar access to multinational corporations' pool of knowledge and talent as Singapore. Researchers suggest that one of the key differences lies in each country's respective national innovation system, which is "the network of institutions in the public and private sectors whose activities and interactions initiate, import, modify and diffuse new technologies."[31] This adds a national policy component to the idea of the business ecosystem introduced in Chapter 5, and suggests how both a nation and its multinational corporation investors can leverage the innovation system for mutual benefit.

However, national innovation is not solely reliant on large multinational corporations. In the development of Singapore's biotechnology and biomedical industries, we see local knowledge being generated through start-up enterprises and their local networks. The Singapore example, much like the earlier examples of "regional advantage" discussed in Chapter 5, suggests that these enterprises can play a key role in the overall success of the innovation system as a whole.

ACCESSING GLOBAL KNOWLEDGE WORKERS

The burgeoning of activity over the Internet since the mid 1990s enables us to see the local versus global dilemma in a different light. Access to talent and other resources is now easier, faster, and more focused. So why do we see differences between organizations and nations in the concentration and quality of their human resources?

Part of the answer may lie in the phenomenon known as "small world networks." These networks have been observed in studies following up on Stanley Milgram's famous 1960s computation that only "six degrees of separation" – six links between existing social contacts – lay between any two people. Milgram also observed that a relatively small number of people were responsible for a relatively large number of these links.[32] The significance of Milgram's observations lie in the larger social consequences.[33] A typical small world network comprises "densely interlinked clusters of nodes, with relatively few links to other clusters."[34] As such, it takes relatively few links between clusters to connect very large populations. Larger, well-connected nodes tend to attract more connections, so once larger nodes have formed, it is harder for others to gain access to other clusters in the network – an idea similar to "the rich getting richer."

Through the action of its small world network, Singapore's Biopolis is able to gain rapid access to global experts, and accumulate talent in the local hub. Having become one of the larger nodes in the global biomedical network, it can continue to attract people and knowledge into its innovation system. We also see the small world network operating in the film-making industry, with producers, directors, actors and crew members forming local clusters, but linked globally to other clusters along with their respective communities of practice. Activation of these links enables these workers to be recruited to successive film projects. Many other examples have been mentioned over the course of this book. The common factor is of local industry clusters or regions being linked to larger global knowledge pools through relatively few connections, but where those few connections provide relatively easy access to the global network.

The World Wide Web itself grew from a small world network.[35] It now plays a major role in facilitating connections within other small world networks across all kinds of industries. It was the advent of the World Wide Web and the Internet that enabled complex network structures to be analyzed and better understood, and led to the recognition of the small world network phenomenon. As knowledge, innovations, and ideas flow through the World Wide Web and the small world networks of our global society, access to global talent at a local level is no longer constrained. As we saw in the virtual world discussed in Chapter 7, distance is not a deterrent to the flow and transfer of knowledge: the small world network phenomenon helps to explain why.[36]

TOOLS FOR GLOBAL KNOWLEDGE WORK

One of the most common tools used by multinational corporations for global knowledge transfer is the rotation of employees through expatriate assignments. In earlier times, these kinds of assignments tended to focus on control and coordination functions. However, as the corporations have decentralized, expatriate assignees have a key role in knowledge transfer between subsidiary and headquarters, as was illustrated earlier in the example of the Acer Aspire computer. Although the success of expatriate assignments varies greatly, they remain an effective tool for multinational corporations to promote the exchange of relevant information between locations, and to combine local and global knowledge. Staff rotation programs can provide a similar function between separate offices, divisions, or areas of functional specialization within the same country.

A number of tools discussed in earlier chapters are also relevant to knowledge transfer in a global context. For example, many industry web-based tools, such as portals, or blogs, readily reach a global network of participants. Cluster mapping processes identify cross-border linkages, where present, and highlight channels for knowledge transfer. Network analysis is also useful for mapping and analyzing the network structure and relational qualities of a multinational corporation within its own network, and with the national environments in which it is situated. Understanding these network attributes, such as network density, centrality, and structural holes, can enable corporations to configure or reconfigure in ways more appropriate to their knowledge requirements.[37]

As we saw in the case of Singapore, nations can develop and nurture national innovation systems, or high-skill ecosystems, in order to promote innovation in specific industries. For example, one approach suggests that in order for ecosystems to thrive they need to have in place four distinct elements: catalysts (such as government or entrepreneurial initiatives), resources (such as high-skilled human and financial capital), a supportive environment (cultural and legislative support) and connectivity (network links within and beyond the nation's borders). Frameworks such as this can provide a basis for examining and developing a region's or a nation's participation in global knowledge work.

SUMMARY

This chapter has considered the particular challenges and opportunities surrounding knowledge and learning in an increasingly global economy. Global companies, as illustrated by the Nokia example, focus on learning from separate pockets of knowledge dispersed around the world. A related global–local dilemma can be addressed from several perspectives, including exploiting local knowledge (Acer), thinking globally and acting locally (ABN AMRO), and being "born global" as happened in the example of PixTech. Knowledge transfer between an organization and its global subsidiaries or global alliance partners highlights the importance of the various industry milieux, recipes and communication systems in which participating organizations operate. However, individuals and communities also participate in global knowledge work, and have far greater opportunities to do so with the presence of the World Wide Web.

Industries have been and continue to reconfigure themselves to take advantage of the dispersed resources, including knowledge resources, available around the globe, as illustrated by the apparel industry's global supply chain. The role of the nation was also considered, this time, in the example of Singapore as a biotechnology ecosystem or national innovation system. The idea of "small worlds" reconnects ideas of global knowledge work to earlier ideas about interpersonal networks (Chapter 2) and industry regional advantage (Chapter 5). Many of the tools and techniques for facilitating global knowledge work have already been discussed in previous chapters, but there are also particular tools to examine any knowledge diamond participant's or any nation's interest in global knowledge work.

QUESTIONS FOR REFLECTION

1 Consider an organization that operates internationally. What is its approach to knowledge sharing and learning, and how is this manifest in the organization's products or services?
2 Using PixTech as an example, what "core competencies" do you think a company may require in order to be successfully "born global"?
3 What features of a country's industry milieu, recipes and communication systems influence an organization's local or global learning? What examples can you suggest?
4 Can you think of examples of (a) key individuals and (b) influential communities who have contributed to global learning activities? How did they do so?
5 What issues of local versus global knowledge exist in your own geographic region or country? How is your region or nation addressing them?
6 What "small worlds" are visible to you? Whom do you know, or know about, that acts as a key node in a small world's network communications?
7 What tools have you used, or seen used, that have contributed to global knowledge work? How useful were they?

NOTES

1 Giddens, A. (1999) *Runaway World: How Globalisation is Reshaping Our Lives*, London, Profile.

2 Adapted from Doz, Y.L., Santos, J. and Williamson, P. (2001) *From Global to Metanational: How Companies Win in the Knowledge Economy*, Boston, Harvard Business School Press.

3 Haikio, Martti (2002) *Nokia: The Inside Story*, Prentice Hall, p. 28.

4 Bartlett, C.A., Ghoshal, S. and Birkinshaw, J. (2003) *Transnational Management: Text and Cases*, McGraw-Hill/Irwin.

5 Ibid. The authors cite other companies such as Acer, Citibank, Hewlett-Packard, PolyGram, and Procter and Gamble behaving similarly.

6 Doz et al., *From Global to Metanational*.

7 Adapted from Trompenaars, F. and Hampden-Turner, C. (2002) *21 Leaders for the 21st Century*, New York, McGraw-Hill; Bartlett et al., *Transnational Management*.

8 Bartlett et al., *Transnational Management*, p. 42.

9 Ibid.

10 Hofstede, G. (1980) *Culture's Consequences: International Differences in Work-Related Values*, Beverly Hills, CA, Sage.

11 Ghoshal, S. and Bartlett, C.A. (1990) "The multinational corporation as an interorganizational network," *The Academy of Management Review*, 15 (4), 603–25.

12 Adapted from Trompenaars and Hampden-Turner, *21 Leaders*.

13 Ibid., p. 342.

14 Adapted from Doz et al., *From Global to Metanational*.

15 Tsang, E.W.K. (2002) "Acquiring knowledge by foreign partners from international joint ventures in a transition economy: learning-by-doing and learning myopia," *Strategic Management Journal*, 23, 835–54. The findings from this study indicate that firms in a joint venture improve their skills of knowledge acquisition through learning by doing.

16 Knight, G.A. and Cavusgil, S.T. (2004) "Innovation, organizational capabilities, and the born-global firm," *Journal of International Business Studies*, 35 (2), 124–41.

17 Gupta, A.K. and Govindarajan, V. (2000) "Knowledge flows within multi-national corporations," *Strategic Management Journal*, 21 (4), 473–96.

18 Fernie, J. and Azuma, N. (2004) "The changing nature of Japanese fashion: can quick response improve supply chain efficiency?," *European Journal of Marketing*, 38 (7), 790–808.

19 Ohmae, K. (2002) *Chugoku Shift: Shifting to China*, Tokyo, Shogakukan.

20 Fernie and Azuma, "The changing nature."

21 Hwang Smith, M. and Weil, D. (2005) "Ratcheting up: linked technology adoption in supply chains," *Industrial Relations*, 44 (3), 490–508. This has been observed particularly in the downstream ends of the apparel supply chain, where improvements in retailing have forced improvements in production.

22   Hendry, C., Brown, J. and DeFillippi, R. (2000) "Regional clustering of high-technology-based firms: opto-electronics in three countries," *Regional Studies*, 34 (2), 129–44.

23   Renowned scholars contributing to our current knowledge and understanding in these areas include Ghoshal and Bartlett, "The multinational corporation;" Hedlund, G. (1994) "A model of knowledge management and the N-form corporation," *Strategic Management Journal*, 15, 73–90; Birkinshaw, J. (2002) "Managing internal R&D networks in global firms: what sort of knowledge is involved?," *Long Range Planning*, 35, 245–67; and Doz et al., *From Global to Metanational*.

24   Parayil, G. (2005) "From 'Silicon Island' to 'Biopolis of Asia:' innovation policy and shifting competitive strategy in Singapore," *California Management Review*, 47 (2), 50–73.

25   Mathews, J. (1999) "A Silicon Island of the East: creating a semiconductor industry in Singapore," *California Management Review*, 41 (2), 55–78.

26   Finegold, D., Wong, P.-K. and Cheah, T.-C. (2004) "Adapting a foreign direct investment strategy to the knowledge economy: the case of Singapore's emerging biotechnology cluster," *European Planning Studies*, 12 (7), 921–41.

27   For triple helix organization, see Etzkowitz, H. and Leydesdorff, L. (2000) "The dynamics of innovation: from national systems and 'Mode 2' to a triple helix of university–industry–government relations," *Research Policy*, 29, 109–23; for network mode of innovation, see Fernie and Azuma, "The changing nature."

28   Parayil, "From 'Silicon Island'."

29   EDB website, www.sedb.com/edbcorp/detailed.jsp?artid=28708typeid=7>, cited in Parayil, "From 'Silicon Island'," p. 56.

30   Finegold et al., "Adapting a foreign direct investment strategy."

31   Ibid.

32   Milgram, S. (1967) "The small world problem," *Psychology Today*, 2, 60–7. As noted in Chapter 2, six degrees of separation relates to the notion that individuals around the world are linked through no more than six connections.

33   Watts, D.J. and Strogatz, S.H. (1998) "Collective dynamics of 'small-world' networks," *Nature*, 393, 440–2.

34   Herman, J. (2003) "The new science of networks," *Business Communication Review*, 33 (6), 22–3.

35   Ibid.

36   Ibid.

37   Ghoshal and Bartlett, "The multinational corporation," provide examples of such network analysis processes applied to MNCs and their location within a local infrastructure.

CHAPTER 9

INTELLECTUAL PROPERTY IN KNOWLEDGE WORK

> [I]ntellectual property has become one of the key areas of
> conflict in the global economy. Conflicts have [included]
> disputes over genetically modified seeds . . . piracy of music
> over the Internet [and] questions regarding the ownership
> of . . . knowledge of the human genome.
>
> **Susan Sell and Christopher May**[1]

Advances in both information technology and genetics have created
new legal and ethical challenges to the practice of knowledge work.
Also, the growing economic value of intellectual property rights has
spurred an upsurge in related activity involving all four participants
of the knowledge diamond. Disputes exist between parties favoring
traditional proprietary protections (patents, copyrights, trade secrets) and
the burgeoning open-source view of intellectual property as a "commons"
to be publicly shared. Individuals, communities, organizations and
countries are choosing sides between these contrasting approaches, with
widespread consequences for how knowledge work is practiced among
these parties.

One way to address underlying disputes is to consider proprietary
and open-source intellectual property approaches as complementary
approaches. For example, companies like IBM that previously had
adopted strictly proprietary intellectual property approaches are also
making strategic use of open-source approaches. The complementarities
between proprietary and open approaches to intellectual property
thus parallel the relationship between more closed and more open
approaches to knowledge work. Each approach to intellectual property
will continue to be a powerful driver of the knowledge economy.

Let us consider the case of Qualcomm.

Qualcomm: creating the CDMA standard[2]

Several years late in arriving, third-generation (3G) mobile phone networks are finally in operation. In the year 2000, the hype surrounding this promising new technology reached such proportions that European mobile operators paid a total of 109 billion euros (then US$125 billion) for licenses to build and operate 3G networks. 3G promised to offer higher performance and more capacity than the existing 2G networks, particularly in extended data communications and Internet access.

Although some uncertainties about the new technology still exist, 3G networks are proliferating. At the start of 2004, there were sixteen commercial 3G networks, and by the end of 2004, around sixty such networks. According to the head of strategy at Nokia, the world's largest handset maker, the second half of 2004 would be seen as "the starting point for global acceleration of 3G." 3G is built on a technology made possible by the observations of scientist Claude Shannon in 1948. This "code division multiple access" technology, known as CDMA, underpins the 3G platform that is expected to dominate the mobile phone industry for the foreseeable future.

Qualcomm is the US company that developed CDMA and brought it to market at the end of the 1980s. Its founder and CEO Dr Irwin Jacobs, former professor of engineering at Massachusetts Institute of Technology, lives modestly and disdains the celebrity enjoyed by other high-tech billionaires. Yet he has, in the words of *The Economist*, "built a company on intellect," an "intellectual-property business in its purest form."[3] Essentially a research laboratory, Qualcomm employs over 7,000 people. In 2000, its revenues reached US$4 billion, the vast majority coming from patents and licensing arrangements. Royalties from Qualcomm's CDMA patents are expected to reach $20 billion a year by 2010, propelling the company into the profitability league of Microsoft.

Jacobs claims that, without his professional research background, he would not have had the confidence to persevere with his vision for CDMA. Despite this, many see his enforcement of Qualcomm's patent rights as dogged, even ruthless. In 1998, he came close to triggering a transatlantic trade war, as Ericsson and Nokia contended that the European 3G system, W-CDMA, did not use Qualcomm's intellectual property. While Ericsson and Qualcomm finally resolved their dispute a year later, Nokia continued to fight Qualcomm's demands for royalties. Qualcomm maintains that it has always offered companies like Nokia and Ericsson more than just intellectual property. As Qualcomm's President, Steve Altman, explained: "What caused us to be a success was that very early on we didn't just license patents, we enabled the manufacturers to get to market quickly."[4]

Jacobs is a passionate believer in the value of brainpower. His focus is on creating the best technology and being properly rewarded for the knowledge vested in it. CMDA has attracted substantial venture capital support, and is continually gaining market share. While the 3G network platform has had a checkered start, largely through differences between key industry players, the future of CDMA is essentially guaranteed, as it has recently become the basis for the new international standard for 3G services around the world.

There is no doubt that Qualcomm has gained massively from its intellectual property. However, Tom Engibous, CEO of Texas Instruments (which supplies most of the chips for GSM mobile phones), has argued that too uncompromising an approach to patent enforcement by Qualcomm could force potential partners away. This was put to the test in 2001, when Jacobs went to China to negotiate royalty payments for the use of its 3G technology. To gain the business, Jacobs had to accept lower royalty payments than Qualcomm gets elsewhere, and those are likely to decrease even further as China develops its own 3G standard. However, there are larger opportunities for Qualcomm from China developing expertise in 3G technology. The arrangement may be fruitful for both parties.

The Qualcomm story illustrates a recent chapter in the unfolding history of intellectual property, defined by the World Intellectual Property Organization (WIPO) as "creations of the mind: inventions, literary and artistic works, and symbols, names, images and designs used in commerce."[5] From a legal perspective, intellectual property is broadly covered by patent, copyright and trademark protections in return for a published account of the intellectual property in question, or by "trade secrets" where the creator chooses not to publicize what he or she has to offer.

The Qualcomm story is also about patents, and so about the balancing of rights between the creator and the consumer. The intent of much patent legislation is to allow creators to benefit from their intellectual endeavors, while at the same time encouraging the dissemination of those endeavors for the greater public good. Typically, the creator is granted protection from competition for a limited period, in return for documenting the endeavor for the long-term benefit of society at large.[6] The Qualcomm story highlights two legislative issues. First, it represents a recent trend in US law – but not necessarily in international law – in favor of the creator rather than the consumer.[7] Second, it illustrates a contemporary emphasis on licensing of other parties to use a patent, rather than embedding the patent in any product of the patent holder's own making.

In this chapter, we will highlight a series of key issues and trends in the generation and application of intellectual property. In doing so, our emphasis will be on factors relevant to our overall interest in knowledge work, and in particular on the participants in the knowledge diamond and their interaction.

INTELLECTUAL PROPERTY AND THE KNOWLEDGE DIAMOND

The Qualcomm story suggests that all four participants in the knowledge diamond – individuals (inventors like Irwin Jacobs), communities (the internal groups of Qualcomm scientists, and, presumably, their external professional attachments), organizations (Qualcomm and its licensees) and the industry (in this case the telecommunications industry) – all influence and are influenced by one another as intellectual property is generated and traded among interested parties. The following examples cover each of the knowledge diamond participants in turn, and speak to a series of contemporary issues.

The individual

Intellectual property often begins with individual creativity, even if the returns to that creativity may often accrue to others who commercialize the results. Qualcomm's CEO Irwin Jacobs was a highly educated engineer, but education is not a necessary precursor of creative works. The following example bears a remarkable similarity to the Napster case discussed in Chapter 1, although the legal ramifications have been different.

DVD-Jon: challenging the entertainment giants[8]

In 1999, a few months after the online music-sharing software Napster was released, a young Norwegian went one step further. Fifteen-year-old Jon Lech Johansen posted his newly created DVD-copying software on the Internet. Two years later Napster was shut down by the US federal court for enabling music piracy. Within eighteen months, Johansen was prosecuted in Norway for a similar breach, but was acquitted. He was to see himself in court again the following year – again to be acquitted.

Cited as "the entertainment industry's worst nightmare," Johansen has almost single-handedly challenged intellectual property regimes across both Europe and the US.[9] Reflecting the sentiment of a huge community of consumers supporting peer-to-peer software for music and movie file sharing, Johansen became something of a folk hero in Norway. Such was his notoriety that supporters printed T-shirts and ties bearing Johansen's software code, and also organized a May Day march, carrying a placard reading "Free DVD-Jon."

Since his court victories, Johansen has continued to pursue his goal of freeing up users' rights as purchasers of online music and movies. He has developed software that removes restrictions on Apple's iTunes, enabling music to be transferred to devices other than Apple's iPods or the cell phones that Apple helped design. He posts his free software tools on his website, called "So Sue Me," where he describes his version of iTunes software as "the fair interface to the iTunes music store."[10]

Johansen avows that he is not a "digital pirate." Rather, he claims his efforts are focused on extending the rights of users who have legally purchased music or movies. His software achieves this by unlocking the digital restrictions often placed on music, such as iTunes tracks that restrict copying to other devices, and are part of what the industry calls "digital rights management." Johansen makes the point that people who buy DVD movies often prefer to copy them onto laptops and other portable devices when they travel. He believes that legal purchasers should have the right to do this.

After leaving school at 16, Johansen worked in the TV and telecommunications industries. At 21, he ran his own software consulting business with his father. After his court cases shot him to fame around the world, however, several significant software companies courted him. He chose southern California as a new base, and started working with a new start-up Internet company called MP3tunes in October, 2005.

MP3tunes founding entrepreneur, Michael Robertson, had also been in conflict with the music industry. He sold his former company, mp3.com, after losing a legal battle over alleged copyright infringement.[11] mp3.com allowed users to upload songs from CDs onto its website, enabling them to listen to music online. It seems that Robertson's new company will continue to challenge existing digital rights practices, focusing on enabling Apple's iTunes to be played on a variety of digital media. Clearly, the entertainment industry's problems are not over yet.

In this case the essential issue is not patents but copyright, and whether DVD-Jon can freely distribute his own programming code. In the early days of copyright protection there would have been little controversy about his doing so. However, it has become increasingly common for claims to intellectual property to be raised by large corporations, based either on the creativity of those corporations' employees (as in the case of Qualcomm) or on the corporation's claim to represent another party. In the Napster and mp3.com legal cases the corporations owned the rights to the songs that could be copied. The question of who owns the knowledge is further complicated by the inconsistency of international law. DVD-Jon won two rounds of legal battles in Norway. Shawn Fanning, the developer of Napster, was less fortunate in the US. We will return to this debate later in the chapter.

The community

Community use of and control over intellectual property goes back to the time of the medieval crafts, where "tools of the trade" were closely guarded, and where access to those tools was available only at considerable cost through elaborate apprenticeship programs.[12] That tradition survives in many occupations today, although there is much greater documentation, and therefore explication, of knowledge than there once was. Occupation still serves as a prominent basis for the sharing and creation of knowledge, often in informal ways. Open-source software development (the Linux example in Chapter 3) or grid-facilitated scientific communities (Chapter 7) are two examples. These kinds of community may be termed *producer communities*, in as much as their task is to work on developing a new product.

In contrast to producer communities are what we have previously described as *user communities*, whose members may often be willing to contribute their efforts without financial compensation. This kind of contribution has been variously called open-source development, open innovation, distributed innovation, user innovation, customer co-design, or customer integration.[13] Open-source software development can involve communities in a dual role as both developers and early users of the software programs. User communities can also be found in other industries, including automobiles (for example, among BMW users), health care (for example, the user communities associated with General Electric's Healthcare Division), and computer games.[14] We saw in Chapter 7, though, with the example of Marvel Comics and the legal action it took against user-generated "avatars," that the work of user communities has not always been welcomed.

The development of Lego Corporation's "MindStorms" game provides a contrast to the Marvel Comics example. MindStorms arose from a joint venture between MIT faculty, students and the Lego company. These joint venturers were alarmed to find that, within two weeks of the product's launch, hackers broke the software code for the game's robots, posted it on the Internet, and collectively wrote a new operating system. Rather than sue the hackers, however, Lego decided to incorporate the hackers' ideas into the next version, and even released a developer's kit to support user community participation.[15] Even more explicitly, the computer game maker Electronic Arts (EA) shares programming tools directly with its customers, then posts their modifications on the Internet, and incorporates selected customer creations into their new games.[16]

Eric Von Hippel of Massachusetts Institute of Technology suggests that user community members are less concerned with financial reward than with the reputation their skills are able to earn.[17] Others note the importance of intrinsic rewards (the satisfaction of "helping out" and identification with the product) and closer attachments to fellow users.[18] These observations relate closely to the three dimensions of community activity – shared repertoire, joint enterprise and mutual engagement – described in Chapter 3. Participation along these three dimensions from user communities can make a key contribution to the next knowledge diamond participant – the organization.

The organization

The preceding section shows how organizations can seek value from voluntary community contributions that lie beyond the organization's jurisdiction. An alternative approach is to draw on the creativity of communities from within the organization's own employees, in some cases where those communities have not been regarded as a likely source of intellectual property revenue. The British health system provides a topical example.

The British health system: tapping the IP of health worker communities[19]

Britain's National Health Service (NHS), a long-standing institution of British socialism, has never been concerned with profit-making ventures – until recently. Over the last few years, various communities of practice in the health sector, including doctors, nurses, technologists, and other specialist groups, have provided a seedbed of significant inventions and innovations which the NHS is now keen to exploit.

Since 2002, the British government has granted permission to its various health service bodies to hold shares in companies set up to exploit discoveries made within the National Health Service. In order to protect and transfer the intellectual property rights of these discoveries, the government has also established state-owned companies charged with this responsibility. The objective is to reward both the inventor and the NHS, while improving patient care and contributing to the national economy.

Given that around 1.3 million people work in the NHS, the potential for knowledge exploitation from its health worker communities is huge. The NHS has been described as Britain's largest untapped source of intellectual property. Moreover, the failure to utilize patents effectively in the past has been a cause of significant decline in the world market share of British medical engineering firms – from 20% to 2% in the last 50 years. In contrast, one hospital in the US (Massachusetts General Hospital, in Boston) had annual licensing income from doctors' discoveries of US$30 million in 2002, based on an intellectual property portfolio of 214 discoveries, 104 filed patents, and four new spin-out companies.

An example of the new approach to intellectual property exploitation in the British NHS is the spin-out company Tayside Flow Technologies, established in 2002. This first spin-out from the NHS in Scotland stems from a small community of doctors specializing in the treatment of vein disorders at a hospital in Dundee. The company's three doctor founders created a leading-edge company that won a million pounds (around US$1.7 million) to commence human clinical trials of an advanced vascular graft system. With a global market worth an estimated $300 million, the potential gains from this one example of the NHS's new approach to intellectual property are immense.

The NHS case shows the potential for community-led innovation to be harnessed by the employing organization. In the formation of Tayside Flow Technologies, we see the role that employee communities can play in developing intellectual capital. In some cases these have been further exploited through spin-offs and new company start-ups. Another example was provided in Chapter 5. Richard Branson, head of the Virgin empire, is well known for harnessing the innovations of individuals and communities by offering start-up capital for good ideas.

The industry

We saw in Chapter 5 how biotechnology companies are heavily dependent on patent royalties or sale of patents to sustain income and research and development resources. At the same time, as the next case illustrates, the biotechnology industry is starting to explore other approaches to innovation and the acquisition of intellectual property.

Open-source medicine: a solution to drug discovery ills?[20]

As biotechnology becomes the more frequent source of new drugs, the economies of drug discovery for pharmaceutical companies increasingly come into question. Traditional drug discovery approaches in pharmaceutical companies were plagued by high costs and long periods to commercialization. For these reasons, there was little incentive for pharmaceutical companies to develop drugs for diseases that afflict the poor, because the likelihood of recouping the costs was slim. It was also argued that the full benefits to patients and companies of traditional pharmaceuticals research was not always realized, because of intellectual property constraints on evaluation of new uses for existing drugs.

Recently, teams of medical biologists, entrepreneurs and health care activists have suggested applying the open-source model, familiar in the development of computer software, to the world of drug development. Open-source approaches have already been used in biotechnology, most notably in the Human Genome Project. Here, potentially large conflicts over intellectual property rights were avoided by the project ensuring that all the resulting data were published in the public domain. In the area of bioinformatics, where biology intersects with information technology, the open-source model is also flourishing. The question now is whether or not open-source approaches can work further downstream – that is, closer to the patient – where development costs are greater but potential benefits more direct.

The question highlights fundamental differences in knowledge-sharing approaches to software and to drug discovery. First, software involves the sharing of code, while drug researchers would be swapping data – potentially with myriad applications. Second, different intellectual property rights apply, and they are protected differently. Software generates copyright automatically, at no cost to the developer. Biomedical discoveries are usually protected by patents, which require time and money to obtain and enforce. Third, software development can occur over a relatively short period, while drug discovery can take years. Moreover much drug research, especially that involving direct contact with patients, raises issues about patient care and confidentiality that do not occur in an open-source environment.

Notwithstanding these challenges, a number of biotechnology and biomedical researchers have successfully applied open-source-type approaches.

For example, a group involved in "not-for-profit drug discovery" places much of its data in the public domain. Unlike open-source software systems, however, there is no enforced requirement for reciprocal sharing of data. Treatments for diseases are expected to be found through this collaborative, distributed approach. Where intellectual property is created, the group has the option to license the treatment to a pharmaceutical company to produce and market.

The open-source approach to biotechnology requires participants to put self-interest aside in the pursuit of innovation and potential downstream benefits. However, in contrast to open-source software, there is still an opportunity to seek a patent, rather than share their results on a communal website. For this reason, some commentators claim the open-source approach to biotechnology and biomedical research may never fully emulate that for software development. They have suggested using a different term, such as distributed, Internet-based collaboration to reflect the differences. Whatever term is used, the software industry's open-source approach to innovation is now being leveraged elsewhere, with the potential to change the broad infrastructure of an industry – that is, its milieu, systems and recipes.

The examples so far have shown how all four knowledge diamond participants – individuals, communities, organizations and host industries – can invest in and be affected by intellectual property. Individuals can either capitalize on or be denied the benefits of their own inventions. Communities – and in particular communities of practice within the same occupation, or communities of user groups within the same industry – are now more broadly recognized for the contributions they can make to intellectual property development. Organizations are changing their traditional views about proprietary knowledge to take better advantage of their internal capabilities. Industries can play host to new kinds of initiatives that invite other knowledge diamond participants to put their intellectual property rights aside. Each of these examples is cast in a changing global context surrounding intellectual property rights, to which we now turn.

A CHANGING GLOBAL CONTEXT

The interdependent experiences of the four knowledge diamond participants discussed above point to a global situation where traditional approaches to intellectual property protection are in a state of flux. Some of the issues underlying these experiences involve individual–organization conflict, contrasting organizational strategies, related national initiatives, open knowledge sharing and interdependent forces, as discussed in the following.

Individual–organization conflict

During the late nineteenth century, individuals' rights to the product of their intellectual labor were ratified in two international treaties. One was the Paris Convention of 1883, covering patents, trademarks and industrial designs, and one was the Berne Convention of 1886, covering copyrights. The two treaties largely cemented a patchwork of separate national legislation which, regarding patents in particular, gave rise to a "golden age of independent inventors."[21]

By early in the twentieth century, things had begun to change. Firms made it a habit to seek out and purchase patents from individual patent holders. Some of those firms began to develop specialized skills in commercial development, making themselves even more attractive to individual inventors. Other inventors founded and developed their own firms. Transportation improvements led to the opportunity to establish patent rights over larger geographic arenas, including international arenas, calling further on the specialized skills that some firms offered. The growing complexity of technology and research and development meant that those could often be more easily funded by a system of limited liability corporations and their stock market investors. The era of large corporation claims to, and political lobbying about, intellectual property rights had begun. However, a relatively clear distinction was maintained between a firm's rights to the work done by employees, and an individual's rights to exercise the skills and expertise he or she developed.

What followed varied from one country to another, but US history provides an illustrative example. Despite the shift of patent rights toward corporations, for much of the twentieth century the application of patent law was relatively lax. Patents were regularly disregarded in the early growth of California's Silicon Valley as both people and technology moved relatively freely between firms.[22] However, a landmark 1986 legal decision came down in favor of the Polaroid corporation, costing rival Kodak more than a billion dollars and eliminating it from the instant photography business.[23] The decision signaled a return to a philosophy "championing protection, exclusion, and opportunities for extracting monopoly rents."[24] Shortly after, that philosophy was affirmed in regard to copyright, as corporations' rights were extended to seventy years after an artist like Elvis Presley's death, or to ninety years after a cartoon character like Mickey Mouse's first appearance.[25]

The reassertion of corporate intellectual property rights has led to a heightening of disputes between individuals and employing organizations. On the one hand, individuals may threaten an organization by misappropriating intellectual property when they transfer their allegiance to another organization. On the other hand, organizations may anticipate breaches by imposing restrictive covenants, or restraints of trade, on their former employees.[26] It is not uncommon for these to be contested in court, at considerable cost to either the former employee or the new employer. An example is the lawsuit brought by Microsoft over the recruitment of its former vice-president and China strategy expert Kai-Fu Lee as the president of China operations for Google.[27]

Contrasting organizational strategies

A larger question concerns the degree of affiliation between communities both internal and external to any particular organization, and the pace at which collaboration among such communities can affect the pace of innovation. As this book goes to press, the contrast between IBM and Microsoft provides an instructive example.

IBM and Microsoft[28]

Flouting accepted tradition in the industry, in 2004 IBM released 500 patents to the public domain, forgoing royalties, and enabling competitors to access its once-proprietary technology. IBM was newly embracing open-source software, particularly that developed by Linux. For example, it donated computer code worth US$40 million to an open-source group called Eclipse, and also made freely available a program called Cloudspace which cost $85 million to develop. IBM, with a research and development budget of over $5 billion a year, and with more patents than any of its rivals, appeared ready to give up almost a billion dollars a year in royalties. Why the shift?

IBM executives believed that patents were stifling innovation, and that collaboration would lead to more innovation, paying for itself in the long run. They also hoped that their initiative would encourage other technology companies to follow a similar path and collaborate on new developments in the industry. IBM's vice-president for standards and intellectual property, Jim Stallings, would like other companies to join IBM in forming a "patent commons," from which bona fide programmers would be entitled to draw without paying royalties. The trend may be catching on, since Sun Microsystems freed more than 1,600 of its patents and its operating system, Solaris 10, for open-source use.

However, one industry giant not following the trend was Microsoft. Ironically, this company reversed its earlier relaxed approach to the protection of intellectual property, and was setting the acquisition of patents as a top priority. Back in the days of Silicon Valley's Homebrew Computer Club, Microsoft founder Bill Gates was not concerned about patenting, and relied on much looser "trade secrets" to protect the company's technology. More recently, obtaining patents and developing its licensing business became "a pillar of the firm's future strategy," according to Brad Smith, Microsoft's general counsel.

With 90% of the world's PCs running on Microsoft's proprietary Windows platform, the corporation sees the growth in open-source software as a serious threat. Spending around US$6 billion a year on research and development, Microsoft planned to increase its patent applications from 2,000 in 2004 to over 3,000 in 2005. Ironically, the law firm advising Microsoft in its intellectual property strategy was the same firm that masterminded IBM's now abandoned strategy. Time will tell what that advice is worth.

Here, we see intellectual property issues influencing knowledge creation and transfer across companies, in this case in the computer industry. IBM and Microsoft, giants in the industry, switched their earlier approaches to intellectual property – but in different directions. Both have taken bold steps that could have far-reaching implications for the development of the computer industry. Their stories illustrate an interesting juxtaposition between community and company participants in the knowledge diamond. On the one hand, IBM has embraced the role that open-source communities can play in innovation in the industry. On the other hand, Microsoft has come to regard those communities as a threat, celebrating instead the control of IP within the boundaries of the company.

National initiatives

As the discussion so far has begun to suggest, the issues of organizational, national and social interests in intellectual property generation frequently overlap. The following case study extends the discussion around the global context for innovation, once more in the biotechnology industry.

China's emerging
biotechnology industry[29]

The Beijing Genomics Institute produces masses of information – 50 million units of genetic sequence a day. With its industrial-scale sequencing operations, the Institute played a key role in the international Human Genome Project. China's government is taking aim at knowledge-based industries, and particularly at biotechnology and the life sciences. The biotechnology industry earned China an impressive 7.6 billion Chinese yuan (around US$912 million) in 2000. However, nearly all of its products, although made in China, were high-tech developments of "rich-country" inventions, introduced when intellectual property rights in China were less strictly enforced.

Originality remains a challenge for many of China's scientists. Yet, China is developing its intellectual property base by luring home some top Chinese scientists trained in Europe and the US. For example, the national research center of the company Beijing Biochip Technology is headed by an engineer and molecular biologist trained in Britain and the US. Similarly, the original director of the Beijing Genomics Institute was trained in Europe and America. Drawing on this director's international links and other scientists involved in the Institute, China has also become involved in the sequel to the Human Genome Project, the International HapMap Project. This was a five-country initiative, launched in October 2002.

Apart from the opportunity to initiate globally important projects, another reason that overseas-trained Chinese scientists are returning home is for the intellectual freedom that they can no longer find in the West. Two prominent examples are the controversial areas of stem cell research and cloning. For both of these fields, different Eastern and Western philosophical traditions mean that scientists returning to China experience fewer imposed restrictions. On the one hand, these differences may raise a barrier to investment in biotechnology by foreign companies and venture capitalists. On the other hand, a freer climate for the generation and sharing of scientific knowledge may give China an edge in further innovation.

The world is starting to see a reversal in the transfer of intellectual property, with Western companies increasingly becoming the licensee, rather than the licensor, of biotechnology products being created in non-traditional countries like China. Another example is Cuba, where new biotechnology developments are also emerging, and original work has been done on a meningitis B vaccine and on a hepatitis B vaccine approved by the World Health Organization for a global vaccination campaign. Several Canadian and European biotech firms are licensing Cuban technology, anticipating significant returns on their investments, as well as access to new developments.

The above illustration adds a global perspective to earlier discussions about the biotechnology industry as it relates to communities of scientists (Chapter 3) and to the development of the industry (Chapter 5). China's entry into biotechnology shows how intellectual property has progressively driven that country's economic development. This began largely by developing "knock-off" versions of already patented technologies and drugs, in an era when intellectual property rights were of little concern. China has also taken advantage of an agreement between China and the US for China to exploit patents registered in the US before 1986, and in some cases up to 1993. As a result, one company, Kexing, has become China's largest biotechnology company, and plans to become one of the world's top ten biotechnology groups within the foreseeable future.[30] The return of Chinese scientists to their home country and the freer intellectual climate they meet there are adding to China's national advantage.

We see similar results in the huge software industry in Bangalore, India, which, since the reduction of restrictions to foreign multinational entry in 1991, has seen the transfer and generation of software engineering knowledge to a vast skilled Indian workforce. Companies that set up in India, such as Motorola and Hewlett-Packard, helped the development of a successful local industry, now exemplified by a number of highly successful Indian multinationals.[31] Moreover, innovative Indian companies appear to be less concerned with profiting directly from the intellectual property they generate than with building bridges and seeking mutual gains with their clients. Business and product development processes are used to help the client leverage its competitive advantage, effectively "tying in" the client to the use of the developer's intellectual property. Both the Chinese and Indian examples illustrate how emerging economies are starting to play very different roles in the global economy. Both countries used to rely on intellectual property embedded in other countries' products, then moved to become imitators and developers of other countries' proprietary technology. Both countries have since become creators of globally important intellectual property contributions.[32]

Open knowledge sharing

The discussion so far in this chapter extends the concept of open innovation introduced in Chapter 4, and – as management scholar Henry Chesbrough has suggested – extends the role of research and development well beyond the traditional boundaries of the firm.[33] Alliances, joint ventures, networks and clusters, both within and across industries, contribute to the collaboration and governance structures through which research takes place and propriety knowledge is created. As we saw in Chapter 8, high-skill ecosystems derive largely from the open knowledge-sharing activities and interactions of their triple-helix participants – that is, government, industry and academia. These ideas reflect a view of intellectual property that is fluid in terms of all of the individual, community, organization, industry and geographic boundaries that it permeates.

In Chapter 3 and 7 we discussed the development of Linux, one of the pioneers in open-source software development. There, we saw the importance of collaboration among individuals within a community of practice, with a strong shared repertoire and mutual engagement in learning, intent on nurturing links among like-minded people throughout the world. It is this dynamic that IBM aims to capture in its own strategy for innovation. Practitioners and academics have long supported the concepts of open systems and collaboration as drivers of innovation. Some observers argue, however, that the enthusiasm for the so-called "softer" aspects of collaboration, concerned with interpersonal relationships and community building, neglects the more pragmatic matters of intellectual property ownership and the returns on research investments. Microsoft appears to be one company that shared this concern.[34]

Since around 1985, large public international web-based databases in the molecular biology industry, known as genomic and proteomic databases, most notably databases called GenBank and Protein Data Bank, have been important repositories for published science research work. The norm among communities of scientists is to publish results in databases such as these, so that others can build on current knowledge. However, companies seek protection to allow them to work on particular genes and gene sequences for the treatment of human diseases. Achieving a balance between these two competing sets of interests is a continuing challenge.

The concept of a research commons (that is, of publicly accessible research) is particularly relevant in science-based industries, and in other areas involving the provision of public goods, such as education, health care, biodiversity, and environmental protection.[35] Companies are free to utilize and contribute to knowledge in this public domain. However, over time, private interests develop around specific aspects of this combined knowledge, which companies concerned may seek to protect as intellectual property. As noted earlier, one area that has created significant controversy is the question of patenting in the genomics industry, even though some mechanisms for knowledge sharing exist. Many scientists argue that the increasing granting of patents to genes and gene fragments should be stopped, on any or all of moral, legal or social grounds.[36]

We see these perspectives of intellectual property protection and open knowledge sharing enacted through the knowledge diamond, illustrated in Figure 9.1.

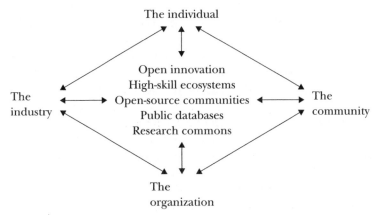

The individual

Open innovation
High-skill ecosystems
Open-source communities
Public databases
Research commons

The
industry

The
community

The
organization

Figure 9.1   Intellectual property and knowledge sharing across the
knowledge diamond

The described shift toward open knowledge sharing clearly raises new
questions for organizations accustomed to a different approach. Next,
we take a further look at how those organizations are responding.

AN INTELLECTUAL PROPERTY PARADOX

The tendency to consider patent protection and open source as mutually
exclusive is commonplace. But an interesting paradox has emerged,
particularly in the technology industries. In the early twenty-first century
there was a huge proliferation of patent registrations and licensing.
At the same time, open-source innovation became the underlying logic
of innovation in several industries. Industries and organizations now
participate through both mechanisms – selling or licensing patents, and
simultaneously engaging in open knowledge sharing. Companies like
IBM, Nokia and Intel have been in the vanguard of this dual strategy.
IBM had the highest number of patents granted by America's patent
office over the twelve years ending in 2004, reaching 3,248 patents in
the final year and 40,000 patents in total. At the same time, IBM has
embraced open knowledge sharing by releasing many of its innovations
to the open-source community to a "patent commons."[37]
    Is it possible to reconcile these apparently opposing approaches to
innovation? Many large companies think it is. First, many see a reliance
on patents and intellectual property rights as an imperative, just to keep
level with competitors. Henning Kagermann, CEO of German software

company SAP, states that, "These are the rules of the game."[38] Second, patents and copyright are also seen as essential to the open exchange of information. Microsoft's director of business development, David Kaefer, suggests that "Patents are a property right that allows the innovation to be exchanged."[39] Similarly, Sun Microsystems' Chief Technology Officer, Greg Papadopoulos, believes that the proliferation of patents is necessary for knowledge sharing, "that has exactly the right outcome. We sit here and exchange patents with each other. Ultimately, that's great: you have a set of companies doing more innovation than they would have otherwise."[40]

Whereas large companies previously developed, controlled and marketed the innovation themselves, participants are increasingly intertwined in the innovation process, and the need for communication and knowledge sharing is paramount. Participants are encouraged to take on specialist roles, as they are rewarded by license fees and other intellectual property rights for their part in the process. These kinds of arrangements provide legal certainty for participants involved in the innovation development.

As we have discussed, open approaches to innovation and knowledge sharing across company boundaries have widespread intellectual property implications. Evidence shows that patents in software and business methods have four times the litigation rates of other products.[41] In their attempts to avoid litigation costs, companies have tended to follow a cross-patenting strategy – both licensing out their own intellectual property and licensing in the intellectual property of other companies. This not only protects a company's existing property, but also promotes innovation through greater knowledge sharing.[42] Whatever the mechanism used for intellectual property protection, there is little doubt that open knowledge sharing also plays an important role. As we have seen in this chapter, all the knowledge diamond participants engage in the web of new knowledge generation. However, finding an effective balance, where the creators of intellectual property are rewarded and open knowledge sharing is encouraged, remains an elusive goal.[43]

TOOLS RELATED TO INTELLECTUAL PROPERTY

This chapter has highlighted how individuals, communities, organizations and industries have engaged in both traditional and new forms of intellectual property. Traditional instruments of intellectual property are patents, copyright, trademarks and trade secrets, all of which have been used by individuals, communities and organizations across numerous industries for centuries.

A range of mechanisms, or tools, are used to support open approaches to innovation, many based on the use of these traditional instruments. Most common is the open-source approach in the software industry, in many cases using shared knowledge without any legal form of protection attached. We also see the use of patent pools, which have also been used in other industries, including sewing machines, aircraft, and radio. Patent pools, and the similar concept of patent commons, allow intellectual property to be accessed and used by a defined community of users, generally on the condition that the subsequent developments are also made available to the community.[44]

With the apparently increasing role of intellectual property in innovation and the proliferation of patents and other forms of intellectual property, we see organizations developing a variety of tools to "keep up with the play." Over recent years, most large organizations, especially in high-technology industries, have created an intellectual property division. For example, Hewlett-Packard has engineers and lawyers working side by side to generate patents and licensing business. Since the division was created in 2002, the licensing revenue for Hewlett-Packard generated by this division has increased from $50 million to over $200 million. Microsoft, which has only recently joined the patenting rush, started a new business in May 2004, called Microsoft Intellectual Property Ventures, to license technology to venture capitalists and start-up firms.[45] Meanwhile, former Microsoft Chief Technology Officer Nathan Myhrvold has since formed a new company, Intellectual Ventures, to provide funds to inventors, patent the technologies they produce, and license these patents around the world. Myhrvold sees his company simultaneously protecting patent rights from infringement and bringing more innovations to the marketplace.[46]

Finally, as noted in Chapter 1, Napster founder Shawn Fanning and others have developed new tools to enable peer-to-peer file sharing of copyrighted intellectual property.[47] These new tools signal fresh attempts to respect intellectual property rights, as well as to facilitate the open sharing of materials. We can expect that other new tools will emerge to address the intellectual property paradox described above. These tools try new ways to protect the rights of the property holder as well as to promote knowledge sharing for greater innovation.

SUMMARY

This chapter has highlighted the important role of intellectual property for all four participants in the knowledge diamond. The examples provided, beginning with the opening Qualcomm example, illustrate the central tension between the rights of the owners of intellectual property and the larger public interest. Individuals (like Lech Johansen), producer communities (like the Linux community), user communities (like the Mind-Storms game user community), and organizations newly interested in intellectual property (like the British National Health Service) can all make a significant impact on the system through which intellectual property and property rights are sustained. Organizations can also pursue contrasting strategies toward patent protection, as was illustrated in the IBM versus Microsoft example, based on contrasting views of the value of open-source approaches to innovation. Whole industries are shifting toward new approaches to intellectual property creation, with the biotechnology industry providing a particular example.

Some nations, like China and India, have been transforming their traditional approaches to intellectual property protection. Meanwhile, both nations and organizations have been experimenting with a more open approach to knowledge sharing. There is an emergent paradox between the parallel growth in patent registrations and open knowledge sharing approaches. All four knowledge diamond participants need to understand their role in intellectual property development relative to other participants, and to remain aware of the tools that facilitate this development.

QUESTIONS FOR REFLECTION

1   What is your reaction to the opening Qualcomm example? What other examples have you seen of intellectual property rights protection by a company, and what is the strategic importance of these rights?

2   How are open approaches to innovation affecting a company or industry that you know? What impact might these approaches have on intellectual property rights, and on the future competitiveness of the company or industry?

3   What examples have you seen of (a) individuals and (b) user communities contributing to a company's intellectual property development? How have intellectual property rights been assigned in those cases?

4   The global innovation arena raises new intellectual property challenges for multinational companies. How can these companies respond to situations where counties with which they collaborate have relatively weak intellectual property protection standards?

5   Which of the described IBM and Microsoft approaches to intellectual property do you prefer, and why?
6   Given the potential for knowledge sharing and creation across the knowledge diamond, how would you advise the company or industry you identified in question 2 to respond? Who will benefit from your advice?
7   What tools have you experienced that either directly or indirectly can influence intellectual property protection or transfer?

NOTES

1   Sell, S. and May, C. (2001) "Moments in law: contestation and settlement in the history of intellectual property," *Review of International Political Economy*, 8 (3), 467–500, p. 467.
2   Adapted from *The Economist* (2003) "Spread betting," June 19, http://www.economist.com/displaystory.cfm?story_id=1841059; *The Economist* (2000) "Qualcomm's Dr Strangelove," June 15, http://www.economist.com/Printer Freindly.cfm?Story_ID=82450; *The Economist* (2004) "Vision, meet reality," September 2, http://www.economist.com/displaystory.cfm?story_id=3150731.
3   *The Economist*, "Qualcomm's Dr Strangelove."
4   *The Economist* (2005) "The Arms Race," October 20, http://www.economist.com/PrinterFriendly.cfm?story_id=5015059.
5   WIPO, http://www.wipo.int/about-ip/en/, accessed November 26, 2005.
6   Khan, B.Z. and Sokoloff, K.L. (2001) "The early development of intellectual property institutions in the United States," *Journal of Economic Perspectives*, 15 (3), 233–46.
7   Sell and May, "Moments in law."
8   Adapted from *Wall Street Journal*, New York, October 15–16 and October 20, 2005.
9   *Wall Street Journal*, New York, October 15–16, 2005.
10 *Wall Street Journal*, New York, October 20, 2005.
11 Ibid.
12 Sell and May, "Moments in law," p. 475.
13 Piller, F., Ihl, C., Fuller, J. and Stotko, C. (2004) "Toolkits for open innovation: the case of mobile phone games," *Proceedings of the 37th Hawaii International Conference on System Sciences*, January 5–8, pp. 1–10.
14 *The Economist* (2005) "The rise of the creative customer," March 10, http://www.economist.com/displaystory.cfm?story_id=3749354.
15 Estola Kari-Pekka, Nokia Research Centre, "Open innovation," http://www.mirror4u.net/dokumentit/Estola17032005.pdf.
16 *The Economist*, "The rise of the creative customer."
17 Ibid.
18 Kogut, B. and Metiu, A. (2001) *Open Source Software Development and Distributed Innovation*, Working Paper 01-08, Philadelphia, Reginald H. Jones Center, pp. 1–38.

19 Adapted from *The Economist* (2003) "NHS and innovation. Healthy profits: making money out of the health service," October 2, http://www.economist.com/displaystory.cfm?story_id=2101517.

20 Adapted from *The Economist* (2004) "Report: an open-source shot in the arm?," June 10, http://www.economist.com/displaystory.cfm?story_id=2724420.

21 Hughes, T.P. (1989) *American Genesis: A Century of Innovation and Technological Enthusiasm*, New York, Viking Penguin. In contrast, the US was at the same time seen as "something of an international plunderer" in being slow to recognize foreign authors' copyright claims: see Kahn, B.Z. and Sokoloff, K.L. (2001) "History lessons: the early development of intellectual property institutions in the United States," *Journal of Economic Perspectives*, 15 (3), p. 234.

22 Rogers, E.M. and Larsen, K. (1984) *Silicon Valley Fever*, New York, Basic, Chapter 5 "Networks," pp. 79–95.

23 Silverstein, D. (1991) "Patents, science and innovation: historical linkages and implications for global technological competitiveness," in A. Cutler, V. Haufler and T. Porter (eds), *Private Authority and International Affairs*, Albany, State University of New York Press, pp. 169–97.

24 Sell and May, "Moments in law."

25 *Wall Street Journal* (2002) "Several justices raise concerns about copyright-extension case," Eastern Edition, October 10, p. B4.

26 Carnardella, M.J. (2004) "Restrictive covenants," *Employment Relations Today*, 31 (1), 109–15.

27 Guth, R.A. (2005) "Microsoft sues to keep aide from Google," *Wall Street Journal*, July 20, p. B1.

28 Adapted from *The Economist* (2005) "Big Blue becomes bountiful," January 11, http://www.economist.com/agenda/displaystory.cfm?story_id=3554542; *The Economist* (2005) "Smart assets," February 17, http://www.economist.com/displaystory.cfm?story_id=3675679; *The Economist* (2001) "An open and shut case," May 10, http://www.economist.com/displaystory.cfm?story_id=620445.

29 Adapted from *The Economist* (2002) "Chinese biotechnology: biotech's yin and yang," December 12, http://www.economist.com/displaystory.cfm?story_id=1491569; *The Economist* (2003) "Biotech in Cuba: truly revolutionary," November 27, http://www.economist.com/displaystory.cfm?story_id=2249479.

30 *The Economist* (2001) "Intellectual property in China: have patent, will travel," June 28, http://www.economist.com/displaystory.cfm?story_id=677617.

31 Prominent examples are the corporations WIPRO and Infosys.

32 Prahalad, C.K. and Lieberthal, K. (1998) "The end of corporate imperialism," *Harvard Business Review*, 76 (4), 68–76.

33 Chesbrough, H.W. (2003) "The era of open innovation," *MIT Sloan Management Review*, 44 (3), 35–41.

34 Microsoft's concern has been somewhat mitigated by its instigation of an "embrace and extend" strategy allowing large customers to access the source code of Windows 2000 and notify Microsoft of bugs and to suggest improvements.

35   Maskus, K.E. and Reichman, J.H. (2004) "The globalization of private knowledge goods and the privatization of global public goods," *Journal of International Economic Law*, 7 (2), 279–320.

36   Ebersole, T.J., Guthrie, M.C. and Goldstein, J.A. (2005) "Patent tools as a solution to the licensing problems of diagnostic genetics," *Intellectual Property and Technology Law Journal*, 17 (1), 6–13.

37   *The Economist* (2005) "An open secret," October 20, http://www.economist.com/displaystory.cfm?story_id=5015177, p. 1.

38   *The Economist*, "The arms race," p. 2.

39   Ibid., p. 5.

40   Ibid., p. 2.

41   Vemuri, V.K. and Bertone, V. (2004) "Will the open source movement survive a litigious society?," *Electronic Markets*, 14 (2), 114–19.

42   *The Economist*, "Big Blue becomes bountiful."

43   Plitch, P. (2002) "The legal theorist: what is intellectual property in the age of PCs and the Internet? Pamela Samuelson thinks she knows," *Wall Street Journal*, Eastern Edition, May 13, p. R12.

44   Ebersole et al., "Patent tools."

45   *The Economist*, "The arms race."

46   *The Economist* (2005) "Voracious venture," October 20, http://www.economist.com/PrinterFriendly.cfm?story_id=5015073.

47   Hansell, S. (2005) "Putting the Napster genie back in the bottle," *New York Times*, November 20, http://www.nytimes.com/2005/11/20/business/yourmoney/20fanning.html?pagewanted=1.

CHAPTER 10

PARTICIPATING IN THE KNOWLEDGE ECONOMY

> We need to remember . . . how big a part of our working life
> we spend learning particular jobs, and how valuable an asset
> in all walks of life is knowledge of people, of local conditions,
> and of special circumstances.
>
> *Friedrich A. Hayek*[1]

An understanding of people, conditions and special circumstances
suggests three perspectives that we will use to summarize this book.
First, to participate in the knowledge economy we need to address three
personal questions: why do we work, how do we work, and with whom
do we work? Variations on these three questions help us to understand
how individuals, communities, organizations and industries participate
in knowledge work. Second, knowledge work arises under specific
conditions related to the degree of alignment or conflict between the
interests of different participants, and how open or closed participants
are to sharing knowledge. Third, a variety of processes are involved
in knowledge work, such as in the making and sustaining of social
connections and the global transfer of knowledge through project
collaborations.

As knowledge work participants, it is important to consider the multiple roles we each play in the knowledge economy. It is also important
to consider how our roles influence and are being influenced by other
participants – individuals, communities, organizations, and industries –
as our work unfolds. By viewing our roles in these multiple contexts, we
can more effectively navigate our own separate journeys as participants
in the knowledge economy.

We now return to the film industry with which we began in
Chapter 1.

The Lord of the Rings

A first for fantasy in Hollywood, *The Return of the King* received an astonishing eleven Academy Awards in 2004, including Best Director and Best Adapted Screenplay. The third of the *Lord of the Rings* movie trilogy had already won four Golden Globe awards, Best Film at the *Empire* magazine film awards, and the Directors Guild of America award for its director.[2] By early 2004, the trilogy had grossed a record-breaking $3 billion in box-office sales.[3] The first two films in the trilogy, *The Fellowship of the Ring* and *The Two Towers*, also won Oscars, and all three films made it into the top ten revenue-generating movies of all time.

The dream of a young New Zealand movie maker, Peter Jackson, the *Lord of the Rings* trilogy was a milestone for the movie industry. Commentators have pointed to Jackson's unique qualities and unconventional style as the keys to the trilogy's success. His passion had always been filmmaking. He learned his craft, and built a modest professional reputation, making a series of low-budget but critically acclaimed films, the first of them released when he was twenty-six years old. By age thirty-three he was completing his first Hollywood-backed film, *The Frighteners*, starring Michael J. Fox. Jackson turned his attention to Tolkien's epic trilogy after learning that the rights for a more modest idea – to film the same author's earlier book, *The Hobbit* – were already taken.

Jackson developed his career as a member of a lively Wellington, New Zealand-based film-making milieu. Its members included long-time friend – and Oscar-winning co-director of *Shrek* – Andrew Adamson, as well as special effects experts Richard Taylor and Tania Rodger, who would become key players in filming the Tolkien trilogy. Since the age of twenty, Jackson was also an enthusiastic member of a worldwide community of Tolkien fans. These included, for example, students at Warwick University who renamed their campus ring road Tolkien Road, a Frodo Society that was formed in northern Borneo, and a Vietnamese dancer in Saigon who used a shield with the lidless eyes of arch-villain Sauron.

The Lord of the Rings was made under a contract between Jackson's New Zealand company, Wingnut Productions, and the Hollywood production company New Line Cinema.[4] New Line Cinema had never attempted anything on the scale of a trilogy of films, to be made simultaneously over seven years, at a budget of $264 million. The trilogy was "a daring undertaking many thought would fail" and where failure "would have sent Jackson's career into a tailspin, and toppled a major studio."[5] A digital and special effects company called Weta, led by Richard Taylor, Tania Rodger and others from the Wellington milieu, was also formed. It developed new technology that gave "life" to digital characters, so that each could act on its own and also react to the environment – a key feature of the *Lord of the Rings* battle scenes.[6]

The New Zealand film-making industry had cut its teeth on a series of earlier films, several of which gained international attention. Among them were Jane Campion's *The Piano* (with young Oscar-winning Anna Paquin), *Once Were Warriors*, and *Heavenly Creatures* (starring a then unknown Kate Winslet). Television series such as *Hercules: The Legendary Journeys* and *Xena: Warrior Princess* took advantage of and helped build expertise for filming in New Zealand's natural environment – with snow-capped mountains, glaciers and dense rainforests all in close proximity. The industry was better prepared for Jackson's trilogy than many might have imagined.

Somehow, everything came together. One commentator noted that "The sheer logistical achievement . . . is prize-worthy: seven years in the making; 15 months of principal photography; nine camera units operating simultaneously; reshoots every year to enhance and refine; the creation of [Jackson's] own studio and special effects house in New Zealand, far away from the Hollywood establishment."[7] The project sometimes saw Jackson supervising up to seven crews simultaneously, by satellite, in locations across New Zealand. Near the end of the project soundtrack composer Howard Shore commented: "It's really bittersweet because we've worked on it for so long and so hard, with great collaboration and true friendship. *The Lord of the Rings* is also our story."[8]

Many of the principals in the making of the trilogy moved on to other projects with their reputations greatly enhanced. The profiles of the main cast such as Elijah Wood, Orlando Bloom, Viggo Mortensen and Liv Tyler – originally chosen by Jackson for their enthusiasm for the Tolkien project – skyrocketed. Peter Jackson accepted an invitation from Hollywood to direct the remake of the blockbuster movie, *King Kong*. That movie would reuse the talents of many of the original *Lord of the Rings* cast and crew.

The making of *The Lord of the Rings* is interesting for several reasons: it captures the dreams of one individual, it unfolds largely outside the glitter of Hollywood, and it emphasizes camaraderie and fellowship rather than expenses and paychecks. It also celebrates the involvement of a great number of players, all working in a shared endeavor, apparently seamlessly. The work drew not only on the remarkable individual talents of Peter Jackson and many others, but also on communities of actors and technicians, new organizations at the cutting edge of innovation, partnership with an independent production company, and a responsive host industry cluster. All four kinds of knowledge diamond participants were clearly in play.

THE KNOWLEDGE DIAMOND AT WORK

Chapters 2 through 5 of this book focused on the separate involvement in the knowledge diamond of individuals, communities, organizations and industries. The *Lord of the Rings* story invites us to reflect back on each kind of involvement, as well as to see how those separate kinds of involvement come together.

The individual

There is little question that the strong personal commitment of Peter Jackson – that is his own "knowing-why" – was the catalyst for the making of the epic trilogy. Jackson was emphatic that the movies should reflect the values woven into Tolkien's writing. As the actors and crew lived by these values over the months and years of filming, the fellowship experienced in the making of the movies paralleled that in Tolkien's story. Jackson was particularly skillful in gathering around him other individuals who shared his enthusiasm for film-making in general, and for *The Lord of the Rings* in particular. In some cases, little-known actors were chosen as much for these attributes as for their acting reputation.

The community

As the ideas of Jackson and his immediate collaborators unfolded, the project started to engage widespread communities – of actors, technicians, animators, computer programmers, and others. Each of these communities became dedicated to the "joint enterprise" of fulfilling its own commitments to the trilogy, in some cases for up to seven years. Communities also worked together effectively in facing the challenges of filming across multiple locations and tying in new technologies, particularly those involving special effects. The reference to "great collaboration and true friendship" seems to be largely a reference to inter-community attachments.

The organization

The main New Zealand companies in the creation of the *Lord of the Rings* movies, Wingnut Productions and Weta, evolved from a regional group of film-making enthusiasts. These companies' cultures reflected their founders' commitment to succeed, and quickly attracted an array of talented and similarly committed workers. Links and relationships across the industry grew, attracting further talent and new supporting companies. The risk taken by New Line Cinema was extraordinary, and out of character with the usual Hollywood approach of spreading its production bets across a range of movie projects.

The industry

Many of the companies involved in the making of the trilogy were involved in, and drew largely on, the emerging Wellington, New Zealand, regional industry milieu. There was also an important inter-cluster link to the Hollywood milieu, home of New Line Cinema, with its specialized capabilities and connections in promotion and distribution. For the filming and production of *The Lord of The Rings*, these two clusters appeared to work together seamlessly, and to the substantial benefit of both parties.

Interdependencies

None of these four participants acted alone. On the contrary, the *Lord of the Rings* story offers numerous examples of individuals (such as Peter Jackson, Richard Taylor, and Tania Rodger), communities (such as the separate occupational communities contributing to the film crew), companies (such as Wingnut Productions, Weta and New Line Cinema) and the established industry (across two continents) interacting with one another toward the eventual success of the movie trilogy. The range of Oscars received speaks loudly for the learning that occurred through the interdependent work of all four knowledge diamond participants. In keeping with these observations, Figure 10.1 re-presents the knowledge diamond, but this time with all six links between diamond participants emphasized.

The film-making industry has not always functioned as it is described in this book. Until the 1960s the so-called "studios" lived up to their name, with all the necessary actors, screenwriters, crew, technicians, even directors, retained as permanent studio employees. The disaggregation into independent film companies, actors and specialist work groups was initially seen as a cost-cutting measure.[9] However, the participants making *The Lord of the Rings* used, and may have improved on, a different film-making recipe. It is a recipe for projects built on productive interdependencies between individuals, communities, organizations and the industry, and invested in the creation of new knowledge on the back of the knowledge previously available.

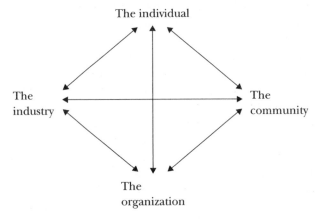

The individual

The industry

The community

The organization

Figure 10.1   The knowledge diamond revisited

WHY, HOW AND WITH WHOM WE WORK

Not only are there four kinds of participant involved in knowledge work, but also there are connections in the way that each participant gets involved in the work. As the previous chapters have shown, each of the participants is frequently engaged in the application of both tacit and explicit knowledge. Each participant is involved in both knowing and learning (or knowledge exploitation and knowledge exploration). Each participant draws on the practices – broadly recognized occupational practices or other specialized practices – through which knowledge work gets done. Each participant also gets involved in the communication across practices necessary for knowledge work to succeed. The quality of this communication will depend on the underlying questions of why, how and through whom knowledge work occurs.

In Chapter 2, we raised the questions "*Why* do we work?," "*How* do we work?" and "With *whom* do we work?" and we introduced a framework of three interdependent ways of knowing to respond to these questions. For example, in the story of Mary we described how Mary's responses traced back to her early knowing-why identification with the acting profession, and to the "Jimmy Stewart theory of acting" she applied in subsequent work behavior. We described how her motivation to "add dimensions" to her character influenced the future jobs and knowing-how skills that she sought. We also illustrated how Mary saw that fellow workers were important not only to help her succeed in her present job, but as knowing-whom contacts for her further career.

In Chapters 3, 4 and 5 we described similar frameworks to cover community, organizational and industry knowledge work, illustrated at the start of each chapter with the stories of the forensic accountants' community, the Intel organization and the UK advertising industry respectively. One way to tie the four chapters together is to see each of the four frameworks responding to the same set of questions. That is, a community's answer to the question "Why do we work?" will relate to the joint enterprise in which the community is engaged; an organization's answer will relate to the culture in which its employees function; and an industry's answer will relate to the industry milieu and the history that lies behind it.

Similarly, answers to the question "How do we work?" will relate to a community's shared repertoire, an organization's capabilities and an industry's recipes. Responses to the question "With whom do we work?" will relate to a community's mutual engagement, an organization's connections and an industry's system of interconnections. These links across the three underlying questions and the four knowledge diamond participants are shown in Table 10.1.

Looking across the separate rows and columns in Table 10.1 can provide an opportunity for preliminary diagnosis. That is, with a particular situation in mind we can look across all four participants in the knowledge diamond – individuals, communities, organizations and the host industry or industries – to anticipate what kind of mutual interests or tensions may emerge. Table 10.1 can also prompt further investigation about the participants, such as the investments of key individuals, communities and alliance partners that a knowledge work project may need to succeed. Some of that success will depend on the particular conditions existing at the outset, to which we turn next.

CONDITIONS UNDERLYING KNOWLEDGE WORK

Any knowledge work situation, or any new knowledge work project, may be characterized by certain sets of conditions. One condition is alignment among the participants involved; another is conflict among the participants; and a third is the balance between closed and open positions on knowledge work that separate participants bring to the situation.

Alignment

Alignment refers to the degree to which separate knowledge work participants have common interests. In the case of the *Lord of the Rings* story, all four kinds of participant appear aligned with one another. Why? To

Table 10.1 Dimensions of knowledge work for knowledge diamond participants

		Dimensions of knowledge work		
		Why do we work?	*How* do we work?	With *whom* do we work?
Knowledge diamond participants	Individuals	*Knowing-why*: individual motivation and identity	*Knowing-how*: individual skills and expertise	*Knowing-whom*: individual relationships and reputation
	Communities	*Joint enterprise*: community goals and mutual accountability	*Shared repertoire*: community tools, concepts and ways of working	*Mutual engagement*: community investments in working together
	Organizations	*Culture*: organizational mission and core values	*Capabilities*: organizational skill and knowledge resources	*Connections*: organizational contacts and network relations
	Industries	*Milieu*: the industry's collective beliefs and values	*Recipes*: the industry's mental models and ways of doing things	*System*: inter-connections within the industry

contribute to the making of a successful movie trilogy and learn from the process. How? By applying and developing the skills and expertise that the participants possess. With whom? With other participants who had been drawn into the film-making project. However, alignment does not occur without effort. Peter Jackson made a particular effort to share his vision for the movie trilogy with other participants, such as the special effects workers eager to enhance their craft, and the actors who were already enthusiastic Tolkien fans.

Alignment has also been portrayed in a number of other stories in this book. For example, the "chemistry in academia" example in Chapter 1 rested on scientists realizing they had a common interest in unsolved research questions. The Intel story in Chapter 4 described how the organization's internal laboratories and manufacturing plants, its external contacts with relevant scientific and technological communities, and its links to other organizations reflected an overall alignment concerning new silicon chip development. The Voicetech example in Chapter 6 reflected alignment among a group of companies intent on producing a novel answering machine, even if one of those companies could not later deliver what it had promised.

Conflict

Conflict refers to the degree of difference, or lack of alignment, between participants' interests. There are other parts to the *Lord of the Rings* story we have not told: of actors and communities left out of the work; of organizations that chose not to join in, or joined in and then got cold feet (as happened with the first production company that contracted to promote the film); or of alternative industry clusters (such as those around Hollywood, California, and London, England) largely missing from the project. Potential conflict also loomed between the artistic goals of Peter Jackson's directorial team and the budgetary concerns of New Line Cinema's business managers.

Elsewhere in this book, a sharp example of conflict is the competing interests of individuals, user communities and music industry companies in the music and DVD file-sharing cases described in Chapters 1 and 9. Inter-community conflict was illustrated in the differences between forensic accountant and mainstream accountant communities described in Chapter 3, and in the differences among the geographically separate communities developing a new Internet business venture or ice hockey rink as described in Chapter 7. Inter-organizational conflict is fundamental whenever organizations participate in the kind of "learning races" described in Chapter 4. Conflict between alternative visions of industry regions is inherent in the contrasting US and European views of business ecosystems described in Chapter 5.

Open versus closed positions

An open position means participants are disposed to share what they know with other participants. A closed position means participants are indisposed to share what they know. In the *Lord of the Rings* example, the overall success of the trilogy-making venture suggests the great majority of participants brought an open approach, perhaps in response to Peter Jackson's enthusiasm for the venture, perhaps because they understood that any other position would threaten the success of the venture, and in turn their own reputations. There seemed a shared understanding of the importance of task completion and inter-community problem-solving – as described near the end of Chapter 3 – that would be required for project success.

Again, all four kinds of knowledge work participant are implicated in individuals' or communities' readiness to share what they know, in organizations' stances on alliances or broader ideas about open-source innovation, and in industry traditions that may or may not put the wellbeing of an industry, or an industry region, above that of any particular firm. Open-source communities are strong advocates of more open positions. Organizations making choices between knowledge exploitation and exploration, or between codification and personalization, or between closed and open approaches to innovation, are all dealing with the contrast between closed and open positions. The Singaporean versus Malaysian electronics industry clusters in Chapter 5 provided an example of relatively open versus relatively closed industry positions in each respective country.

A number of writers would argue that interaction of the three conditions, that is of alignment, conflict, and contrasting open versus closed positions, can be healthy.[10] The argument goes that this interaction gives rise to a clash of ideas and subsequent synthesis, or what was in Chapter 1 referred to as a kind of "creative abrasion" through which further innovation occurs. To address that issue further calls for a fuller review of the processes underlying knowledge work.

PROCESSES BEHIND KNOWLEDGE WORK

This book has highlighted a number of forces that contribute to the processes through which knowledge work unfolds. Some principal ones include making and sustaining connections, the evolution of projects, collaboration over the web, contributing to global knowledge work, developing intellectual property, and the use of knowledge work tools. We review each of these processes in the following.

Making and sustaining connections

In Chapter 2, we described how individuals developed interpersonal relationships through either bridging (making new relationships) or bonding (sustaining existing relationships). In Chapter 3 we extended the argument to describe how communities developed closure (through interpersonal bonding of their members) and brokerage (through further bridging activities of their members). In Chapter 4, we described how Intel acted as a broker in promoting technology research activities. In Chapter 5, we described how regional brokerage and closure contributed to the relative openness of the Singaporean versus the Malaysian electronics industry.

Each of the knowledge diamond participants contributes to the making and sustaining of connections as knowledge work unfolds. Interpersonal bridging and bonding can occur on behalf of not only the individuals involved, but also the communities, organizations or industries those individuals represent. In the other direction, people representing either industry or organizational positions can make new inter-community or interpersonal connections at the same time.

The evolution of projects

The film-making examples used to introduce Chapters 1 and 10 provide graphic illustrations of how knowledge work can unfold through successive industry projects. The sequential project stages of variation, selection and retention, first mentioned in Chapter 1, were further examined in the example of Ericsson in Chapter 6. A series of four case examples in Chapter 6 further illustrated how the three stages can give rise to alternative patterns of project performance and project learning. Projects are also associated with learning landscapes that shape the protocol, knowledge boundaries and autonomy associated with project development. Projects further make use of boundary objects that provide a shared language and level of concreteness, and thereby facilitate knowledge transformation among project participants representing distinctive knowledge communities and specialized expertise.

Projects serve as meeting-grounds for all four knowledge diamond participants. They also provide opportunities for all four participants to come together, to share knowledge, and to provide or receive learning to other participants. The learning is then carried forward into new project opportunities.

Collaboration over the web

The Teltech example in Chapter 7 described how Teltech supported client company innovation by providing virtual access to its geographically dispersed technical experts and specialized databases. The Linux community described in Chapter 3 provided the first of several examples of a community connected in virtual rather than physical space. Advances in web infrastructure, such as grid computing, provide new opportunities for virtual collaboration among scientific communities. Organizations use the web in virtual product testing by providing customers with virtual experiences of products and services. Much of the interplay between local and global knowledge work, described in Chapter 8, takes place over the web.

The web adds to the possibilities for people to make and sustain connections, either on their own behalf or on behalf of the larger groups those people may represent. The web also broadens the range of projects that knowledge diamond participants can join, and therefore the learning opportunities that each participant can experience.

Contributing to global knowledge work

In Chapter 8, we described Nokia's transformation to become a global organization. This kind of organization can evolve from local beginnings, or can be "born global" – as was the case for the flat-panel display manufacturer, PixTech. International travel by people like Mary (Chapter 2), who established the first Federal Express office in China, can directly affect the global circumstances of both organizations and industries. Global organizations mediate among industry regions represented in their countries of operation. Links between industry participants can be altered through knowledge work arrangements, as happened in the reconfiguration of the apparel industry's supply chain. Industries also respond to the particular efforts of host nations, as illustrated in the examples of Singapore and Malaysia (Chapter 8) and China and India (Chapter 9).

Global knowledge work is part of the everyday reality facing all four knowledge diamond participants. The availability of global talent, and the accessibility of it over the web, create widespread opportunities to leverage local knowledge, and thereby to broadly restructure work arrangements across national boundaries. There is also far greater collaboration across these boundaries than once (not too long ago) used to be the case.

Developing intellectual property

The Qualcomm story in Chapter 9 is an example of an organization that generates most of its revenue from intellectual property licensing. The conflict between the developers of file-sharing software and the recording industry, covered in Chapters 1 and 9, reflects competing intellectual property claims. Communities are increasingly relevant after the example set by open-source software communities, the availability of collaborative software, and the increasing involvement of user communities in new product development. Conflicting national legal positions on intellectual property, in particular between the US and other countries over the relative claims of the rights of property holders versus those of consumers, will continue to influence future developments.

Intellectual property affects all of us, often in multiple roles as providers, consumers and interested parties in the litigation relating to property rights. What were once simple ideals of encouraging innovators to share their ideas for the greater public good have now become contested issues of global significance. All four kinds of knowledge diamond participants are involved.

Using the knowledge work toolkit

Tools have always been available to help people deal with particular challenges and processes in their work. What is different in the contemporary era is the power of information technology to provide common tools, and to coordinate work across different locations. Examples across previous chapters include the reach of the web for interpersonal communication and community building, the role of knowledge portals for organizations, the opportunities for cluster mapping for industries, more sophisticated tools for project management, imaging tools for remote medical diagnosis, and patent repository and search tools.

These tools can serve to foster broader collaboration among knowledge diamond participants. They reinforce the significance of the second meaning of "knowledge at work" described in Chapter 1. That is, knowledge does its own work as it gets transmitted through the various channels that the described tools provide. The challenge for each of us, whatever knowledge diamond participant we represent, is to appreciate what this broad, frequently global, knowledge transmission can mean and what opportunities it creates.

PLAYING PARALLEL ROLES

We address this last section of the book directly to the reader. You are likely to be in the process of doing, or to have done, most of the following: finishing formal education, and using that education to get a start in the world of work; gathering early experience, and making important choices about the direction of your career; building relationships with peers, mentors and eventually protégés; developing an occupational specialization, and community building within that occupation and with other interest groups; being employed by at least one but probably several organizations and playing a part in one or more industries; establishing a home, developing a social life, starting a family, and extending your ties in the geographic area where you work; being politically active in a national economy; and contributing to a market-driven international economy. Along the way, you will be playing parallel roles as an individual worker, a community member, an organizational employee and an industry collaborator.

It has been common for writers to focus on the prospective conflict between an individual and an organization.[11] It has also been common for human resource management writers to emphasize the benefits of "alignment" from the organization's perspective, that is of everyone pulling for the organization's greater good.[12] However, these perspectives can be limiting in the knowledge economy. You play more roles than the individual careerist or the organizational good soldier, and the knowledge economy does not unfold through tidy, long-standing, employment arrangements. You can do better by seeing your own work from multiple viewpoints – by placing yourself in each corner of the knowledge diamond to see your own, your community's, your organization's and your industry's economic interests. Doing so can help you make more informed choices as your work proceeds.

Your career will also involve a series of knowledge work projects, each drawing on your own and other people's knowledge, and providing new learning opportunities. You will be collaborating over the web, and taking advantage of the access provided to outside resources and knowledge specialists. You will be contributing to global knowledge work and its shifting arrangements. You will be a provider and consumer of intellectual property, either on your own or on another party's behalf. In all of these activities, placing yourself at each successive corner of the knowledge diamond can help you see your own work in a broader context.

A FINAL MESSAGE

In the opening chapter of their popular book *The Social Life of Information*, John Seely Brown and Paul Duguid talk about the significance of what they call the "social periphery" around work, that is the "communities, organizations and institutions that frame human activities."[13] We fully agree with those authors' sentiments, and have sought to provide an integrative model – the knowledge diamond – that reminds you of the nature of that periphery in your future knowledge work. The processes described above will continue to gain importance as web-facilitated, globally coordinated knowledge work expands.

Steve Jobs once said about Apple, "It doesn't make sense to hire smart people and then tell them what to do."[14] Similarly, it doesn't make sense for the authors of this book, and others who have helped bring it about, to attract smart readers and then tell you what to do. However, we sincerely hope that this book leaves you better able to decide for yourself. Good luck in your own knowledge work!

QUESTIONS FOR REFLECTION

1   Can you apply Table 10.1 to a knowledge work situation with which you are familiar? What conditions of alignment, conflict, and open and closed positions among the participants do you see?
2   Looking at the same situation as for question 1, which of the following processes are relevant and how:
    • making and sustaining connections
    • the evolution of projects
    • collaborating over the web
    • contributing to global knowledge work
    • developing intellectual property
    • using the knowledge work toolkit?
3   Can you draw on some of the main ideas in this book to describe the kind of knowledge work you would like to be doing five years into the future?
4   Given your answer to question 3, what can you do over the next six months to help you prepare for the future you describe?

NOTES

1   Hayek, F.A. (1980) *Individualism and Economic Order*, Chicago, Midway Reprint/University of Chicago Press, p. 80. Original article in *American Economic Review*, 1945, XXXV (4), 519–30.
2   BBC News (2004) "*Rings* is third biggest film ever," http://newsvote.bbc.co.nz/mpapps/pagetools/print/news.bbc.co.uk/2/hi/entertainment/.
3   TheOneRing.net (2003) "The *Lord of the Rings* gamble pays off," December 12, http://www.theonering.net/perl/newsviews/1/1071277639.

4 TheOneRing.net (2004) "Master replicas to introduce LOTR line," October 2, http://www.theonering.net/perl/newsviews/8/1076447871.

5 Mueller, M. (2003) "Why rings director deserves Oscar," BBC News, December 17, http://news.bbc.co.uk/go/pr/fr/-/2/hi/entertainment/3324035.

6 Snider, M. (2004) "*Rings* takes special effects to another level," *USA Today*, February 10, http://usatoday.printthis.clickability.com/pt/cpt?action=cpt&title=USATODAY.com+.

7 Mueller, "Why rings director deserves Oscar."

8 *The Canadian Press* (2004) "Composer Howard Shore writing more for *Lord of the Rings*," February 9.

9 Bohn, T., Stromgren, R. and Johnson, D. (1978) *Light and Shadows: A History of Motion Pictures*, 2nd edn, Sherman Oaks, CA, Alfred.

10 Leonard, D. and Swap, W. (1999) *When Sparks Fly: Igniting Creativity in Groups*, Boston, Harvard Business School Press; Chatzel, J. (2003) *Knowledge Capital: How Knowledge-Based Enterprises Really Get Built*, Oxford, Oxford University Press; Thite, M. (2004) *Managing People in the New Economy: Targeted HR Practices That Persuade People to Unlock Their Knowledge Power*, Thousand Oaks, CA, Sage.

11 For example, Roberto, M.A. (2005) *Why Great Leaders Don't Take Yes for an Answer: Managing for Conflict and Consensus*, Upper Saddle River, NJ, Pearson Education.

12 See for example Rothwell, W.J. (2005) *Effective Succession Planning: Ensuring Leadership Continuity and Building Talent from Within*, New York, AMACOM.

13 Brown, J.S. and Duguid, P. (2002) *The Social Life of Information*, Boston, Harvard Business School Press, 2nd edn, p. 5.

14 Davenport, T.H. and Prusak, L. (1998) *Working Knowledge*, Boston, Harvard Business School Press, p. 50.

ABOUT THE AUTHORS

Robert DeFillippi is Professor of Management and Director, Center for Innovation and Change Leadership, Suffolk University, Boston, USA. His scholarly writings focus on project-based organizations and careers as vehicles for knowledge creation and dissemination and his empirical research spans high technology and cultural industries. Additionally, he is Book Series Editor for *Research in Management Education and Development* and Associate Editor for the *International Journal of Management Reviews*.

Michael Arthur is Professor of Management at Suffolk University, Boston, USA. His work focuses on the relationships among careers, communities and employment arrangements in the knowledge-based economy. His previous books include *The Boundaryless Career, The New Careers, Career Frontiers*, and *Career Creativity*. He has written widely for the academic and professional journals, and is a developer of the "intelligent career card sort"® (ICCS®) intended to help people manage their careers in contemporary times.

Val Lindsay is Associate Professor in International Business and Head of the School of Marketing and International Business at Victoria University of Wellington, New Zealand. Her research work focuses on the international strategy of firms, the knowledge-based dynamics of networks and clusters in relation to international performance, and services internationalization. She is a reviewer for a number of international business and management journals, and has consulted widely for businesses and government organizations on international strategy.

BIBLIOGRAPHY

Allen, T. (1984) *Managing the Flow of Technology: Transfer and the Dissemination of Technological Information with the R&D Organization.* Cambridge, MA: MIT Press.

Allen, L. (1993) *Introduction to Type® and Careers*; all Palo Atto, CA, CPP, Inc.

Amin, A. and Cohendet, P. (2004) *Architectures of Knowledge.* Oxford: Oxford University Press.

Amundson, N.E. (2003) *Active Engagement: Enhancing the Career Counseling Process,* 2nd edn. Richmond, BC: Ergon.

Anklam, P. (2005) Social network analysis in the KM toolkit. In M. Rao (ed.), *Knowledge Management Tools and Techniques.* Oxford: Elsevier, pp. 329–46.

Argyris, C. and Schön, D. (1974) *Theory in Practice: Increasing Professional Effectiveness.* San Francisco: Jossey-Bass.

Argyris, C. and Schön, D. (1978) *Organization Learning: A Theory of Action Perspective.* Reading, MA: Jossey-Bass.

Arthur, M.B., Claman, P.H. and DeFillippi, R.J. (1995) Intelligent enterprise, intelligent careers. *Academy of Management Executive,* 9 (4), 7–22.

Arthur, M.B., DeFillippi, R.J. and Jones, C. (2001) Project-based learning as the interplay of career and company non-financial capital. *Management Learning,* 32 (1), 99–117.

Arthur, M.B., DeFillippi, R.J. and Lindsay, V.J. (2001) Careers, communities, and industry evolution: links to complexity theory. *International Journal of Innovation Management,* 5 (2), 239–55.

Arthur, M.B., Khapova, S.N. and Wilderom, C.P.M. (2005) Career success in a boundaryless career world. *Journal of Organizational Behavior,* 26, 177–202.

Atkinson, R.D. (2003) *The Innovation Economy: A New Vision for Economic Growth in the 21st Century.* Washington, DC: Progressive Policy Institute.

Awad, E.M. and Ghaziri, H.M. (2004) *Knowledge Management.* Upper Saddle River, NJ: Pearson Prentice Hall.

Axelrod, R. (1984) *The Evolution of Cooperation.* New York: Basic.

Ayas, K. and Zeniuk, N. (2001) Project-based learning: building communities of reflective practitioners. *Management Learning,* 32 (1), 61–76.

Barney, J. (1986) Organizational culture: can it be a source of sustained competitive advantage? *Academy of Management Review,* 11, 656–65.

Barth, S. (2005) Self-organization: taking a personal approach to KM. In M. Rao (ed.), *Knowledge Management Tools and Techniques*. Oxford: Elsevier, pp. 347–61.

Bartlett, C.A., Ghoshal, S. and Birkinshaw, J. (2003) *Transnational Management: Text and Cases*. New York: McGraw-Hill/Irwin.

Barton, D. and Swap, W.C. (2005) *When Sparks Fly: Igniting Creativity in Groups*. Boston: Harvard Business School Press.

Bateson, G. (1980) *Mind and Nature: A Necessary Unity*. London: Bantam.

Becerra-Fernandez, I., Gonzalez, A. and Sabherwat, R. (2004) *Knowledge Management*. Upper Saddle River, NJ: Pearson Prentice Hall.

Bell, D. (1976) *The Coming of Post-Industrial Society: A Venture in Social Forecasting*. New York: Basic.

Best, M.H. (2001) *The New Competitive Advantage: The Renewal of American Industry*. Oxford: Oxford University Press.

Birkinshaw, J. (2002) Managing internal R&D networks in global firms: what sort of knowledge is involved? *Long Range Planning*, 35, 245–67.

Bohn, T., Stromgren, R. and Johnson, D. (1978) *Light and Shadows: A History of Motion Pictures*, 2nd edn. Sherman Oaks, CA: Alfred.

Bowes, B.J. (1999) *The Easy Resumé Book: A Transferable Skills Approach*. London: Bowes.

Brady, T. and Davies, A. (2004) Building project capabilities: from exploratory to exploitative learning. *Organization Studies*, 25 (9), 1601–21.

Brady, T., Marshall, N., Prencipe, A. and Tell, F. (2002) Making sense of learning landscapes in project-based organizations. In P. Love, P.S.W. Fong and Z. Irani (eds), *Management of Knowledge in Project Environments*. Oxford: Elsevier Butterworth-Heinemann, pp. 197–217.

Bresnen, M., Goussevskaia, A. and Swan, J. (2005) Embedding new management knowledge in project-based organizations. *Organization Studies*, 25 (9), 1535–55.

Brown, J.S. and Duguid, P. (1991) Organizational learning and communities of practice: toward a unified view of working, learning and innovation. *Organization Science*, 2 (1), 40–57.

Brown, J.S. and Duguid, P. (2002) *The Social Life of Information*, 2nd edn. Boston: Harvard Business School Press.

Buchel, B. and Raub, S. (2001) Media choice and organizational learning. In M. Dierkes, B. Antal, J. Child and I. Nonaka (eds), *Handbook of Organizational Learning and Knowledge*. Oxford: Oxford University Press.

Burt, R.S. (1992) *Structural Holes*. Cambridge, MA: Harvard University Press.

Burt, R.S. (2005) *Brokerage and Closure: An Introduction to Social Capital*. Oxford: Oxford University Press.

Campbell, D. (1969) Variation and selective retention in sociocultural evolution. *General Systems*, 16, 69–85.

Canadian Press (2004) Composer Howard Shore writing more for *Lord of the Rings*. *The Canadian Press*, February 9.

Capek, P.G., Frank, S.P., Gerdt, S. and Shields, D. (2005) A history of IBM's open-source involvement and strategy. *IBM Systems Journal*, 44 (2), 249–57.

Carlile, P.R. (2002) A pragmatic view of knowledge and boundaries: boundary objects in new product development. *Organization Science*, 13 (4), 442–55.

Carmel, E. and Tija, P. (2005) *Offshoring Information Technology: Sourcing and Outsourcing to a Global Workforce.* Cambridge: Cambridge University Press.

Carnardella, M.J. (2004) Restrictive covenants. *Employment Relations Today,* 31 (1), 109–15.

Castells, M. (2001) *The Internet Galaxy.* Oxford: Oxford University Press.

Chandler, A.D. (1990) *Scale and Scope: The Dynamics of Industrial Capitalism.* Cambridge, MA: Harvard University Press.

Chatzel, J. (2003) *Knowledge Capital: How Knowledge-Based Enterprises Really Get Built.* Oxford: Oxford University Press.

Chesbrough, H.W. (2003) *Open Innovation.* Boston: Harvard Business School Press.

Chesbrough, H.W. (2003) The Era of Open Innovation. *MIT Sloan Management Review,* 44 (3), 35–41.

Child, J. (2001) Learning through strategic alliances. In M. Dierkes, A.B. Antal, J. Child and I. Nonaka (eds), *Handbook of Organizational Learning and Knowledge.* Oxford: Oxford University Press, pp. 657–80.

Coers, M., Gardner, C., Higgins, L. and Raybourn, L. (2001) *Benchmarking: A Guide for Your Journey to Best-Practice Processes.* Houston, TX: American Productivity and Quality Center.

Collins, H. (2003) *Enterprise Knowledge Portals: Next-Generation Portal Solutions for Dynamic Information Access, Better Decision Making, and Maximum Results.* New York: AMACON.

Cook, S.D.N. and Brown, J.S. (1999) Bridging epistemologies: the generative dance between organizational knowledge and organizational knowing. *Organization Science,* 10 (4), 381–400.

Daft, R.L. and Lengel, R.H. (1984) Information richness: a new approach to managerial behavior and organizational design. In B.M. Staw and L.L. Cummings (eds), *Research in Organizational Behavior,* vol. 6. Greenwich, CT: JAI, pp. 191–233.

Daft, R.L. and Lengel, R.H. (1986) Organizational information requirements, media richness and structural design. *Management Science,* 32 (5), 554–71.

Dalkir, K. (2005) *Knowledge Management in Theory and Practice.* Oxford: Elsevier Butterworth-Heinemann.

Davenport, T.H. (2005) *Thinking for a Living.* Boston: Harvard Business School Press.

Davenport, T.H. and Prusak, L. (1998) *Working Knowledge.* Boston: Harvard Business School Press.

Davenport, T.H. and Prusak, L. (2003) *What's the Big Idea?* Boston: Harvard Business School Press.

Davies, A. and Hobday, M. (2005) *The Business of Projects.* Cambridge: Cambridge University Press.

Davis, G.B. and Nauman, J.D. (1997) *Personal Productivity with Information Technology.* New York: McGraw-Hill.

Davis, G.B., Collins, R.W., Eirman, M. and Nance, W. (1991) *Conceptual Model for Research on Knowledge Work.* Management Information Systems Research Center Working Paper 91-10. University of Minnesota, Minneapolis.

De Janasz, S.C., Sullivan, S.E. and Whiting, V. (2003) Mentor networks and career success: lessons for turbulent times. *Academy of Management Executive*, 17 (4), 78–91.

DeFillippi, R. (2001) Project-based learning, reflective practices and learning outcomes. *Management Learning*, 32 (1), 5–10.

DeFillippi, R. (2002) Information technology and organizational models for project collaboration in the new economy. *Human Resource Planning*, 25 (4), 7–18.

DeFillippi, R.J. and Arthur, M.B. (1996) Boundaryless contexts and careers: a competency based perspective. In M.B. Arthur and D.M. Rousseau (eds), *The Boundaryless Career*. New York: Oxford University Press, pp. 116–31.

DeFillippi, R.J. and Arthur, M.B. (1998) Paradox in project-based enterprise: the case of film-making. *California Management Review*, 40 (2), 125–39.

DeFillippi, R. and Arthur, M. (2002) Career creativity to industry influence: a blueprint for the knowledge economy? In M.A. Peiperl, M.B. Arthur and N. Anand (eds), *Career Creativity: Explorations in the Remaking of Work*. Oxford: Oxford University Press, pp. 298–313.

Delbecq, A. and Weiss, J. (1988) The business culture of Silicon Valley: is it a model for the future? In J. Weiss (ed.), *Regional Cultures, Managerial Behavior and Entrepreneurship*. New York: Quorum.

Department of Trade and Industry (1998) *Building the Knowledge-Driven Economy*. White Paper. London: DTI.

DeSanctis, G. and Monge, P. (1999) Introduction to the special issue. *Organization Science*, special issue on "Communication Processes for Virtual Organizations," 10 (6), 693–703.

Dess, G.G., Lumpkin, G.T. and Taylor, M.L. (2005) *Strategic Management*, 2nd edn. New York: McGraw Hill, pp. 133–7.

Dodson, M., Gann, D. and Salter, A. (2005) *Think, Play, Do*. Oxford: Oxford University Press.

Dolliver, M. (2002) I'll trust you not to be very trustworthy, buster. *Adweek*, 43 (32), 17–20.

Doz, Y.L., Santos, J. and Williamson, P. (2001) *From Global to Metanational: How Companies Win in the Knowledge Economy*. Boston: Harvard Business School Press.

Drucker, P. (1959) *Landmarks of Tomorrow*. New York: Harper Collins.

Dyer, J.H. and Nobeoka, K. (2000) Creating and managing a high performance knowledge-sharing network: the Toyota case. *Strategic Management Journal*, 21, 345–67.

Ebersole, T.J., Guthrie, M.C. and Goldstein, J.A. (2005) Patent tools as a solution to the licensing problems of diagnostic genetics. *Intellectual Property and Technology Law Journal*, 17 (1), 6–13.

Eby, L.T., Butts, M. and Lockwood, A. (2003) Predictors of success in the era of the boundaryless career. *Journal of Organizational Behavior*, 24 (6), 689–708.

Engwall, M. (2003) No project is an island: linking projects to history and context. *Research Policy*, 32, 789–808.

Ensher, E.A., Murphy, S.E. and Sullivan, S.E. (2000) Boundaryless careers in entertainment: executive women's experience. In M. Peiperl, M. Arthur, R. Goffee and T. Morris (eds), *Career Frontiers: New Conceptions of Working Lives*. Oxford: Oxford University Press, pp. 229–54.

Etzkowitz, H. and Leydesdorff, L. (2000) The dynamics of innovation: from national systems and "Mode 2" to a triple helix of university–industry–government relations. *Research Policy*, 29, 109–123.

Favreau, M. (2005) *The Future of Portable Computer and Communication Devices.* Norwalk, CT: Business Communications Company, Inc.

Ferguson, C. (2005) Pacific Rim group evolves into international model of collaboration. *National Partnership for Advanced Computational Infrastructure: Archives.*

Fernie, J. and Azuma, N. (2004) The changing nature of Japanese fashion: can quick response improve supply chain efficiency? *European Journal of Marketing*, 38 (7), 790–808.

Finegold, D., Wong, P.-K. and Cheah, T.-C. (2004) Adapting a foreign direct investment strategy to the knowledge economy: the case of Singapore's emerging biotechnology cluster. *European Planning Studies*, 12 (7), 921–41.

Friedman, T.L. (2005) *The World Is Flat.* New York: Farrar, Strauss, and Giroux.

Fuller, S. (1992) Knowledge as product and property. In N. Stehr and R.B. Ericson (eds), *The Culture and Power of Knowledge: Inquiries into Contemporary Societies.* Berlin: de Gruyter.

Gallivan, M.J. (2001) Striking a balance between trust and control in virtual organizations: a content analysis of open source software case studies. *Information Systems Journal*, 11, 277–304.

Garcia-Lorenzo, Lucia (2004) From networks to networking: implications of a social practice for organizing and knowledge sharing. *Coalitions and Collision: 11th International Conference on Multi-Organizational Partnerships, Alliances and Networks*, June 23–26, Tilburg, The Netherlands.

Gates, B. (1999) *Business @ the Speed of Thought.* Chatham: Penguin.

Gherardi, S., Nicolini, D. and Odella, F. (1998) Toward a social understanding of how people learn in organizations: the notion of situated curriculum. *Management Learning*, 29, 274.

Ghoshal, S. and Bartlett, C.A. (1990) The multinational corporation as an interorganizational network. *The Academy of Management Review*, 15 (4), 603–25.

Gibson, C.B. and Cohen, S.G. (2003) *Virtual Teams That Work.* San Francisco: Jossey-Bass.

Giddens, A. (1999) *Runaway World: How Globalisation is Reshaping Our Lives.* London: Profile.

Gladwell, M. (2002) *The Tipping Point*, 2nd edn. Boston: Little Brown.

Goleman, D. (1998) *Working with Emotional Intelligence.* New York: Bantam.

Gomes-Casseres, B. and Spar, D. (2002) *Xerox and Fuji Xerox: Update 2002.* Case 9-703-009. Boston: Harvard Business School.

Gosh, B.C. and Taylor, D. (1999) Switching advertising agency: a cross-country analysis. *Marketing Intelligence and Planning*, 17 (3), 140–6.

Grabher, G. (2002) The project ecology of advertising: tasks, talents and teams. *Regional Studies*, special issue, 36 (3), 245–62.

Granovetter, M. (1974) *Getting a Job: A Study of Contacts and Careers.* Cambridge, MA: Harvard University Press.

Granovetter, M. (1992) Problems of explanation in economic sociology. In N. Nohria and R.G. Eccles (eds), *Networks and Organization*. Boston: Harvard Business School Press.

Grant, R. (1996) Toward a knowledge-based theory of the firm. *Strategic Management Journal*, winter special issue, 17, 109–22.

Grant, R. (2002) *Contemporary Strategy Analysis*. Malden, MA: Blackwell.

Grant, R.M. and Baden-Fuller, C. (2004) A knowledge accessing theory of strategic alliances. *Journal of Management Studies*, 41 (1), 61–84.

Gribble, C. (2005) *History of the Web Beginning at CERN*. hitmill.com.

Grove, A.S. (1996) *Only The Paranoid Survive*. New York: Doubleday.

Grutter, J. (n.d.) *Making It Beyond Today's Organizations*. Palo Alto, CA: CPP, Inc.

Grutter, J. and Lund, S.L. (n.d.) *Making It In Today's Organizations*. Palo Alto, CA: CPP, Inc.

Gupta, A.K. and Govindarajan, V. (2000) Knowledge flows within multinational corporations. *Strategic Management Journal*, 21 (4), 473–96.

Guth, R.A. (2005) Microsoft sues to keep aide from Google. *Wall Street Journal*, July 20, B1.

Haikio, Martti (2002) *Nokia: The Inside Story*. Prentice Hall.

Hakim, C. (2003) *We Are All Self-Employed: How To Take Control of Your Career*. San Francisco: Berrett-Koehler.

Hall, R. (1992) The strategic analysis of intangible resources. *Strategic Management Journal*, 13, 136–9.

Hamel, C. and Prahalad, C.K. (1994) *Competing for the Future*. Boston: Harvard Business School Press.

Hamm, S. (2005) Linux Inc. *Business Week*, January 31, 60–8.

Hammer, A.L. (1993) *Introduction to Type® and Careers*. Palo Alto, CA: CPP, Inc.

Hammer, M. (2004) Deep change: how operational innovation can transform your company. *Harvard Business Review*, April, 85–93.

Han, Y. (2004) A transaction cost perspective on motives for R&D alliances: evidence from the biotechnology industry. *Journal of the American Academy of Business*, 5 (1/2), 110–15.

Hansell, S. (2005) Putting the Napster genie back in the bottle. *New York Times*, November 20.

Hansen, M.T., Nohira, N. and Tierney, T. (1999) What's your strategy for managing knowledge? *Harvard Business Review*, March–April, 106–16.

Harvard Business Review (2005) *Appraising Employee Performance*. Edited Collection. Boston: Harvard Business School Press.

Hayek, F.A. (1980) *Individualism and Economic Order*. Chicago: Midway Reprint/ University of Chicago Press. Original article in *American Economic Review*, 1945, XXXV (4), 519–30.

Hedlund, G. (1994) A model of knowledge management and the N-form corporation. *Strategic Management Journal*, 15, 73–90.

Heires, K. (2005) The blogosphere beckons: should your company jump in? *Harvard Management Communication Letter*, 2 (4), November.

Hendry, C., Brown, J. and DeFillippi, R. (2000) Regional clustering of high technology-based firms: opto-electronics in three countries. *Regional Studies*, 34 (2), 129–44.

Herman, J. (2003) The new science of networks. *Business Communication Review*, 33 (6), 22–3.

Higgins, M.C. (2002) Careers creating industries: some early evidence from the biotechnology industry. In M.A. Peiperl, M.B. Arthur and N. Anand (eds), *Career Creativity: Explorations in the Remaking of Work.* Oxford: Oxford University Press.

Higgins, M.C. (2005) *Career Imprints: Creating Leaders across an Industry.* San Francisco: Jossey-Bass.

Higgins, M.C. and Kram, K.E. (2001) Reconceptualizing mentoring at work: a developmental network perspective. *Academy of Management Review*, 26 (2), 264–88.

Higgins, M.J. (2004) *Developmental Network Questionnaire.* Case Study 404105. Boston: Harvard Business School Press.

Hislop, D. (2003) The complex relations between communities of practice and the implementation of technological innovations. *International Journal of Innovation Management*, 7 (2), 163–88.

Hofstede, G. (1980) *Culture's Consequences: International Differences in Work-Related Values.* Beverly Hills, CA: Sage.

Houghton Mifflin (2000) *The American Heritage Dictionary of the English Language.* Boston: Houghton Mifflin.

Howkins, J. (2001) *The Creative Economy.* New York: Penguin.

Hughes, T.P. (1989) *American Genesis: A Century of Innovation and Technological Enthusiasm.* New York: Viking Penguin.

Hwang Smith, M. and Weil, D. (2005) Ratcheting up: linked technology adoption in supply chains. *Industrial Relations*, 44 (3), 490–508.

Iansiti, M. and Levien, R. (2004) Strategy as ecology. *Harvard Business Review*, March, 69–78.

Ibarra, H. (2003) *Working Identity.* Boston: Harvard Business School Press.

Inkson, K. and Arthur, M.B. (2001) How to be a successful career capitalist. *Organizational Dynamics*, 30 (1), 48–61.

Jones, C. and DeFillippi, R.J. (1996) Back to the future in film: combining industry and self-knowledge to meet the career challenges of the 21st century. *Academy of Management Executive*, 10 (4), 89–103.

Jones, C. and Lichenstein, B.M.B. (2000) The "architecture" of careers: how career competencies reveal from dominant logic in professional services. In M. Peiperl, M. Arthur, R. Goffee and T. Morris (eds), *Career Frontiers: New Conceptions of Working Lives.* Oxford: Oxford University Press, pp. 153–76.

Kahn, B.Z. and Sokoloff, K.L. (2001) History lessons: the early development of intellectual property institutions in the United States. *Journal of Economic Perspectives*, 15 (3), 233–46.

Kanter, R.M. (1989) *When Giants Learn to Dance.* New York: Simon & Schuster.

Kanter, R.M. (2001) *Evolve! Succeeding in the Digital Culture of Tomorrow.* Boston: Harvard Business School Press.

Kearns, D.T. (1990) Leadership through quality. *Academy of Management Executive*, 4, 86–9.

Keegan, A. and Turner, R.J. (2001) Quantity versus quality in project-based learning practices. *Management Learning*, 32 (1), 77–98.

Keller, R.T. (2001) Cross-functional project groups in research and new product development: diversity, communications, job stress, and outcomes. *Academy of Management Journal*, 44, 547–55.

Khan, B.Z. and Sokoloff, K.L. (2001) "The early development of intellectual property institutions in the United States," *Journal of Economic Perspectives* 15 (3), 233–46.

Khanna, T., Gulati, R. and Hotria, N. (1998) The dynamics of learning alliances: competition, cooperation and relative scope. *Strategic Management Journal*, 19 (3), 193–210.

Kidder, T. (1981) *The Soul of a New Machine*. Boston: Little Brown.

Kirsner, S. (2005) What's cost of pact not to compete? *The Boston Globe*, September 19, E5.

Knight, G.A. and Cavusgil, S.T. (2004) Innovation, organizational capabilities, and the born-global firm. *Journal of International Business Studies*, 35 (2), 124–41.

Kodama, F. (1992) Technology fusion and the new R&D. *Harvard Business Review*, July–August, 70–8.

Kogut, B. and Metiu, A. (2001) *Open Source Software Development and Distributed Innovation*. Working Paper 01-08. Philadelphia: Reginald H. Jones Center.

Kotter, J. (1997) *The New Rules*. New York: Free.

Langford, C.H., Wood, J.R. and Ross, T. (2003) Origins and structure of the Calgary wireless cluster. In D.A. Wolfe and Meric S. Gertler (eds), *Clusters Old and New*. Montreal: McGill–Queen's University Press, pp. 161–86.

Lawrence, T.B. (1998) Examining resources in an occupational community: reputation in Canadian forensic accounting. *Human Relations*, 51 (9), 1103–31.

Leonard, D. and Swap, W. (1999) *When Sparks Fly: Igniting Creativity in Groups*. Boston: Harvard Business School Press.

Leonard, D. and Swap, W. (2005) *Deep Smarts*. Boston: Harvard Business School Press.

Leonard-Barton, D. (1992) Core competencies and core rigidities: a paradox in managing new product development. *Strategic Management Journal*, 13, 111–25.

Leonard-Barton, D. (1995) *Wellsprings of Knowledge*. Boston: Harvard Business School Press.

Levinson, D.J. (1978) *The Seasons of Man's Life*. New York: Knopf.

Levitt, B. and March, J.G. (1988) Organizational learning. *Annual Review of Sociology*, 14, 19–40.

Levy, S. (2001) *Hackers: Heroes of the Computer Revolution*, rev. edn. New York: Penguin.

Lindkvist, L. (2005) Knowledge communities and knowledge collectivities: a typology of knowledge work in groups. *Journal of Management Studies*, 42, 1189–1210.

Lindsay, V.J. (2005) The development of international industry clusters: a complexity theory approach. *Journal of International Entrepreneurship*, 3, 71–97.

Lucier, C. and Torsilieri, J. (2001) Can knowledge management drive bottom-line results? In I. Nonaka and D. Teece (eds), *Managing Industrial Knowledge*. Thousand Oaks, CA: Sage, pp. 231–43.

MacCormak, A. and Herman, K. (1999) *Red Hat and the Linux Revolution*. Case 9-600-009. Boston: Harvard Business School.

Maister, D.H. (1997) *Managing the Professional Service Firm*. New York: Simon & Schuster.

March, J.G. (1991) Exploration and exploitation in organizational learning. *Organization Science*, 2 (1), 71–87.

Markus, M.L., Manville, B. and Agres, C.E. (2000) What makes a virtual organization work? *Sloan Management Review*, 42, 13–26.

Marshall, A. (1890) *Principles of Economics*. London: Macmillan.

Marshall, N. (2004) *Managing Knowledge Spaces: Coordinating across Talent, Teams and Territory*. Workshop presentation, June 22. Falmer: University of Sussex Freeman Innovation Centre.

Martin, P. (2001) The technological evolution. *Financial Times*, December 24, 17.

Maskell, P. (2001) Towards a knowledge-based theory of the geographic cluster. *Industrial and Corporate Change*, 10 (4), 921–43.

Maskus, K.E. and Reichman, J.H. (2004) The globalization of private knowledge goods and the privatization of global public goods. *Journal of International Economic Law*, 7 (2), 279–320.

Mason, J. (2005) From e-learning to e-knowledge. In M. Rao (ed.), *Knowledge Management Tools and Techniques*. Oxford: Elsevier.

Mathews, J. (1999) A silicon island of the East: creating a semiconductor industry in Singapore. *California Management Review*, 41 (2), 55–78.

Maznevski, M. and Chudoba, K.M. (2000) Bridging space over time: global virtual team dynamics and effectiveness. *Organization Science*, 11 (5), 473–92.

McHugh, J. (1998) For the love of hacking. *Forbes*, August 10, 1–12.

McQuade, K. and Gomes-Casseres, B. (1992) *Xerox and Fuji Xerox*. Case 9-391-156. Boston: Harvard Business School.

Milgram, S. (1967) The small world problem. *Psychology Today*, 2, 60–7.

Mintzberg, H. (1987) Crafting strategy. *Harvard Business Review*, 65 (4), 66–75.

Mirvis, P.H. (1997) "Soul work" in organizations. *Organization Science*, 8 (2), 193–206.

Moon, J.Y. and Sproull, L. (2000) Essence of distributed work: the case of the Linux kernel. *First Monday*. http://www.firstmonday.org/.

Moore, G. (1996) Some personal perspectives on research in the semiconductor industry. In R.S. Rosenbloom and W.J. Spencer (eds), *Engines of Innovation*. Boston: Harvard Business School Press, pp. 165–74.

Moore, J.E. (1993) Predators and prey: a new ecology of competition. *Harvard Business Review*, May–June.

Mutch, A. (2003) Communities of practice and habitus: a critique. *Organization Science*, 24 (3), 383–401.

Nachira, F. (2002) *Toward a Network of Digital Business Ecosystems Fostering the Local Development*. Discussion Paper. Information Society Technology Specific Programme. Brussels: European Commission.

Nachira, F. (2005) The role of business ecosystems in the promotion of research in Europe. In *The Emergence of Novel Organisational Forms in the Globalising Planet: Toward the Business Ecosystem?*, July 6–9, Brindisi, Italy.

Nelson, R.R. and Winter, S.G. (1982) *An Evolutionary Theory of Economic Change*. Cambridge, MA: Harvard University Press.

Newell, S., Robertson, M., Scarbrough, H. and Swan, J. (2002) *Managing Knowledge Work*. London: Palgrave.

Ohmae, K. (2002) *Chugoku Shift: Shifting to China*. Tokyo: Shogakukan.

Orlikowski, W.J. (2002) Knowing in practice: enacting a collective capability in distributed organizing. *Organization Science*, 13 (3), 249–73.

Overland, M. (2005) A tale of two countries. *Chronicle of Higher Education*, November 11, 52 (12), A 42–A45, 3p, 5c.

Overland, M. (2005) Malaysia's stagnation. *Chronicle of Higher Education*, November 11, 52 (12), A43–A45, 3p, 5c.

Parayil, G. (2005) From "Silicon Island" to "Biopolis of Asia": innovation policy and shifting competitive strategy in Singapore. *California Management Review*, 47 (2), 50–3.

Parker, P., Arthur, M.B. and Inkson, K. (2004) Career communities: a preliminary exploration of member-defined career support structures. *Journal of Organizational Behavior*, 25 (4), 489–514.

Peiperl, M.A. (2001) Getting 360° feedback right. *Harvard Business Review*, 79 (1), 142–7.

Peters, T. (1999) The Wow Project. *Fast Company*, May, 116–28.

Piller, F., Ihl, C., Fuller, J. and Stotko, C. (2004) Toolkits for open innovation: the case of mobile phone games. *Proceedings of the 37th Hawaii International Conference on System Sciences*, January 5–8.

Pink, D. (2002) *Free Agent Nation: The Future of Working for Yourself*. New York: Warner.

Plitch, P. (2002) The legal theorist: what is intellectual property in the age of PCs and the Internet? Pamela Samuelson thinks she knows. *Wall Street Journal*, Eastern Edition, May 13, R12.

Polanyi, M. (1966) *The Tacit Dimension*. London: Routledge and Kegan Paul.

Porter, M.E. (1990) *The Competitive Advantage of Nations*. New York: Free.

Porter, M.E. (1998) Clusters and the new economics of competition. *Harvard Business Review*, 76, 77–90.

Powell, W.W., Koput, K.W. and Smith-Doerr, L. (1996) Interorganizational collaboration and the locus of innovation: networks of learning in biotechnology. *Administrative Science Quarterly*, 41, 116–45.

Prahalad, C.K. and Hamel, G. (1990) The core competence of the corporation. *Harvard Business Review*, 68 (3), 79–91.

Prahalad, C.K. and Lieberthal, K. (1998) The end of corporate imperialism. *Harvard Business Review*, 76 (4), 68–76.

Prencipe, A. and Tell, F. (2001) Inter-project learning: processes and outcomes of knowledge codification in project-based firms. *Research Policy*, 30, 1373–94.

Prencipe, A., Davies, A. and Hobday, M. (2003) *The Business of Systems Integration*. Oxford: Oxford University Press.

Prichard, C., Hull, R., Chumer, M. and Willmott, H. (2000) *Managing Knowledge: Critical Investigations of Work and Learning*. London: Macmillan.

Putnam, R.D. (1993) *Making Democracy Work*. Princeton, NJ: Princeton University Press.

Qu, L. and Pao, S. (2005) Tools for tapping expertise in large organizations. In M. Rao (ed.), *Knowledge Management Tools and Techniques*. Oxford: Elsevier, pp. 365–77.

Quinn, J.B., Baruch, J.J. and Zien, K.A. (1997) *Innovation Explosion*. New York: Free.

Raider, H.J. and Burt, R. (1996) Boundaryless careers and social capital. In M.B. Arthur and D.M. Rousseau (eds) *The Boundaryless Career: A New Employment Principle for a New Organizational Era*. New York: Oxford University Press.

Rao, M. (ed.) (2005) *Knowledge Management Tools and Techniques*. Oxford: Elsevier.

Raymond, E.S. (1998) *The Cathedral and the Bazaar: Musings on Linux and Open Source by an Accidental Revolutionary*. Sebastopol, CA: O'Reilly.

Read, B. (2005) Lectures on the go. *Chronicle of Higher Education*, October 28, A39–A42.

Reed, R. and DeFillippi, R.J. (1990) Causal ambiguity, barriers to imitation and sustainable competitive advantage. *Academy of Management Review*, 15, 88–102.

Richardson, G.B. (1972) The organization of industry. *Economic Journal*, 82, 883–96.

Rickards, T. (1999) *Creativity and the Management of Change*. Oxford: Blackwell.

Roberto, M.A. (2005) *Why Great Leaders Don't Take Yes for an Answer: Managing for Conflict and Consensus*. Upper Saddle River, NJ: Pearson.

Robinson, D. and Miner, A. (1996) Careers change as organizations learn. In M.B. Arthur and D.M. Rousseau (eds), *The Boundaryless Career*. New York: Oxford University Press, pp. 76–94.

Rogers, E.M. and Larsen, K. (1984) *Silicon Valley Fever*. New York: Basic.

Rothwell, W.J. (2005) *Effective Succession Planning: Ensuring Leadership Continuity and Building Talent from Within*. New York: AMACOM.

Salk, J.E. and Simonin, B.L. (2003) Beyond alliances: towards a meta-theory of collaborative learning. In M. Easterby-Smith and M.A. Lyles (eds), *The Blackwell Handbook of Organizational Learning and Knowledge Management*. Malden, MA: Blackwell, pp. 253–77.

Sapsed, J. and Salter, A. (2004) Postcards from the edge: local communities, global programs and boundary objects. *Organization Studies*, 25 (9), 1515–34.

Sapsed, J., Bessant, J., Partington, D., Tranfied, D. and Young, M. (2002) Teamworking and knowledge management: a review of converging themes. *International Journal of Management Reviews*, 4 (1), 71–85.

Sapsed, J., Gann, D., Marshall, N. and Salter, A. (2005) From here to eternity? The practice of knowledge transfer in dispersed and co-located project organisations. *European Planning Studies*, special issue on "Knowledge Management and Innovation in Urban and Regional Development," 13 (6), 831–51.

Saxenian, A. (1994) *Regional Advantage*. Cambridge, MA: Harvard University Press.

Saxenian, A. (1996) Beyond boundaries: open labor markets and learning in Silicon Valley. In M.B. Arthur and D.M. Rousseau (eds), *The Boundaryless Career*. New York: Oxford University Press, pp. 23–39.

Scarbrough, H., Swan, J., Laurent, S., Bresnen, M., Edelman, L. and Newell, S. (2005) Project-based learning and the role of learning boundaries. *Organization Studies*, 25 (9), 1579–600.

Schmidt, H. (1999) From ascribed to earned trust in exporting clusters. *Journal of International Economics*, 48, 139–50.

Schwenk, H. (2002) Real-time CRM analytics: the future of BI? *KM World*, 11 (2), February.

Sell, S. and May, C. (2001) Moments in law: contestation and settlement in the history of intellectual property. *Review of International Political Economy*, 8 (3), 467–500.

Senge, P.M. (1990) *The Fifth Discipline*. New York: Doubleday.

Senge, P.M., Kleiner, A., Roberts, C., Ross, R.B. and Smith, B.J. (1994) *The Fifth Discipline Fieldbook: Strategies and Tools for Building a Learning Organization*. New York: Doubleday.

Sennett, R. (1998) *The Corrosion of Character: The Personal Consequences of Work in the New Capitalism*. New York: Norton.

Silverstein, D. (1991) Patents, science and innovation: historical linkages and implications for global technological competitiveness. In A. Cutler, V. Haufler and T. Porter (eds), *Private Authority and International Affairs*. Albany, NY: State University of New York Press, pp. 169–97.

Smeds, R., Olivari, P. and Corso, M. (2001) Continuous learning in global product development: a cross-cultural comparison. *International Journal of Technology Management*, 22 (4), 373–91.

Snider, M. (2004) "Rings" takes special effects to another level. *USA Today*, February 10.

Spender, J.C. (1989) *Industry Recipes: An Enquiry into the Nature and Sources of Managerial Judgment*. Oxford: Blackwell.

Sproull, L. and Kiesler, S. (1986) Reducing social context cues: electronic mail in organizational communication. *Management Science*, 32 (11), 1492–512.

Starbuck, W.H. (1992) Learning by knowledge-intensive firms. *Journal of Management Studies*, 29 (6), 713–40.

Stewart, T.A. (2003) *The Wealth of Knowledge: Intellectual Capital and the 21st Century Organization*. New York: Random House.

Stone, B. (2003) *Blogging: Genius Strategies for Instant Web Content*. Berkeley, CA: New Riders.

Sullivan, D. (2004) *Proven Portals: Best Practices for Planning, Designing, and Developing Enterprise Portals*. Boston: Addison Wesley.

Sydow, J., Lindkvist, L. and DeFillippi, R. (2004) Project-based organizations, embeddedness and repositories of knowledge. *Organization Studies*, 25 (9), 1475–90.

Tapscott, D., Ticoll, D. and Lowy, A. (2000) *Digital Capital: Harnessing the Power of Business Webs*. Boston: Harvard Business School Press.

The Economist (2000) Qualcomm's Dr Strangelove. June 15.

The Economist (2001) An open and shut case. May 10.

The Economist (2001) Intellectual property in China: have patent, will travel. June 28.

The Economist (2002) Chinese biotechnology: biotech's yin and yang. December 12.

The Economist (2003) Biotech in Cuba: truly revolutionary. November 27.

The Economist (2003) NHS and innovation. Healthy profits: making money out of the health service. October 2.

The Economist (2003) Spread betting. June 19.

The Economist (2004) Biotechnology: on the mend. May 13.

The Economist (2004) Report: an open-source shot in the arm? June 10.

The Economist (2004) Vision, meet reality. September 2.

The Economist (2005) An open secret. October 20.

The Economist (2005) Big Blue becomes bountiful. January 11.

The Economist (2005) Smart assets. February 17.

The Economist (2005) The arms race. October 20.

The Economist (2005) The rise of the creative customer. March 10.

The Economist (2005) Voracious venture. October 20.

The Economist Intelligence Unit (2005) *The 2005 e-Readiness Rankings*. London.

Thite, M. (2004) *Managing People in the New Economy: Targeted HR Practices that Persuade People to Unlock Their Knowledge Power*. Thousand Oaks, CA: Sage.

Thomas, L.B. (1998) "Examining resources in an occupational community: reputation in Canadian forensic accounting," *Human Relations*, 51 (9), 1103–31.

Torvals, L. and Diamond, D. (2001) *Just for Fun: The Story of an Accidental Revolutionary*. New York: HarperBusiness.

Trompenaars, F. and Hampden-Turner, C. (2002) *21 Leaders for the 21st Century*. New York: McGraw-Hill.

Tsang, E.W.K. (2002) Acquiring knowledge by foreign partners from international joint ventures in a transition economy: learning-by-doing and learning myopia. *Strategic Management Journal*, 23, 835–54.

UK Department of Trade and Industry (1998) *Building the Knowledge-Driven Economy*, White Paper.

US Census Bureau Foreign Trade Statistics (various dates) *US International Trade in Goods and Services*. APS Office of Public Affairs.

Uzzi, B. (1996) The sources and consequences of embeddedness for the economic performance of organizations: the network effect. *American Sociological Review*, 61, 674–98.

Vemuri, V.K. and Bertone, V. (2004) Will the open source movement survive a litigious society? *Electronic Markets*, 14 (2), 114–19.

Von Hippel, E. (2005) *Democratizing Innovation*. Cambridge, MA: MIT Press.

Wall Street Journal (2002) Several justices raise concerns about copyright-extension case. Eastern Edition, October 10, B4.

Wankel, C. and DeFillippi, R. (2005) *Educating Managers through Real-World Projects*. Greenwich, CT: Information Age.

Watts, D.J. and Strogatz, S.H. (1998) Collective dynamics of "small-world" networks. *Nature*, 393, 440–2.

Weick, K. (1979) *The Social Psychology of Organizing*. New York: McGraw-Hill.

Weick, K.E. (1996) Enactment and the boundaryless career. In M.B. Arthur and D.M. Rousseau (eds), *The Boundaryless Career*. New York: Oxford University Press, pp. 40–57.

Wenger, E. (1998) *Communities of Practice: Learning, Meaning and Identity*. Cambridge: Cambridge University Press.

Wenger, E., McDermott, R. and Snyder, W.M. (2002) *Cultivating Communities of Practice*. Boston: Harvard Business School Press.

Wheelwright, S.C. and Clark, K.B. (1992) *Revolutionizing Product Development*. New York: Free.

Windeler, A. and Sydow, J. (2001) Project networks and changing industry practices: collaborative content production in the German television industry. *Organization Studies*, 22 (6), 1035–60.

Wingfield, N. and Smith, E. (2003) Microsoft plans to sell music over the web. *Wall Street Journal*, 11 (17).

Wingfield, N. and Smith, E. (2003) With the web shaking up music, a free-for-all in online songs. *Wall Street Journal*, 11 (19).

INDEX

Note: page references in bold refer to tables; page references in italics refer to figures.